To P.

THE ADVENTURES OF JOY CHRONICLES **BOOK 4**

PATHS *of* FREEDOM

JOURNAL OF GALACTIC ROMANCE AND GLOBAL EVOLUTION

Love, & Joy - to you

6/23/19

By Joy Elaine

www.JoyElaine.com

The Adventures of Joy Chronicles Book 4
Paths of Freedom
Journal of Galactic Romance and Global Evolution

Published by Joy Books

ISBN-13: 978-1535112314
ISBN-10: 153511231X

DEDICATION

Dedicated to Helena and all those who are embracing new lives.

ACKNOWLEDGEMENTS

Thanks to members of the Joy Councils for your continued encouragement and assistance.

Thanks to George Verongos, editor and Angela Phillips, cover design/graphic design.

Thanks most of all to those of you living on Earth who are adding your hopes, dreams and good wishes for humanity (including yourself, of course) and Earth to our transmissions. Hold the vision for a magical journey to the 8th dimension while enjoying all the views along the way.

Storyline Participants for Paths of Freedom

Aton—an embodiment of the essence of our Sun; member of the Joy Council and married to Gaia
CEV—Council for Earth Vigilance—a collective of ninety-four energy beings now most frequently known as the Swizzlers
Changkolar Kimreenah—member of a plot in the Fantrah Universe to overthrow all the Joy Councils; became an ascended master with Liponie's "assistance"
Charlie (Charlie Brown)—number one Swizzler (CEV)
Chu—the name of a reptilian species living on Earth (many are underground). They have the ability to appear as human and are inimical to humanity
Comahlee—a genie who attempted to help us with Liponie's birthday party
Commander Ashtar—non-dual master supporting the graceful elevation of Earth; member of the Joy Council and Supreme Commander of the Ashtar Command
Conch—a Tibetan monk who lived to be 140; he ascended and is now located in an ascended master temple
Cory—a sentient crystal in my soul lineage; she and Liponie are in love
Emmon—Tonas's father
Esthra—the angel guide I speak with most frequently
Firona—Tonas's mother
Gaia—embodiment of the essence of Earth and Joy Council member married to Aton
Hosemelia—a non-dual world in our universe; Tonas created a crystal place on it for us to enjoy
Inoh—representative of a collective of energy beings located inside a space in Earth that Liponie called Equinox; we assist them to rewrite when, where and how they were brought to Earth
Isis—guardian of Earth and humanity, member of the Joy Council and mate of Osiris
Jewel—her essence incarnated into a crystal and then embodied, with Liponie's assistance, at the Joy Council; she appears to be about six years old and is my sister
Joyyahl Kindar—Council Presence from the Corena Universe
Kamala Shrow—Universal Presence from the Joeshrahnah Universe

Liponie—genie from Andromeda assisting me with pranks and Joy Council work; member of the Joy Council
Melchizedek—ascended master assisting me with playing the violin and member of the Joy Council
Ohniuh Comb—Council Presence from the Porneeseesee Universe
Osiris—guardian of Earth and humanity, member of the Joy Council and mate of Isis
Queen Kahleah—an Atlantean of great importance in my soul lineage who gave me some of her genetic attributes
Rosebud—boy fairy married to Sheliah
Sananda—ascended master and member of the Joy Council
Sharinah—a member of Changkolar's harem and the key to peace in the Fantrah Universe; she changed her name to Helena once she was safely at our Joy Council
Sheliah—a fairy I frequently visit; she is married to Rosebud
Skipper & Trigger—Charlie's horses
Swizzlers—also known as the CEV; those who chose names in this book are: Chuckie (21), Manley (23), Toby (36), Jory (47) and Bruce (57)
Thoth—a non-dual being and member of the Joy Council
Tonas—member of the Joy Council and a Supreme Commander of the Ashtar Command
Toshi—an energy being who embodied into a crystal in order to radiate a vision of the culmative
True Heart—(Konishewah) librarian for a pre-historic Native American tribe and member of the Joy Council
Yarah Homma—Emissary from the Inseanahrah Universe
Zahseet—Council Presence from the Zhorin Universe; a large portion of her world, Horeeshna, is water
Zeezzz—formerly a crystal and Cory's mother; she is an emissary to the stars, moons, suns, and planets who are considering embodying

Dragons:

Chiros—male dragon—and Migda are dragon mates
Joyous—first female dragon born on Earth in this timeline—August 9, 2014—Chiros and Migda are her parents
Kira—a female dragon who is Woonfred's mate
Woonfred—member of the Joy Council

Representatives and their universes who join the Joy Council in this book:

Bizzarah Nahcoomeeuh—Emissary for the Fantrah Universe
Champignon Defratross—Representative from the Keylonas Universe
Hehtarnew Johnrah—Representative from the Mystos Universe
Hermeenah Veelowsh—Council Presence for the Lowmahteese Universe
Kemper Findarian—Councilman from Astrenoid Universe
Nohdahwah—Chief Council for the Nestus Universe
Pronestos Optheos—Councilman from Hellipicore Universe

NOTE TO READER

Read this book start to finish and enjoy the journey. Enhance your personal evolution and the elevation of Earth by participating in the work of the Joy Councils. Turn to page 377, read the Mission Participation Directives and join the greatest adventure of your life.

CHAPTER ONE

January 16, 2015

"'You have designed a complete package for the evolution of all stars, worlds and planets.' I heard that on January eleventh and we were shown the end result on the twelfth, but I don't know what the elements of this package are. Will I be able to get any help from my future self?"

Sananda replies that I will be able to get pieces of the package even though many things have not happened yet; however, he advises me that my future self will not give me any information.

I go to the Fifth Realm at the near completion and choose to connect with every council and every being involved in the formulation and design of the evolution package. I ask them for their pieces of the culmative project with the intention of handing this package to Charlie at the council when I finish my list of items to examine.

"Yesterday, I heard someone ask me, 'Does anyone know who you are?'"

Sananda informs me that Charlie asked me that question and the answer is, "Some."

"Some what?"

"You are doing a tremendous amount of work that is directly affecting the species that you have been referring to as the you-know-who's. (I have avoided asking the name of this species because I haven't wanted to say it out loud.) I am now requesting an upgrade to your shields from some of the councils of light. I've just returned from the Joy Council with additional assistance for you from the CEV. The piece they gave me is linked, not to you as Joyce on Earth, but to the Joy Council. The new shields you now have make it so that the energy of that species cannot cross through. They can know who you are but that is all."

I feel safer with this extra protection in place, but then I realize that if the you-know-who's are aware of my identity, they probably also know about my children and perhaps my brother and his family. After I share that concern with Sananda, he says that he has requested protection from the Ashtar Command for those individuals.

I emphasize that from the beginning of my work I want my sons, brother and his family to be untouchable, impervious, invisible, sovereign, safe and untrackable. Sananda replies that he has assurances from a legion of angels that my family is safe. (Tonas later adds an enhancement of this work for me by making it appear that I am already an "incorruptible, under protection and impossible to interface with.")

This morning I saw a vision of a young boy who looked like a ten or twelve-year-old version of my son Mike. He was in the midst of a group of people, all of whom were looking at me, but he was staring at me quite intently. I show Sananda what I saw and ask him if this was Mike.

"No, this was another son."

"John?"

"No."

I'm starting to cry as I realize that this boy is a son I will have in the future. My mind is racing as I try to digest this magnificently astounding, utterly amazing bit of knowledge. I want to talk to someone, but I can't tell Tonas. What if it's not his child? It must be his child. My mind has gone into a loop of, "Tell Tonas, don't tell Tonas, tell Tonas, you absolutely can't say a word of this to Tonas." Now I know how he must feel when he knows things that he can't tell me. Maybe he already knows about this. I'm going to speak with Esthra after I've had time to assimilate this news.

At the Joy Council:

Tonas sounds effusive as he greets me and immediately begins to speak about the culmination as a "confirmation that everything his life has been about is relevant."

I just can't talk about this right now because I'm loaded down with boxes of pictures from my parents' home. Mother saved every piece of paper she ever received and every picture she ever took. It has been a staggering job going through everything and I'm feeling overwhelmed by trying to sort the pictures out.

"Do I have my arms loaded with things?"

"You should have gotten yourself a big shopping cart."

"Let me put it down because I want to speak with Liponie."

After I hear his laugh, I say hello and announce that I have a project that's going to be the most difficult thing he's ever done. As soon as those words leave my lips, I burst into laughter as I realize how silly my declaration sounded. There are thousands of pictures, there are duplicates, there are undated photos, very faded photos, and photos of unknown people in boxes, CD's and photo albums. (I brought my pictures along, too.) There are letters I wrote to my parents while I was in college; there are all the cards and letters I ever sent Mom and Dad as well as all the cards I received as a baby and growing up. I threw boxes and boxes of these things away but there's still so much left; this seems like a monumental job to me but maybe it won't be for Liponie.

He says, "I will wear my big boy pants then."

"I'm going to help you with it, but not right now. I want to put all of these pictures in albums. I can go through them with you to put them in some kind of order."

Tonas reminds me that Liponie can make all this happen in an instant.

"Liponie, I'm not disparaging your abilities, but can you really fix all this?"

"In an instant. I can create councils of crystalline in an instant."

"It's just that this has been so difficult for me. Some of these I may not want."

He advises me not to throw anything away and asks me to leave this with him. I do, with relief.

"I also brought a set of china and some sterling silver."

These are things my mother had that I don't really have room for and I want Liponie to recreate them so that we can use them for the council. I'm also going to have him create a set of Fiesta Ware to use. I don't have any of that with me, but there is one piece at my parent's home that I picture in my mind for him. He assures me that he can recreate all of this beautifully.

"I thought the pictures would be a really hard job, but maybe not."

"My dear, one day I will give you a little bit of a primer on the life of a genie."

"Could we add Osiris and Charlie please, because I want to discuss genies."

Charlie says, "Hello, Mother."

I love hearing him call me that. After I return his greeting, I ask Osiris how genies are created. He answers me by saying it depends, then he reveals that Liponie is the first of all the jinn.

"Oh, Liponie, I'm going to pin a little medal on you. Here, Number 1."

Liponie chuckles and titles himself Liponie the first.

"Liponie, I know you can do everything that is going to come up, so this is not a question of me doubting your abilities in any way. I want to uplift the genies."

"What do you mean by this?"

"I have a feeling that they could be involved in our project and that this would be a gift for them and for us. I might be wrong, but if they have a smidgeon of your creative abilities…"

Liponie wants to know what a smidgeon is and I explain it means a little bit.

"I would like to help Comahlee. I don't know if he will be a candidate for this or not because he doesn't seem to have what you have. It's not that you can give people what you have, but maybe you can inspire the genies to be involved in the creation of whatever we have to create. I'm assuming that we'll have to have places for all the beings who want to embody to exist upon."

"And you believe that I will require assistance?"

"No, I'm not saying you're not up to it. I have a picture of genies wandering through the universes…"

Here, Osiris interrupts to tell me that most of them are owned by someone, usually by the person who created them. I point out that Liponie managed to become free. Osiris explains that this was because the one who created him died.

"I don't like the idea of anybody being owned. That's slavery. Mr. Lincoln went through this with the slaves in the South. There was a war over it to free the people who had been slaves, and while I don't want to have a war, slavery is not part of the evolutionary plan."

Addressing Mr. Lincoln, I ask him to be a consultant on this issue. He points out that people who are in a position to free others are often held accountable for stirring the pot if they do so. I agree that's a valid point and ask anyone else who has had experience with this kind of issue to please assist. Liponie asks if I want the council to get involved in emancipating his brothers and sister. I agree that's what I'm planning.

"I have one sister. She was created by a feminine; it was quite comical."

"Are people still creating genies?"

Liponie says he doesn't think there has been a new one in millions of years. I ask Osiris if he knows how many genies there are; he doesn't. I inform the council that I'm leaving this issue with them, because, at some point, all the genies are going to be free.

Osiris mentions that the different councils would know of the genies. "Then, perhaps, we could call in the owners of these jinn and make the request for them to be allowed to emancipate if they wish. It will be interesting."

"Slavery, in any form, is something that we will release from all the universes."

Osiris says that will happen in any event and my rejoinder is that I would like to prod that along a little bit.

Before I move to a completely different subject, I ask if the people imprisoned in crystals are still being rehabilitated. Charlie answers that the council is still working with them.

"This morning I saw an open envelope. Half of it was empty but the other half had several packets of seeds in it. Let me see if I can give the information about this to you."

Liponie says they are important, but not seeds at all. "They are simply taking on the symbol of a seed so that they might resonate with your mind as something to be planted. I believe that they belong on Earth. It will be simple for us to expand this onward, do you not think, Charlie?"

"Yes, Mommy, I think this is true. If we can do this for our world, we can do this for more worlds. It is the seed of a bridge—on one side is the 4th dimension and on the other side is the 5th dimension."

"How do we plant them?"

"I think they belong circulating in the air so that the freedom can be smelled and sensed and drawn into the body and felt."

"I like the sound of that."

"Let us work with this for a moment."

Then I hear Charlie's group voice say they have prepared the evolution. They also prepared for the universes that still have some duality. "There are elements within the air that are breathed. We must integrate this into the different substances that are taken in within the different universes. For Earth, the taste of freedom will be within the air. We will be breathing the higher dimensions; I believe that we should make these seeds so that they begin to flower and guide the bridge to create from the 5th into the 6th dimension as well. When the dimension is crossed into the 5th, we can recalibrate this to influence the 6th dimension. We are complete."

With the main council:

"I don't know about you, but if you watched what happened the last time I was here, it was tremendously moving for me. As Tonas shared with me, it's an affirmation that, by golly, we're going to do it somehow. Can you give me some feedback about the reactions of people in the other universes?"

Sananda says he believes great understanding was raised through what unfolded during the celebration; however, the individuals involved in decision-making positions for the undeclared universes—deeply dual—have left our council. He assumes that the reason they left is that they are choosing to meet in council within their own universes to gain some kind of acceptance and support of the decision to join.

"But they all had a chance to see what is going to happen, right?"

"Everyone from every universe was represented. They have seen and they have left. We all believe this is good."

"What's happening in the Nordahnee Universe?"

"It is still in a bit of a conflict and yet they are speaking, so it is back and forth. It is what you would expect for something like this. Plany is held in high esteem and our team is working with everyone who wishes to hear their voices."

The next item I address is helping souls who want to embody to do so. Charlie says that one option is through individuals who become pregnant, although those numbers are shrinking. He also points out that many individuals are choosing to be just energy.

"Do you think even those beings would want to see what it's like to have a body?"

"I think we can set a council in presence. There are many who are embodied as planets and stars and we are very anxious to assist them to find their voices. We heard a few of these. I like the post office idea. Someone suggested a dating conglomerate where different stars and moons can be doing what you call 'speed dating.' We have been doing our research."

"I've never experienced anything like that, but before I became involved with this work I did try a couple of online dating programs where you can put in information about yourself. Other people can read about you to see if you might be compatible with them. I ended up with matches of guys with long beards standing in front of their Harley motorcycles—definitely not of interest to me. Does anyone have a thought about how to proceed with this monumental task?"

Sananda says they've had some discussion on this subject. The plan is to put together a program so that individuals will have the ability to see what, for example, Aton and Gaia created for themselves. "The first experience would be to create in each universe a place for these individuals to embody and we would need to show them what the embodiments could look like. Then we can put Liponie in charge of a party; what you call a 'mixer.'"

Liponie exclaims that he can do it.

"I know you can. I think it would be fun for you and Cory to do that together."

"It would be a way for her to learn a little bit about these things and she could show individuals what is possible. I understand there was a great deal of resistance with her mother. She loves me now; it is because of you."

I suggest that Zeezzz might enjoy having some quarters here and Liponie agrees to speak with her about what she would like. In the course of our brief conversation about accommodations, I learn that Liponie doesn't even have any! His excuse is that he's always busy somewhere. Then I learn that he's been meeting Cory in her quarters in order to, as he says, experience sexual intercourse; they got the book Gaia created.

"Liponie, couldn't you write a masterpiece of a manual on that?"

"Not ever have I experienced this. Cory and I are virgins, and we have decided we are going to make many blue babies."

"Oh, good, I love you so much, Liponie."

"My love for you is endless, my dear."

"Do we have any idea what kind of places we need to create for people to embody upon?"

Tonas says he suggested something like the meeting places we had during World War I and II where individuals would come and dance. "Liponie did not like this idea because he said many of these individuals would be learning their legs. He is using Inishimora as the example; he wants the beings that embody to have sensory experiences."

Osiris asks me if there is a special celebration that is upcoming and I mention Valentine's Day. He says the children—the Swizzlers—are already making valentines. His suggestion is that we have a special lover's dance in order to give the planets, suns and stars a chance to connect; our universe could become the image for all others to model!

I love the idea of a dance like this! With my approval, Osiris agrees to work with the council on it.

"I had a thought the other day about a certain anniversary that's coming up. I wondered if any of the non-dual planets have restaurants. Are there restaurants on Lyra?"

Tonas says he doesn't know of any, but there probably will be some before this is over if Liponie has anything to do with it. I offer an explanation of how students on Earth can sometimes move into their communities to experience plying their skills, under supervision, of course. My idea is that if the students on Inishimora are learning how to cook or to build things, a chance to do those activities outside of the academy could enhance their studies.

Tonas says he loves the idea and they could have counselors to assist. I think dining in a restaurant on Lyra would be an extraordinarily delicious experience.

"I want to know about the Native American people who are in my genetic lineage. I know that on my mother's side there is Kickapoo and on my father's side there is Shawnee and Chickasaw. Sananda, do you have any of that kind of information?"

Sananda answers that those genetics are present within me and they are the primary ones I have.

"Who was the Native American woman many generations back on my father's side?"

"Ah, Coocoosha, which I think means 'Little Bird.' She was Shawnee and seven generations back."

"I might want to talk to her sometime."

"She is dead, and so it will be a simple matter for you to speak with her."

You'd never hear advice like that given anywhere on Earth—at least not legitimately. Here it's easy, as long as I take a translator with me into the Fifth Realm.

I start to leave but Charlie reminds me we haven't sent out the seeds. We do the transmission very quickly and I advise everyone to take a nice deep breath.

With my genetics team and Gaia:

I ask if there's anything to do with my energy channels because I heard something about the left channel opening soon. Aton explains that my orbs are opening up my energy channels and they will continue to evolve until I am in the 8th dimension.

"I also saw a very small door that I've not seen before in my head. (I know that sounds odd, but odd seems to be the rule rather than the exception for my internal experiences.) Is that another level of awareness?"

"It is more than that. It is an opening to the gates of what can be considered infinite awareness."

Of course, I want to know if there's anything to do, but Aton says to just watch it happen. This is part of my advancement, which, he says, is only in the chrysalis stage.

I mention to Gaia that a lot of my orchids are dying. I think they have some kind of rot, but I don't want to use chemicals on them. She says they are trying very hard to assist me and suggests that they could release their responsibility to me.

"I don't want them to die for me. Why are they doing that?"

"They wish to be a part of assisting you. They are a part of me, after all, just as you."

"So many of the little ones have died and I'm sad to see them go."

"My dear, enjoy these and enjoy their life. Know that they are not dying; they are simply experiencing their life. You are holding the reins very tightly with your need for them to be a certain way. They are trying very diligently to offer you a conclusion to this. That is, they are offering you what you are in the greatest fear of."

"I'm afraid of them dying, so they die?"

Gaia agrees that my orchids are trying to give me what I'm giving most of my energy to. This is very unsettling news, of course. I've really got to turn my focus to seeing healthy orchids; otherwise, I'll have an empty greenhouse.

Alone with Esthra:

"Esthra, I saw a future son of mine, but I'm not going to ask you about him. I know you won't tell me."

I should use this strategy more often, because Esthra says he will tell me everything about him.

"His name is Brillian."

"And is he with Tonas and me?"

"This I will not say. Although who else could it be, my dear?"

"I don't know what I'm going to do. I have no clue about the part of me that is at the council all the time."

"It is not necessary for you to be of concern."

"Why did I get that he is a champion?"

"He is. Fold the time, and you will see it. He is a brilliant champion, and he stands beside you strong."

I ponder this for a moment because it is incredible information. Then I add that I want to have a little girl, too.

"That will not be a problem. There are a great number of little ones in your future. Why are you weeping? It is so silly for me to tell you these things to make you cry. I will say to you that Brillian is what you can consider to be a child after your heart. Naturally, he is the first of the offspring of his father."

"I can't tell any of this to Tonas."

"Yes, this would be an overture. How are you enjoying your dear association with Liponie?"

"Did you peek into the future when you told me about him?"

"I know of the future, and so, how could I not know of him. You have made him with your heart. You have created him as much so as Gogosha himself."

"He has such a big heart, Esthra."

"Ah, but he did not."

"Well, I want us to help *all* the genies."

"If you will help all of the genies, you will help them as you have Liponie. You helped him to come into his own awareness of what is possible when you put yourself and the needs of yourself in alliance with the needs of the one that you love. Liponie loves you, my dear."

"I love him very much."

"To him you are more than Joy. To him, you are the best friend he never had. Everyone wants something from Liponie; expects something from him. You expect something from him, but you do not tell him how to do it. You allow him to have his individuality and to create, and in doing so you have created him to be a person. He is not a jinn with you, he is an important part of the team."

"Yes, and he's a dear friend."

"And he knows it. Naturally, you will make him Godfather of Brillian and Brillian will love him."

This is all the future information I can handle right now. I thank Esthra for it and bid him goodbye.

CHAPTER TWO

January 19, 2015

"I've been going through my notes of things I heard in 2000 and 2001 and I'm curious about this statement, 'The Koll are people who have been embedded for a long time.'"

Sananda explains that these people live in South America and they are similar to the aboriginals.

"That fits because twice in the last two days I've heard the words, 'South America!' I also heard someone there say, 'We're ready to go.' What does embedded mean?"

"They were put in the jungle in such a way that no one knows they are there. I believe they wish to be extracted. By the way, their name is Kolah, not Koll. Let me find out what council is overseeing them; if they were put in that spot, then someone is watching them. As soon as the 4th dimension is gone, their job is complete. They are doing something very unique; they are living in two separate realities. They're living on their world and they are also living here. They've been here for over 100,000 years and they don't die. I suggest that you speak with the council because they could get trapped in the 4th dimension when it leaves."

"November 19, 2001, I saw a huge dragon facing me and holding a crystal ball in its claws. Then it lifted its head straight up to the sky, breathed out fire, threw the crystal ball, breathed fire all around again and flew off. It was a very dramatic scene but I have no idea what it meant."

"The dragon is one of the ones you know. The crystal ball represented everything that is linked to the old reality of 4D; throwing it was similar to a ribbon cutting ceremony. This was a female dragon named Migda."

"That's Joyous's mother!"

"You saw the ceremony, but I think you should still suggest this to them. This signifies that they are also free of the past and the old story because 4D was linked to 3D. This will be a big dragon celebration."

It's interesting that just when I think my old notes aren't relevant anymore—due to all the rewriting I've done for my life—I'm drawn to look at them again and discover work to do *now*. I love the synchronicity of happenings like that.

"May 26, 2002, I heard someone speaking, but I could only remember the last sentence which was, 'Laughing on the flames of good and bad.'"

Sananda explains that this was instruction from Archangel Chamuel, who has been one of my biggest teachers. "The complete teaching was, 'The journey of life is a journey with experiences that can be judged as good and even less than good. The path to fulfilling the journey in grace is to laugh and to remember joyfulness even when the flames are painfully treating you to the experiences of change. Remember that, in the end, all will be viewed as laughing on the flames of good and bad.'"

Even though, at the time, I couldn't remember all the words Chamuel told me, I remembered feeling very good after his teaching. Laughing on the flames of good and bad sounds like it could be a great title for a book; maybe I'll write it someday.

With Osiris, Tonas, Charlie, Isis, Gaia and Aton:

Tonas says they have been waiting patiently. I advise them to be ready because I believe in a matter of days all the universes will be part of our council. Tonas is excited that we will have the full quorum, but right now I have another situation to address.

I inform the group that two nights ago I heard, "'You are choosing to find the one holding the final piece that will bring peace to the Fantrah Universe.' Last night I heard a woman named Sharinah say hello to me. I believe she is the final piece, but I'm also sure she is in danger from someone named Changkolar."

Charlie knows of this man and says his full name is Changkolar Kimreenah; he's someone of high stature in the Fantrah Universe and he is also difficult. That figures.

"Last night I came to you, Osiris and Tonas and asked you to help me with the bad dream I had." I relate the exact details of my dream and suggest that perhaps this actually happened to Sharinah. Even if it didn't, I know she's reaching out to me for help.

Charlie says that we will be able to communicate with her through me. He believes this is the only secure way to speak with her and that any other form of communication will cause her to be murdered.

I'm not sure how I'm going to do that kind of communication, but I will. When I mention to Charlie that I felt him trying to talk through me a couple of days ago, he explains that I'm becoming a transmitter. "This is an exciting experience for you. Aton will, of course, take full credit."

Laughing, I reply that I don't care who takes credit as long as I can do what I'm supposed to be doing. "How do we move forward with this?"

Charlie wants to know if I can allow Sharinah to speak out of my mouth. Before I can answer, he asks Osiris what to do and Osiris gives me the go ahead. I've felt people speaking through me in the past, but I've never attempted to initiate a conversation. As soon as I open to this, a torrent of words, tones, gasps and sounds I would never make during normal conversation pour out of my mouth. My lips move faster than I ever thought possible. I can feel that Sharinah is really scared.

Charlie warns us that this information must be kept only among those within this room. I answer that I don't know what I said and Charlie explains that she is in fear for her life. Osiris says that she told us that her husband is communicating with the other universes. "He and individuals in his groupings wish to create a coalition to break through the Joy Council; they are against our actions towards unity. This is important information, Tonas."

"Yes, but this is a delicate situation. If we interfere between the communications of these it will be as if we are not allowing them to make their decisions."

I emphasize that she wants help, help, help, help. "Help her!"

Osiris says that if we remove her from her position with Changkolar all could be lost. "She is the pinnacle and the one who can bring us information. We must find out which universes are involved in this coalition. If any of them are part of the Joy Council we must know this."

Her voice comes from me again. Once she gets started she doesn't want to stop and these words sound even more emphatic than her first transmission.

"It is as if they have used the Nordahnee Universe as an idea. They are in collaboration with one faction in Nordahnee. She tells us also with the Keylonas Universe, Mystos and the Hellipicore Universe."

It's interesting that none of the words that came through me sounded anything like those names. Osiris says it's good to know this and that it is important to watch these individuals that have unified within Nordahnee.

"Is there some way to protect her without calling attention to her?"

Osiris feels it would be a disaster to bring the Fantrah council member, someone named Bizzarah, into the loop.

Sharinah speaks briefly through me. I don't know how she's managing it, but she must be listening to our conversation.

Osiris suggests that we secretly remove Sharinah from her position and bring her to our sanctuary. She speaks very rapidly again. Osiris advises her to be of no concern, saying, "Liponie can create an exact replica of yourself. We will find someone who is willing to go 'under the covers' on this and carry the embodiment of you into position. I believe Liponie can assist us on this. Liponie, help me."

I have never heard or even imagined that Osiris would ask anyone for help.

Liponie's answer is, "I can create that any of us looks like Sharinah, and it will be easy for me to come in as a rain cloud, rain upon her, shrink her into a little particle of water, carry her off and then rain the replica into position."

Normally, I would be agog at this description of his abilities, but I'm too wrapped up in how to help this woman to comment. I remind the group that Sharinah's substitute will also need to be able to act like her. Liponie agrees that is important and asks Sharinah, through me, if we could extract a little bit of her genetic material as well as her story from her. He adds that it will be easy for him to replicate her and he believes that he is the only one who can do it.

"But then we'd have two of her, wouldn't we?"

"No, one will be me. I will take on the vision of her; I am a quick study."

"Oh, OK, but Liponie, I don't think I could make it if something happened to you. You must be very careful."

"Hmm, I think you misjudge how strategic I can be, my dear. It will be very simple. I will not rain myself down upon her; instead, we will confiscate her."

Liponie asks her if she wishes to receive sanctuary and immediately she answers an affirmative through me. He assures her that he will watch after her little offspring as well. Then he states that perhaps we can mop this up quickly with him in her position. He asks her how often she is with Changkolar. From her reply, Liponie says that Changkolar keeps her with him every moment; that is why she can be so helpful. "The only thing is that I must make a boundary. I must keep him from being amorous with me for I have pledged myself to Cory."

Immediately, she speaks through me and Liponie says, "Ah, this is the answer. He has a harem." More words come from her via me. Liponie says he can make himself less attractive so Changkolar would turn to someone in his harem. He adds that Sharinah said she is required to be with him even when he is with another woman. When she comments about this her tone is one of disapproval, and something like the word "bleck" comes out of my mouth.

I say that I think she's had enough of this guy.

Liponie agrees with me. He adds that Changkolar keeps her with him always because he wishes to keep his genetic strain pure. He explains that this won't matter because he's going to create great flatulence for himself which will be very unattractive to Changkolar. I find myself laughing as Sharinah gabbles something that must be approval.

"Liponie, make sure she has told you everything you need to know so that you can do this safely."

"The moment I have Sharinah in presence she must give me what you would call a 'supreme upload.'"

"Can she do that through me?"

"It is possible. Sharinah, let us have the opportunity now; please make the transmission."

"OK, I'm just going to open up to her."

Although I can't feel that I'm doing anything in particular that is different, Liponie tells me this is working. He laughs and then says, "I have all that I need. Now, of course, this is where my jinn comes in, for I will be making an immediate exchange. One moment she will be in presence, and the next moment she will be me. We will use this in the toilet; he does not follow her in there." Sharinah comments with what sounds like agreement.

There's about ten seconds of silence and then I hear a woman's voice say, "Oh, thank you. There is nowhere in the world of my life that I would be able to leave, to hide or to be, and I know that I am safe here."

I greet her with something that sounds like what she's been speaking through me. Tonas offers to take her to my quarters to help her settle in and asks Sananda for something in SVH that would cloak her energy from the very beginning.

Sananda replies that he will assist her and offers to escort her to my quarters. He asks permission to use my clothing and I readily agree. He suggests we should call her by a new name; then asks me for my recommendation.

When I ask her what name she would like, she says she is not accustomed to thinking for herself and it was a very big endeavor for her to break through to me.

I suggest Helena. That's a combination of Helen of Troy's name and my middle name, Elaine.

She repeats it and says, "I *love* this name! I am Helena. I will keep this name forever. How will you keep me safe?"

"We are resolving the wars in the universes and then we or you can do something about this man who has been treating you like a slave."

"I belong to him."

"No, you belong to yourself."

"I like these new teachings."

"No one owns anybody, Helena. This is the new way to be."

Sananda asks her to come with him and adds that they will discuss some courses she might take for personal empowerment. I'm grateful we were able to rescue this woman, but celebrating is out of the question until Liponie is back.

My next suggestion is that we need to help the Kolah, and that they told me they are ready to go. Tonas wants to know if they are ready to go in this moment. I say I don't know, but I do know they don't want to be trapped in the 4th dimension. Tonas explains that they were also connected to the 3rd dimension and that it was difficult for them when that dimension left us. Charlie adds that if they are still on Earth when the 4th dimension leaves, they would be split between themselves and would not have the opportunity to ascend.

Tonas says that if they had the full measure of themselves on Earth, he believes they could pull themselves out of being "wired" into Earth. He could then transport them to their world, Telerow.

Charlie confirms that they are in the jungles of South American and adds that Tonas is correct. "We have done the maths. I like this expression; it is funny. It is imperative that the part of themselves on their star be integrated into the part of themselves on Earth. From that position it will be easier for them to step away. Wiring them into Earth was the only means for them to be able to coexist with humans and to be a part of Earth in its transition."

Charlie tells me he is communicating with the emissary from Telerow, and adds that the "energies must be brought through on the threads that connect to everything. This will take us a little time, Mommy. This must be very well timed." Five seconds later he says they are ready. I'm always fascinated by how quickly everyone can complete an action here.

Charlie adds that our transmission from the Joy Arrows to these few hundred individuals must be flawless. "They are in agreement with this. Once they are complete, it will be for Tonas to arrange transportation."

Tonas says that, instead of Inishimora, he will use a smaller, cloaked ship. Charlie adds that there are beings watching them who wish to trap them in the 4th dimension. Their pick up must be within seconds of when both parts of them are integrated here.

I am once again amazed at the situations that keep coming up in this work. I never expected to experience on the job training for covert operations!

Tonas suggests that all of this be made invisible, and offers to use ships from the fleet as a distraction. "We could wave our ships a little bit to those in watchfulness. Here we are! Come and get us. We can make it look like we mean business. I know exactly where several of the nests are, and this is where we will send the ships."

"Nests?"

"There are quite large complexes under the ground that can be as big as cities."

I realize that Tonas is talking about the "you-know-who's." I finally give up my reluctance to ask him their true name and learn they call their species Chu.

"They are actually beneath some of the major cities. Are you familiar with Denver? We shall put a ship there and over Las Vegas, one over New York and Frankfurt. Give me a few minutes to make my arrangements. We will ask for only those around the council table to be present. Please think of some kind of distraction to bring all of the others to another place. Charlie, what do you have?"

"I can take them on my train."

Tonas reminds him there isn't room for everyone. I suggest that we bring Migda to the council so that I can speak with her about the vision of her I had fourteen years ago. Tonas says he needs at least five minutes and suggests that we have Woonfred give an overview of the dragon population for all to watch before Migda comes. "Perhaps you can ask those around the council table to remain and ask all others to find their way to the great hall."

Charlie adds that having an understanding of what will happen with the dragons will help them with an understanding of the species of their worlds as they are elevating. I hadn't thought about the species that would be returning to the other worlds; that would be interesting to find out. Then I remind myself that I don't even know all the species that will return to *our* world.

With the full council, I ask the core group to remain while I direct everyone else to move to the great hall along with Woonfred who will be giving them a dragon history lesson. Charlie says he has the transmission ready but we need to wait for the signal from Tonas.

Now seems like a good time to ask Mr. Lincoln to share his thoughts about the work we've been doing.

"I view the full measure of what is accomplished from this council. It is like a star of liberation. In fact, if I was still president, I would add that star to the flag. It is, indeed, a time when the world is reminded of what is possible when everyone is in the full awareness of their value. It does not matter their color or species, looking upon all of you here, it is now brought to my attention that it is not all about humanity. It is about the hearts of each of us. We, together, and in our own universes and worlds throughout are as if one beat of a heart after another, together beating to create the full life experience of that one that we *all* are a part of. What we are doing here is creating the greatest experience ever known, for there is no other culmative in the full measure of the everything. This is the very first time that every heart and every mind will be on the same focus. It takes the one tribe vision and expands it beyond anything ever known."

"You lived in a difficult time and we have our own challenges in this time. I'm going to be appreciative of your expertise with letting people know that they are free. Everyone is free, even if they think they are not and no matter their circumstances. That was one thing that one of the writers who survived the concentration camps understood. In the most severe conditions of imprisonment and starvation this man knew he was free and he survived that ordeal."

"Freedom is in the heart."

I reply, "It is in the heart and then the mind accepts that."

"Another item on my agenda is assisting the genies. I didn't know until recently that the majority of them are owned. Osiris, were you able to find out how many genies there are?"

He doesn't know the exact number but there are many. All were created to be of service. I say that I don't understand why, if a person had the ability to create a genie, they would even need one.

"Initially, they were created as a toy for children. A babysitter bred and created to be of service, never, ever thinking of themselves. Liponie has been free to experience and we have been the beneficiary of this. We have been able to experience, along with him, the joy of his personal expansion. And now to have him experience the love of a partner is quite an innovation."

"Is Comahlee owned?"

"Comahlee is free. They become free when they are cast aside."

This is just sounding worse and worse. The idea of anyone being considered a toy and then cast aside is deeply repugnant to me. I ask Osiris if he has any idea of the number of genies who are free. He says he doesn't but he will find out. He also informs me that since they were bred to be of service, they are often, as soon as they become free, captured and used by beings of duality. Although they were primarily created on non-dual worlds, they have a desire to explore, and if they choose to explore a world of duality, that's when they are captured.

Osiris tells me another distressing fact. "Many times these dear jinn have been used beyond any sensibility, for when they are used in a dual world it is not in friendship."

"I want to have some kind of a place for the genies who are free. Could there be an expansion of Inishimora?"

I hear Tonas whisper that he is back and I ask everyone to hold that thought.

Charlie says we are ready and asks permission to telepathically transmit what we are going to do to those around the table. I agree, then check with Tonas to see if he's ready to act as soon as the transmission goes out. He tells me the distraction has already begun. Charlie hands me the transmission in a sphere and I send it out in record time, finishing with, "Go!"

Tonas says it is done, and I immediately go for a high five, hopefully, with someone. Tonas adds that Charlie and his gang are geniuses because they left behind holograms of the individuals. Then Charlie suggests we send out a false transmission that hints it would be valuable to leave the Kolah on the 4th dimension because important information could be extracted from them energetically. He reminds me that the Kolah left here are holographic and adds that they will turn into "popsicles" (melt).

Tonas announces that the Kolah are now home on Telerow in their full measure of presence and they send their greetings and their gratitude. I ask Tonas to thank them for their many years of their service, and that we would be open to their suggestions if they have any ideas that might assist us. He tells me that although they are emancipated from their service, they are willing to put this into their thought. "If there is anything they understand, it is Earth."

Tonas says we are through with the intrigue. I'm not going to correct him, but we are only through with a small bit of intrigue. My blue friend is impersonating, or rather, being, a woman in another universe and I'm worried about him. Rather than dwell on that right now, I ask if there is a way for me to talk with Migda. Gaia says we can bring her here through a transmission of heart from her dimension.

Midga's voice sounds as big as Woonfred's when she says, "Greetings to you and gratitude to you!"

"Greetings, Migda! I'm going to tell you about a vision I saw of you several years ago, but I want Woonfred to hear this too."

Woonfred says he is back, but he also says that he can sense something was done in his absence. Then he tells me he received a transmission so I don't need to explain. I go on to relate the dragon vision I told Sananda about earlier in this session. Migda agrees the dragons will celebrate when the 4th dimension is no more.

"Though our reality does not hold the measure of that story any longer, it is in the history of our previous reality. This will be a great moment and thank you for the vision that I will now be in readiness to bring forth."

"The other big news is that someday I'm going to write a book for children about dragons. I want to ask you if dragons like to sit on buildings so that they can see what people are doing."

Woonfred says that is what they prefer. "We have visions of excitement of what it would be like to taste one."

"Oh, I can't put that in a children's book!"

"I was telling you the truth. It was, after all, the 3rd dimension."

"But I want to talk about dragons as they are now; for example, did Migda sit on her egg to keep it warm or is anything like that necessary?"

I know the picture of a dragon sitting on an egg is ridiculous, but I want to make sure my facts are correct.

I hear him laugh and then he asks, "Do you think that she, at the size she is, would be able to sit upon an egg?"

"No, but do you have to keep it warm?"

"We are cold-blooded."

"So all you have to do is watch it?"

"We do not watch it always; we put the egg in a safe place. None would *dream* of eating a dragon egg."

"Do you have to eat anything in particular to be able to breathe fire?"

"Human beings… I am joking. We have glands that create an incendiary that allows us to breathe fire. We are of magic!"

"Do dragons have different color eyes?"

"Golden eyes are the most common. There are those with green, brown and black eyes. There is, very seldom, a color of blue. In your story you might wish to include an exciting adventure of the little boy with his dragon. The dragon is constantly sending fire out of its nose and out of its mouth, so the little boy gives him ice cream cones to keep the fire in his mouth. I only mention this because I had a dream about that awhile back. I was the little dragon and the little boy who was my friend gave me ice cream. I could not make fire for a long time after the ice cream."

"That is cute; I haven't figured out exactly what I'm going to say, but thank you for the idea."

"It is quite believable."

"Yes, it is."

"Tonas, I'm wondering if we can find out all the genies who are free and either expand Inishimora or have another ship where they can be tutored. I would like for them to be a part of creating the places where the stars and planets will be meeting. I want them to be having fun, rather than being used as servants or toys."

"I think it is a wonderful endeavor. Ultimately, they will all wish to be empowered just as our dear Liponie."

"The other thing is that if we're going to have a restaurant on a planet, it might be nice to start with something simple like a soda fountain. I figured out the other day that food has never been a big deal for people who live on non-dual planets because they have never had to have it to survive."

"Absolutely."

"Those of us who need it to stay alive have developed many eclectic tastes for different types of food. I think it will be fun for those people who have just been thinking of food as an occasional part of a special ceremony, to have the chance to become 'foodies.' Let's have a little pastry shop and an ice cream parlor—something that the Inishimora students would be able to do since they probably haven't been preparing five-course meals.

"My dear, you are always directly on track with these ideas. Everyone who has experienced this enjoys it very much."

"I want to thank all of you for your wonderful work today. Charlie, my regards to you and the team; we chalked up two more victories."

Privately with Tonas:

I'm sure he won't tell me anything he's seen of our future and I *can't* say anything about the person I recently saw in my future. Even so, I feel like I have to say *something* or I'll burst. He asks how he can help me.

I nonchalantly comment that I'm seeing more and more things in the future.

"Are they bringing you happiness?"

"They are very startling. Have you been peeking in the future?"

"A little bit, but not recently."

Rather than continuing a conversation about the future, Tonas points out that nobody has noticed Liponie's absence yet and suggests we don't bring it up. I agree to this plan, but remark that I hope he will be safe. Tonas reminds me that Liponie is magnificent.

Relieved that I didn't feel compelled to divulge any details about the future, I bid Tonas goodbye.

CHAPTER THREE

January 20, 2015

At the Joy Council, Tonas says he did not expect me in "this form." When I ask him what I'm wearing, he only tells me I am beautiful as always. At least I don't think I'm wearing my pajamas.

I ask to have the core group join us. When they are in presence, I say that last night I saw a table full of sparkly jewels, and I know it is some kind of solution.

"Sananda here, my dear, I wonder if these jewels are encoded with some kind of game plan. Perhaps Liponie has these and he is transmitting through them."

As soon as Sananda mentions this possibility, I know that Liponie put something for me in the jewels, and I ask the Creator to help me show my friends all the details of the message.

Sananda says the conspirators have a detailed plan to disrupt everything we are doing, and, even worse, it would work. "Liponie is an excellent interloper. He is most assuredly on the theme. There are five, and perhaps six, people who are involved in this conspiracy. Liponie thinks there is one who hasn't revealed himself yet. It is possible that those of duality are playing with both shoes."

When I ask him what that means, he explains they are waiting to see who will offer them the most to gain. He adds that we are going to reassess the universes that have joined our council, especially those who came on in the beginning, and assures me that the emissaries from those universes are tried and true.

I ask how we can let Liponie know I got his message. Sananda says he would know I have given them the information. I want to know how Liponie would know something like that.

Sananda's excellent answer is, "Because he is Liponie, my dear. Do you not think that he would put some little message in to himself that the message has been accessed? He is quite a genius."

I realize that's exactly what he would do and I'm able to release some of my concern about our communication capabilities. I certainly don't feel prepared for this kind of situation. Maybe I should have watched more spy movies or read more mystery novels. Then I realize that very little, if any, of that kind of information would help me in the types of situations I'm liable to encounter here.

"Bizzarah Nahcoomeuh (emissary for the Fantrah Universe where Changkolar lives) is not a part of this conspiracy. If he were to join the council, there would be more individuals focused on the positive. This could tip the access. We must strategize; Charlie and the council can sift through the details of the plan Liponie sent us."

"Hermeenah Veelowsh spoke through me the other night and said that she was pledging to the council. Has that happened yet?"

"You received the request and you accepted it. Ah, I apologize; you were not here as you are now."

"Right, so I wasn't sure if that was a future event or not."

Sananda agrees that this is curious and I tell him I have to be careful about what I say to the full council in case I'm talking about something that hasn't happened yet. He goes on to reassure me that we can now easily find strategies to discount and limit the successes of the conspirators. When I ask what they were planning, he tells me they were going to use espionage to take over the council members in universes that are of duality.

"I want to make sure there is a representative from all of the indigenous tribes that we can speak with at the council. If any of these tribes want to help us or if they want to leave Earth, we need to know. This would include the Reindeer people and the Dogon. I'm sure there are many others I don't know about. Charlie, can you give us any intel on this?"

"There are several more, of course. We will make an assessment. I believe it is important to understand how they were integrated into their positions."

"If they can assist us or we can assist them, we want to know that."

Osiris now tells me that they are concerned about Helena; it seems she has fallen into a very deep depression. I ask if she is worried about her children. He says that might be part of it, but he believes she has never had any kind of freedom. Sananda adds that she cannot even make a decision about what clothes to wear.

I decide to speak with her and ask Tonas and Sananda to take me to her. We enter my room quietly and Sananda says, "Helena, we do not wish to bother you, but Joy wishes to welcome you personally."

"I do, and I want to thank you for the very brave action that you took. They are telling me that you are feeling very discouraged at this time and I want to reassure you about a few things. First of all, your children are safe and secondly, you are a wonderful woman. Probably no one has ever told you that and maybe you've never had a chance to even have a thought of your own. Now is the time, where, if you will let us assist you, you can move into a feeling of joy and power that is your true nature. Although I've not been to the extremes of being controlled as you have, I have been in situations where I was afraid to dream and hope and I had no plans for the future at all. People that I loved and trusted helped me, and I want to tell you that we are those people for you."

"I do not know how to be. I was given to Changkolar at the age of six suns."

"You've never had to think about doing anything other than what you were told. Is that correct?"

"Indeed, it was important to create no imbalance. It was my position to make all in happiness."

"The good news is that you don't have to do that anymore and never will have to again."

"But I don't know how to do anything else."

"I know, but the exciting thing is that now you can learn other things. Sananda will help and the part of me that stays here will help you also." We go on to discuss other people who might help Helena. Sananda suggests Cory since she is also learning how to create a new identity.

Helena voices a despondent sounding "yes" and adds that she is not worried about her children since they are like Changkolar. I hear her sob and exclaim, "I am alone!"

"No, you have ninety-four million people here ready to help you."

Tonas suggests that she might walk with me in my garden. He adds that Cory is learning how to make many Earth foods including

French toast and French fries and that perhaps Helena could put on an apron and do those things with her.

Helena says she does not think that is allowed. She has never been "allowed to be of any action that would appear to be of lesser stature."

"Wait a minute. Take a look at where you are. There is no one here named Changkolar and he will *never* be here if I have any say in that."

"Thank the gods."

"This is a new place and I think that has thrown you off of your stride. My request is, this not an order, but I'm asking you to assist me by learning some of these new things and finding something that you enjoy. Will you help me that way?"

"Of course, I am so grateful to you I will do anything for you."

"The name of this council is the Joy Council and I know that all of us hope you can find something that *you* enjoy."

Tonas is inspired to suggest that she spends an afternoon with Charlie. "Dear Helena, we have little children here that are genius and they have the purest of hearts. I do not believe that you know what fun is. Do you know what fun is?"

I am chuckling because no one could resist Charlie's irrepressible enthusiasm and joy in experiencing everything.

"I do not." She answers.

I explain that any experience that makes you laugh is fun, and if she rides on Charlie's train she might have fun. She says she will do this for me, and while that was not the enthusiastic reply I was hoping for, I realize it's a beginning. I describe Charlie's appearance as striking—he's very thin, orange-colored and has green hair. She says she has seen him.

"He's existed since the beginning of creation, but he's like a child because he never had a body before."

"Ah, that is just like me. I've never had a life before."

"He wants to do everything and try everything he can possibly try. Helena, can we have him join us?"

"Of course."

Immediately, I hear, "Hello, Mommy!"

I always feel happy when I hear his little boy voice and I return his greeting. After I introduce him to Helena, he says he saw her yesterday.

I explain that she is having a little trouble getting used to being free, and she doesn't know what to do or how to be. I add that I thought he might want to talk with her, show her around the council, and maybe even give her a ride on the train.

Charlie begins to reel off suggestions: riding bicycles, playing orchestra instruments or swimming in our water park. He wants to know if Helena has a swim costume. Before she can get completely overwhelmed, I ask Charlie to remember that everything is new for her and he shouldn't try to do everything in one day. I suggest that he just guide her in finding one or two things she would like to try. He agrees to this plan, and I assure Helena that Charlie is not only wonderful, he is trustworthy.

Helena now speaks to say that she is receiving something in her mind from the blue man. "He says he has some things to tell you and that you will understand."

"What is it?"

"He says that he is giving Changkolar everything that he wants. What does this mean?"

"He did that with his original owner who ended up dying; obviously, he overdid some of his interests. I know Liponie won't kill him outright, but I believe Changkolar will take his desires to an extreme. That will be his undoing. Tell Liponie I love him, to be careful and that I got his message in the jewels."

"He knows that you received the message, and he wishes you to know that this man has a great appetite for things that he wishes." Helena adds that she thinks something very big is playing out but she doesn't understand what it is.

Rather than do any explaining, I ask her to enjoy her time with Charlie and say that I'll speak with her again soon. Before I leave, she asks me what a swimming costume is. I explain what it is, and that, if she wishes, Charlie could teach her how to swim.

"Today is a day to have fun, Helena, and Charlie will be an expert in showing you how to do that."

She says, "I am so happy to have you, Charlie. I am alone."

"Not anymore!"

"Thank you, Joy."

"You're welcome."

CHAPTER FOUR

January 21, 2015

I ask Sananda to join me in the SBT, because Liponie sent me some information last night. After I open up and transmit the messages I received, he explains that Liponie has become very reluctant to use Helena as an intermediary unless it's an emergency. "Using her to communicate might compromise him since he's discovered that their technology is far superior to what he initially understood. He also suggests that the council keeps you in a conscious understanding of what the information is that he brings through because of the way your mind works. When they receive, they need to also explain some of the high points to you."

"Last night I recorded myself humming a little tune. It's only three seconds; do you think it might be a message?"

"A message could easily be carried in music."

"I'll play it for the council. I also heard a woman's voice say the name, 'Coohkwalah.'"

"That was Liponie telling you that individual is one of the conspirators on the council in the Lowmeesha Universe. He gave you lists of people involved and said he would give you more later."

"There's something about the planet Zhollah."

"Council member Graneesha is aware that there is something strange going on and she wants to know what to do. Another of their council members, Leneras, told her he was approached by a conspirator and she transmitted that to you.

At the Joy Council, Tonas says they were not expecting me. I explain that there's lots going on and ask the core group to join us. Once they are in presence, I tell them about Graneesha, Leneras, and the conspirator named Coohkwalah. I let them know that Liponie has given me information and then I play the three seconds of humming I recorded last night. I'm not too hopeful that there is any information in it, but why would I record such a thing if there wasn't?

Tonas says they were able to receive it and it is a transmission.

"What was it?"

"We are extrapolating. Hmm, it is the dates of what you would consider an incursion."

"I tried to communicate with Liponie last night and since I could feel him block it, I set up an SVH protocol for myself to keep me from trying to contact him." Then I tell the group I'm opening up for a transmission from Liponie. After a few moments, I hear Sananda say, "What we are now aware of is that several council members from nearly every dual world that is a member of our council have been approached. None of the higher positions in the councils have been approached. Liponie is telling us that these individuals are moving very swiftly."

At this moment, I hear a loud noise that I can find no source for. Feeling spooked, I report this to Sananda and he immediately suggests I add more security measures. I move into the SBT since that is the safest place my energy body can be. Two measures I implement are: (1) a reflection that my "feet" have always been only in the 25th dimension and that I am interacting with the lower dimensions from there, and (2) any attempts to interact with me or anything/anyone that is a part of my reality in a negative way will always be and have been shifted into a hologram.

After completing that work, I realize that we need to do something like it to support every member in the Joy Councils. I move back to the Joy Council, show them the work I did for myself and ask Charlie to create something similar for council members. He says they are preparing a program for everyone who is embodied. "This will be something we can offer all councils; we will put this in the past as part of our initial offering."

When I ask Tonas if there's anything additional the Ashtar Command can do, he says their hands are tethered for assisting the other council members since they have the right to interact in such a way.

"I want my friends and family and everyone who assists us in any way to be protected. I'm still kind of worried about that."

"We are working diligently to enhance, my dear. This was unpredicted."

"The actions that I would like to take to address this situation are of duality—find these guys and lock them up—and not possible, but don't you think we need to do something rather than just standing by and waiting for them to do their worst?"

"I believe it is important for you to speak with the head of each universe's council. We can call a special private meeting where it will be with our core group. These individuals will not need to know about Helena or Liponie's work."

"If I say something I shouldn't say, someone tell me and I'll roll back and mute it."

We draw the leaders of each council in the universes that are part of our affiliation into a separate room where I explain to them that we have a situation going on that it is headed by a group of conspirators in the Fantrah Universe. "There are many people in that universe who are very divine, but there are also some people who are enjoying experiencing some of the heavier parts of duality. Their intent is to infiltrate and overthrow the Joy Councils. We know that you are all on the up and up, but you have people in your groups who have been approached." I mention the names that were told to me. Then I offer those before me protection that starts even before the Joy Council began and ask Charlie to explain it for them.

"It is a bubble of protection for yourself and for each of your council members which begins even before your first breath. This gives all of you the opportunity to enhance your life experience and be free of this infiltration into your ranks. There could be, perhaps, damage or persuasions to council members to bring them into the conspirators' ranks. Each of your councils is a target except for those of you of the non-dual worlds.

Our idea is to create a field of non-duality for each of the council members to exist within; this will elevate your understanding of what is truth. It is offered to each member of your council. We suggest that those who refuse such an offer will be the ones asked to leave the council.

To accept, there must be some action taken. Perhaps those who accept shall wear a special Badge of Honor that will support their sovereignty and includes this protection. If an individual has been compromised and they choose to be a party to this protection, it will invalidate that they were compromised. Your council will be as if a non-dual. This has been prepared and is offered by Sananda. Each of you may accept this if you wish. Each of you will be required to create a badge for each of your council members. This badge states that they are of pure intention and choosing to be a part of the elevation and transformation; the badge is shaped like the Joy Arrow."

Sananda greets them and says this is just a "wrinkle," not a "great wave of desperation." He adds, "This experience is a part of the journey to elevation. Your alliance with this council offers you an opportunity to step into the stream of a vision for all of what is to come." He directs them to "view the screen" and when they have an affirmative he gives them the badge to place on their clothing. He offers one to Charlie and me. Then he gives them badges for all the members of their councils and asks them to explain what we have told them today. He mentions some of their members may leave the council and says that is their choice. "Hold the greatest vision for the evolution of your world. We are allowing these individuals to have their experience, and yet, we are choosing not to participate in that experience. They will be playing by themselves, you see."

Laughing, I share an Earth expression that perhaps some will grasp the gist of. "We're going to take our ball and go home."

Sananda tells me none here were aware of an incursion and they are grateful to us.

Back into privacy with the core group:

"Liponie, if you need to tell us anything additional, let it flow through me… Here it is."

Tonas says we have the full plan as well as a list of those who have agreed to be a party. "Through the Badge of Honor these individuals will have to make a choice. Liponie is suggesting that they are afraid to interface with Earth itself as well as our universe. They prefer, instead, to weaken the focus. I believe it is not possible for us to transmit to Liponie at this time, and yet, I do know that he will have some awareness of the Badges of Honor very soon."

I ask if there's anything else we can do to be proactive and Tonas suggests we involve Ashtar. When I agree that's a good idea, Tonas invites him to join us and telepathically informs him of what has transpired.

Ashtar responds, "This explains the shift in the energy force I was feeling. Thank you for allowing me to be a party to this. Naturally, we can do nothing."

"That's scary for me."

Before I can continue, he says, "Oh, my goodness, I did not mean this! What I mean is they have the privilege of deciding whether they wish to be in conspiracy or not."

I explain about the noise I heard and say, "I want to feel completely safe! Things keep coming up that make me feel like I'm not quite safe."

"Indeed, you can believe me when I say that from what I have seen of this offering, you are held in great sovereignty. Believe me, that you have even greater sovereignty than any human of Earth."

"I don't want any stumbling blocks to interfere with the work we are doing."

"I believe that what you have received accomplishes this. It would be good planning to have your Vigilance Council watching for needed updates, though it appears what you have is very comprehensive. I cannot imagine anyone with any technology being able to burst the bubble that has been created by them."

"OK, Charlie, can you be a watchdog?"

"Of course, you are my mommy."

Tonas adds that he is ever vigilant, and it is good that everything was stopped in time. "If there is a problem for you, we will extract you. Ah, this would bring you great joy because you would immediately stomp on my foot."

This gives me a chance to laugh and lighten up, although I don't know why he thinks I would want to do something like that.

With the full council:

"We've just been doing a little bit of housecleaning. In the meantime, we've become aware that there are a bunch of indigenous tribes that are ready to 'get the heck out of Dodge.' This is an expression we use when people are ready to leave town. Whoever is working with them, can you tell us where things stand?"

Osiris says the indigenous tribes that have not been integrated into the human population are ready to be extracted at the timing that best fits their purpose. He adds that many of them have a desire to be an instrument to the very last moment and that will require some staging.

I want to know if any wish to leave now. Charlie answers that there are forty-four tribes who are ready to evacuate and return to their original home. "They are all over in the different places where there is rain in the forests."

"We have less and less rainforest so maybe it's just as well that they leave."

"This has been a definite problem for them. I have already formed the preparation; everything is ready for Tonas."

"The Chu might get a little suspicious if you keep wagging your ships at them, Tonas. Our expression is, 'Fool me once, shame on you. Fool me twice, shame on me.'"

"What do you suggest? What is another diversion?"

I briefly consider asking Gaia for a little earthquake, but quickly realize that's too drastic. "Gaia or Osiris, do you have a suggestion that wouldn't rock our boat?"

Osiris says there are individuals who are aware of some of the nests. His idea is to send out a notice that one of those places is to be raided. He sounds like he is relishing this plan when he tells us that even though there won't actually be a raid, the warning would cause the Chu to prepare for it. In the meantime, we could do the extraction.

Ashtar advises it would be simple to energetically set off some of their alarms rather than sending any kind of notice. I like that idea even better and we both chuckle at the idea of the consternation this trick will cause the Chu. I ask him if he knows about the high five. He answers that, of course, he is aware of the 5th dimension.

"Nope! Charlie, are you near me?"

"Yes, Mommy."

"All right, here we go. 1, 2, 3, whack!"

"I am very confused by this and yet I understand that it is, perhaps, a human ritual?"

It seems like council members forgot this gesture; obviously, not used anywhere but Earth. Since it's something I'd like to be able to use occasionally, I give a couple sentences of explanation before moving back into business.

Ashtar suggests we wait to do the high five until after we have accomplished the extraction. I ask what to do now. Sananda addresses me in a lowered voice and suggests I clear the room of those who are from dual worlds. In a polite voice, I make that request. Tonas had stepped out for a moment to prepare the diversion and I hear his voice say he is back. He adds that now these people will feel they've missed out on something and, "maybe they will feel the call to join. Ashtar is returning also and he will be taking care of the alarms."

"Should I roll back so that we didn't reveal this plan to the people who left?"

Sananda has the idea to make an automatic muting of information when we wish to cloak what is happening from the people observing. "We can explain that this is part of our important procedures. I will move to the past and have this put in place by Liponie." Immediately, he tells me that this is done and that we are choosing that that conversation was unheard. He advises me that, in the future, we must remember to ask for muting when we feel it is needed.

Charlie hands me the transmission. After we send it out, Tonas informs me that it is opportune to extract multiple tribes at once. There are holograms in place to make it seem as if they are still here. He adds, "How do you feel about us creating a vision that they are becoming extinct, for if there are no more trees for them to live beneath, how can the hologram work?" I agree that is a good idea and suggest that perhaps the tribes who are remaining need extra protection. He explains that many of these individuals are quite ruthless in their own protection.

Tonas asks Sananda about the possibility of creating holograms that would allow attempts of negative interference to seem to take place. Sananda interrupts and then apologizes for interrupting by saying, "I was running off with my excitement and wanting to slap the hands of everyone…" he pauses, and I briefly wonder if he's considering chastising some of us, but then he adds, "…in gleeful celebration. We have had success, and so if we may all 'high' and the 'five' please." I'm laughing when he asks, "May I 'five' you, my dear?"

"Yes, here goes!"

"My thought is that perhaps we can start a rumor that these individuals are becoming ill and dying off so that over the next months it will seem that they are smaller in number and that they are no longer compatible with Earth. In doing so it would perhaps cause them to be less attractive to the individuals who would ill use them."

I agree with that plan and remind them that we need to keep looking ahead in an attempt to keep our good guys safe until that is no longer necessary to do.

Ashtar says he can give me his five now. "It has been a safe extraction. They are still scrambling to figure out why their alarms are ringing. This will give them something to do. Gaia, if you will please reflect some kind of strange energy burst on the planet that could perhaps have something to do with Aton's Sun-spotting. This will give them an answer for it and they can shrug it off. We can use this in the future as well if we cover our steps now."

"How many people were there in the forty-four tribes we extracted?"

"May I answer you, my dear?"

"Who is this speaking?"

"I am your precious." (Tonas)

"You know, your voice sounds a lot like Sananda."

"He will like that very much."

"Well, he's a sweetie, too. So, how many were there?"

"There were nearly 2,709. I say nearly because there was one who was newly pregnant."

"Would any of them be interested in having a representative here, and, if not, I still would like to thank them for however many millennia they were here assisting Earth."

"None of the forty-four tribes are interested in participating. They wish to give their great thanks for the opportunity. I was trying to explain the 'high five' but they are unaware. They wish to thank us for our assistance; they are now wishing to move on with their experience of personal evolution on their world in preparation for that short span of time before the culmative."

"Let's keep our fingers on the pulse of this. I want us to be aware of tribes who wish to leave and immediately know when/if something ill-favored does start happening to any of them."

"It is, to me, an honor to assist them in this way."

"OK, that was Tonas, right?"

"Hmm, I believe I must change my voice so that you will recognize me. I will begin all of my communications with you with, 'Precious, baby heart.'"

"No, thank you. Good work today; I'll be back tomorrow. I'd like to meet with Tonas and Charlie in private for a moment."

Private meeting:

"Not, my precious baby heart?"

"No, not my precious baby heart, you silly man!"

"You are so dear to me."

"Charlie, was Helena able to keep up with you?"

"Mommy, she is like a baby, afraid to do anything. I was very gentle with her. I let her sit beside me on my train. She did not want to drive, but I kept her beside me and held her hand and she was feeling safe."

"Oh, good. Thank you, Charlie."

Charlie reports that since Helena feels very alone, Marilyn and others are taking turns staying with her. He also believes that if I spoke with her it would give her confidence, because I'm so powerful. That adjective takes me aback since I don't think of myself that way at all. I answer him by remarking that most of the time I'm just trying to find my way.

Helena joins us, I say hello and ask her to hold out her hand. After shaking it, I explain that is one way people of Earth greet each other. Her "OK" sounds very hesitant.

"Or if we really like the person we throw our arms around them and give them a big hug, like this!" And I demonstrate.

"Oh, that is frightening."

I should have realized that my exuberance would frighten her. I offer an apology and explain that we just finished some really important work. "How did you like the train ride?"

"Little Charlie, you are very sweet, but it was very frightening. You drove very fast."

"Oh, I didn't think about that. Well, what part did you see that you would like to visit?"

"Cory has suggested that we put on the aprons. I do not know what an aprons is, but I am willing to don it if it is of help to anyone."

"It is something to put on so your clothes don't get food on them when you are working in the kitchen."

"Oh, she would wish me to work?"

"Cory likes to cook, so to her it's not work, it's fun. You will just need to experiment with things to find out if you like them or not. Sometimes you may not like something the very first time you try it, and that's OK if you really hate it. But if you think you *might* like it, then I suggest you try it for a little longer, since everything is new to you. We don't want to make you do things you really don't want to do."

"Thank you."

"It's very important for you to understand that we just want you to have a chance to pick out something *you* might like. It's just that if you don't know about something, you wouldn't be able to choose it."

"Ah, I see. Cory was explaining to me that it is a cultural experience to cook. She tells me it is…fun. (This is obviously a word Helena has never spoken.) She wishes for me to make something that holds food. This Cory is very creative."

"She's experimenting with a lot of new things now; however, when she first came to the council she sat in a chair looking like a big iceberg with eyes peering out of it for a long time."

I hear Helena giggle and she says, "What are you saying? Ice?"

"She didn't have arms or legs or anything but two eyes staring at people."

"She told me she was resistant, and yet at the same time she saw the cause as good and wanted to be a part of it."

"I don't know if you're ready to know about what we are doing; maybe you are because you were so brave to contact me. We are working to assist all of the universes, all of the planets and all beings to be free."

"I have been told this. It is hard to believe."

I ask her if she would like to see what will happen in about three hundred years and explain that it will show her what all of us are working towards.

"I would indeed. There is so much of this relationship of all of you that is very unique. I have never truly experienced this. Your little child here looks nothing like you. He appears to even be of another species and he seems to have such emotion of heart. We have nothing like this, even with our children. I am witnessing this among all of you, the great esteem and kindness and pleasure of just being together. It is clearly a new experience for me."

"You are part of our family now."

"That would not mean anything on my world. It means something here though, I feel."

"Yes it does. It means one for all and all for one and we love you."

"This love, I do not know it."

"I'm just learning more of it myself. I have two grown up children on Earth that I love. But Tonas tells me that there is a love that the worlds of non-duality have that is the greatest thing ever. Your heart is fully open and you know that you are one with all that is. There is one energy through all the universes, and it is love."

She says that is a lot to take in; I admit that it's also a lot for me to grasp.

"I want to thank you for my time with you, Charlie. I believe that I am ready to isolate a little bit to heal my fears of all of you. You are so demonstrative."

"Is it all right to have someone with you in your room?"

"They are very kind to me. I think I do not wish to drink any more tea."

"It is important that you let people know what you want or don't want. Say, 'I'd like to do that more, or I don't care to do that, thank you.'"

"Ah, these things were decided for me. This will be new learning for me."

"Take your time. We don't want to force you to do anything. We just want you to try things at your own pace."

"Thank you for your patience."

"You're welcome."

After she leaves, Tonas says he doesn't understand why the women think they must have tea as they are communicating. He adds, though, that he has enjoyed it. His idea of what might help Helena the most is to show her some sweet projections of Earth cultures.

I hear Charlie's excited voice suggest, "Disney, Mommy, Disney!"

"Work with Tonas on that Charlie. Remember she's really new."

"She is a little flower, Mommy. I do not want her to wilt."

"She'll be strong one of these days. Thank you, Charlie, for your help."

Calling Osiris into presence, I ask him how the captured genies are restrained. He tells me they are not restrained, but they are owned. He adds that the only true safety for a genie, and sometimes not even then, is to be on a non-dual world.

I state that I don't want the genies that are being mistreated to have to stay in those situations. His idea is that genies that would be willing to collaborate with us could show the owned genies the possibility of emancipation.

After a little more discussion, we decide it's important to keep our focus on the current situation. Osiris suggests that when Liponie returns we can make him the "poster" genie.

"Did you find out the number of genies on dual worlds?"

"In this universe alone there are more than 2,000."

"I'll be back tomorrow."

Osiris says, "You are loved, my dear."

CHAPTER FIVE

January 22, 2015

Meeting with Tonas, Charlie, Osiris, Isis, Sananda, Ashtar, Gaia, Aton and Isis:

"I have a stair-step vision and a big picture from Liponie in my head, and I heard two musical notes last night. Here are the two things from Liponie and also the two notes. I don't remember them but maybe you can get them."

Sananda reports that Liponie feels that the point of escalation will be in four days. "We will meet it with a full block, for we are working with each of the councils now. What Liponie believes is, if all are in presence, ready and wearing their emblazoned stamp so that they are fully brought into collaboration with the light path, then we will easily know those who are not in compliance.

The Nestus Universe and the Lowmahteese Universe wish to join; Liponie has been very instrumental in this. He wants you to know that there is what he would consider to be a child's plan afoot. These are advanced individuals, and although they have great technology, they are stretched too far. They are trying to put themselves in all of the universes and they cannot touch our universe, Chailee."

I share with the group that last night I got the names of two people, Zarrah and Kolaska, who are supposedly freedom fighters but are actually working both sides of this game. Sananda agrees that is important information and wonders how many others would be working both sides. I didn't get any more information about that sort of thing, but I have a feeling that perhaps Liponie gave me more information to share. After I open up to that possibility, I find myself humming a few notes, some la, la, lah's and some musical ha, ha, ha, ha's.

Sananda asks me to open up fully and allow the information that was transmitted to me to open to each of the council. Then he chuckles and informs us that Liponie has created a shiny stone so that all who wish to become part of Changkolar's conspiracy may rub upon it to receive great powers. "They are coming from many places to rub upon this stone, for every time they do, they receive what they want, what they desire and hope for themselves. Liponie believes that if everything that they desire is brought to them, they will be carried away by it, and perhaps they will all wish to fight one another to be the guardian of the stone. At this time, Changkolar has the stone in his possession. We do not have the full story, but we do know that they are all making plans to steal it. The stone is becoming the most important thing to all of them."

Liponie is brilliant; I really think this divide and conquer plan will work. I ask the group if they got the big picture that I was supposed to keep in my head.

"It is the big picture that he wishes all of us to focus upon, including all of the councils that are wearing their badge. This vision can be transmitted through the arrow; it is the vision of unity and a happy ending to this story."

I'm more than ready for an ending to this drama, and I really want Liponie out of that situation as soon as possible.

"Liponie also revealed that he is off the hook for intimacy. He has allowed Changkolar to have ninety or more of these spaces to conquest women."

"I don't understand what you mean."

"Changkolar rubs the stone and keeps creating more and more harems; he now has ninety of them. Each of these delightful creatures that are being created for him is wearing him out. He is very sexually driven."

I leave unvoiced my thought that that seems to be a bit of an understatement.

"Aton, there's lots of happenings going on in my head. Several days ago I saw a double rainbow going from the right side of my head up to the middle."

Aton explains that this will continue until it develops itself into the full arc and adds that I will be seeing many beautiful things.

"I believe several of the things I've seen recently are in the future. I'm not complaining about this, but it is a little bit challenging since I don't know what to do about the information. Do I wait for these things to happen or is there a way to speed them up so that they are not two or three years in the future?"

Sananda offers that that is the quirk in receiving something from the future. "You might say to yourself, 'Hmm, well I can put that aside and when I notice it come along I can prepare for it.' You might also decide it is something that must be addressed so that it can be supported to be created. It is a difficult situation for you, and yet I am celebrating that you are having these experiences from the future."

"The other thing that I saw, Aton, which was really interesting, was a little white dot in my mind. I got that it was the touch of the Sun."

"Ah, let me look into you. This is very advanced. Of course you will develop this. This is something that all individuals of a non-dual world have. It is like plugging in to boost your battery. It only takes a short time for a non-dual being on Earth to deplete their energies; their abilities become sluggish. This connection is something that boosts the orbs."

"So the Sun does the boosting?"

"Yes. I did not expect this until you were fully within the 8th dimension and so there are many cuckoos for you."

"Many what?"

"Oh, no, sorry, it is the kudo."

I ask Gaia for an update on Sheliah and learn that she has decided that ninety-four babies are enough for now. Through my laughter, I manage to comment that that is a lot of babies. Wondering how Rosebud managed ninety-four birthing experiences, I ask if he was able to get used to the births.

Gaia explains that he never became accustomed to the event and that Sheliah brings a chair for him now.

When I think of Sheliah and Rosebud, I feel so tender towards them, especially Rosebud. I remember when he was brand new and him saying how much he loved it that Sheliah dressed him like a flower. I can just picture him slumping over in his chair each time Sheliah lifted a new baby from a blossoming rose. Oh, Rosebud…

"Do all the council members who are part of the Joy Council now have their badges?"

Charlie answers, "Mommy, I wish for you to know that it was most genius of Sananda for we weeded the garden of the councils; some left from almost every council that was of duality. It was an opening of the eyes for everyone."

"Now we know that everyone on the councils is legitimate."

"We believe that Liponie is working to support the shift in this. As soon as he has made his work as comprehensive as we believe he will, there will come a time when there is no thought of overtaking the universes. It will always simply be that they will want their rock to rub upon."

"I just wish he could be back now. It's like having part of yourself gone when he's not around. Everybody has a special place in my mind and in my heart, and he has a big hunk of both."

"And Cory is very worried about him. I saw her cry, Mommy."

"Liponie told me that he is as safe as a 'pea in a pocket.'"

"Oh! I do not understand this."

"You know how a pea is snuggled in its pod with the other peas?"

"Oh! It is not the urine!"

More laughter as I realize what Charlie was trying to visualize. Yuck.

It's time to inaugurate the two new universes. Tonas suggests we do the Lowmahteese Universe first. The Council Presence for that universe is Hermeenah Veelowsh and Chief Council Nohdahwah is from the Nestus Universe. I start to move to the Lowmahteese Universe, but Charlie tells me they don't know where Liponie put the council buildings he made for the universes who hadn't yet joined. Osiris suggests he could make a preparatory space to use until Liponie returns. I've been feeling like I can do something and tell him I'm just going to open up to the possibilities. "Hmm, I think that would be where Liponie would put something like that."

Osiris remarks that he can feel that the buildings have been positioned. Now that I'm sure they exist, I can just intend to go to wherever they are. Sananda informs me he has the badges, so I take him,

Osiris and Tonas through the gate with me to the Lowmahteese council building.

Hermeenah welcomes us and says, "It was as if by magic when, all of a sudden, we are in this big, pink, structure of crystal."

"That's because Liponie is a magician."

These two inaugurations are slightly different than the previous ones we have done. When we finish the transmissions, Sananda telepathically transmits the information about the Badges of Honor that council members will wear. I guide them to view their screens. Those who accept, automatically have the badge emblazoned onto their clothing. He adds that, "It is honored if you do not accept, but this indicates to us that your alliances are elsewhere and we release you from the council."

Hermeenah adds that she feels as if she has been reborn. "I am within that place of non-dual even now. It is a glorious feeling; it is magnificent!"

I gate our group to the Nestus Universe and follow the same procedure. The only difference is that Nohdahwah asks those to leave who were not willing to wear the badge. I ask him for a moment of privacy and then reveal that there is a deep conspiracy connection with the Fantrah Universe in his universe. When he asks what to do about it, I advise him to carry on as usual. "You and your council members are safe; the work we just implemented will assist you and we have been working to encourage the conspiracy to fold in upon itself. We think this will be a short-lived situation."

He remarks that they have been at war for a long time. I reply that it's time to quit.

"You will be enjoying all the work we're going to do in the future; thank you for joining us."

"We feel very neutral at this time; we are drunk with it."

I'm ready to gate us back and, just for fun, I ask them to hang on. I guess that was good advice, because Osiris says he had no idea traveling like this would be like a roller coaster ride. I remind him that he's been on a gate trip with me before, but he says it was never like this. This time it was like riding on a stream of light. It's so interesting to me that I don't feel a thing when I move this way. Perhaps I will when I'm able to also move my physical body this way; hopefully, I won't get—can't call it carsick—gatesick?

Last night I also became aware that the Ashtar Command quickly quelled an attack in the Ahkahnay Universe. After I offer Tonas my congratulations, he explains that the command took very forward focus and honored each of the individuals who were choosing to create havoc. I ask him for the details of what happened.

"They had intentions to vaporize the council itself. Each of these councils is under our protection, and so, unfortunately, those individuals did find themselves in what you would call battle with the Ashtar Command. It is a poor choice to do such a thing since our technology is far superior to any of these individual worlds."

"What happened to them?"

"Over four thousand were brought into a special counseling; they are no more in conflict."

"Who does the counseling?"

"We have individuals whose passion in life is to assist individuals to recognize their own true spirit. This is a simple enough exercise because they are receiving their transmissions in stasis. We are not re-formatting them; we are allowing them to learn. Sometimes it takes a long time.

The other thing you must know, my dear, is that we never stop. We may eat and revel and listen to the children when they play, but until Liponie is back with us he is being supported by our thoughts and our hearts. I have my own fingers in the game, but will not speak about this."

"I really do miss him. I imagine it has to be difficult for Cory."

"She has been very sad."

Private meeting with Tonas, Cory, Helena and Charlie:

"Cory, I want you to know that Liponie has told me he is very safe and that miracles are coming. I know it's hard to be without him. Tonas, can you bring her up to speed on what he's doing?"

I hear her burst into laughter and say that Liponie is so clever.

"Helena, have you been able to keep up with Cory? She's been keeping you very busy I heard."

"She has indeed. I wish for you to know that I have discovered what the fun is." She adds, "Today we made chocolate dipped cherries and strawberries. The most fun of all was to see the joy and the rapture on the faces of those who tasted them."

I agree that giving and seeing how people love what you give is a wonderful experience.

"Have you had a chance to watch any movies?"

"Yes, I saw *Gidget.* It was very interesting because Liponie has made a special place to surf and Gidget surfs. Your little one has given me that as the homework, to watch *Gidget.* I have watched her already, but I am not ready to do the surf."

"It is good that you spoke and said what you prefer not to do."

"Yes, and there was another that was very curious. It was something called *Mr. Ed* and it was a talking horse."

"Those were shows that were popular many years ago."

"I loved it! I loved it! It was wonderful, and the flying noon (nun) was amazing! She had a magic hat and she could ride in the air with it. It was very interesting."

"It sounds like you are having fun."

"I have discovered this fun; I have never experienced it before."

"This can be your life from now on. Don't worry about any little bumps you hit because we're all riding together in this beautiful Joy Vehicle."

"I never want to go back, Joy, please. I am asking for sanctuary."

"You have it."

CHAPTER SIX

January 23, 2015

At the Joy Council, Tonas informs me that we have an emissary from the indigenous people who wishes to speak with me in front of the council. Before I enter the full council, I ask the core group to join us. When they are present, I explain that this morning I experienced Liponie looking through the "rolodex" of my soul lineage in order to understand the mannerisms and societal rules of the ones who are instigating the conspiracy. I add that he lined up seven individuals and it might be helpful for them to know what he discovered.

Sananda asks me to "fire away." I'm not positive I can give him the information, but I intend to open up and show the group what I have. Sananda says he can see what Liponie is interested in and asks me to release the transmission I have for them. I didn't know I had a transmission, but I am able to release that also.

Sananda laughs and then says, "My dear, what we now understand is that these individuals are very sensual; Liponie wishes for you and all of us to know that this issue is moving very swiftly to an end. Without leadership, there is no incursion. Changkolar has made the request that Liponie was waiting for; this is something Liponie has witnessed before. Changkolar has asked to be capable of being constantly aroused, and that the experience of the culmination of the act will last for an extended period of time. Liponie believes this is the beginning of the end for Changkolar for he is already into more than thirty-six hours of constant excitement. His body can do this for perhaps another three days before it will no longer be able to exist. The reason Liponie was looking through your lineage was to try to find a loophole to make the offering of the magic stone stimulate an idea that would allow these other individuals to have such fun, if they wish."

I remark that this is unfortunate for Changkolar. Sananda contends that neither Changkolar nor Liponie feel that way. "Liponie is again in the role of party planner. It is very easy for him to create beings that are as if robotic; the women he has created are not actual alive beings."

I suppose Sananda is right in that Changkolar considers this the ultimate party. This news does help me release most of my concerns for Liponie's safety.

"What is the name of the indigenous person who will be speaking with me?"

Tonas explains that the man's name is Oongarrah and he is an emissary from all of the indigenous tribes that have been assisted. He has brownish skin and is about the size of a nine-year-old human. As a precaution, I ask if there is anything else I need to know before I step into the council. In a matter-of-fact voice, Tonas informs me that the emissary is not wearing underpants. In hopes that he might be wearing a shred of clothing, I ask Tonas if the man is wearing *anything*. As I suspected, I'm told, as we would say, that the emissary is wearing only his birthday suit.

"Now I'm embarrassed, Tonas. (I can feel myself blushing.) You should have waited until I was through speaking with him to tell me that. Hold on while I compose myself for a moment. I'll just pretend that he has a little bit of clothing on."

"I wished for you to know in the event he embraces you, my dear."

"Oh, well, I'm not really feeling things, either."

With the full council:

"Oongarrah, thank you for waiting very patiently to speak to me and to our council, please do address us." After a short period of silence, I find myself speaking softly in what, I assume, is his language. I ask him if it is possible for him to speak to us in English.

"I am being translated. I wish for you to know that there are many roads leading to the same destiny. Sometimes the destiny may appear to be somewhat different in the beginning, but, surely, as the time is reaching its final moments of the *true* achieving of the goals, that destiny, however it has changed or evolved, becomes the story that you live by. When we chose to make our position and place on Earth it was, for us, a very easy decision to make. All of you here, and you, Joy, must know that we knew of this day. We knew that you would exist, Joy, more than a hundred years of thousands past. Before you were born and before you grew to be the Great One who resides and is in position on your throne there before me. More than a hundred of thousands, and yet here you sit, in that same vision that we knew was the possibility of the destiny of us. We knew that perhaps we would forfeit our lives to undertake such a mission. The one thought that held for us that flavor of returning to our home was our vision of this council that we saw so long ago.

More than a hundred of the thousands of years we knew that this Command of the Ashtar would be an instrument for extricating us from the bindings that held us to Earth, and so we allowed ourselves to be bound. We allowed ourselves to be and to act as if we were of Earth. Many times we forgot who we were; many times we became someone that we were not; many times we then remembered and we made changes and hoped never again to fall into those traps of the dimensional fields that would lead us to such visions of the illusions of the experiences that we would perpetuate and create into the story of our lives.

You did indeed create this council; you did indeed extricate us, and it is now that we spend the remainder of our experience of existence cleansing ourselves from that story. We cleanse ourselves not to cast away the vision of what we were prepared to do, for that part of ourselves did know its mission and we did successfully achieve it. It is to move into the purity of our former selves and to hold that story of the hundred of thousands of years as a part of our destiny and our history that intertwined with Earth and with you.

We wished you to know, Joy, that many times it was the vision of Great Father that brought us back to our awareness of self. That it was through that which you transmitted to the hearts of us that allowed us to remember our true makings. As eternals on Earth, it was a long stead for us to exist in such primitive conditions, and yet, it was our honor and privilege. Now that it is complete, we wish to remind you that the others that are on Earth that are waiting for their time will also carry a similar story to our own. They, too, connect very deeply with the heart of Earth, with humanity, with the animal kingdom, with Gaia, and with the purpose that you hold.

We are in gratitude. I wish to offer you now my humble staff. I realize that it is not the shiny sword that you have lying beside you, though to me it is a powerful tool that leads and did lead us to that release which now has freed us from our purpose. We wish for you to have this as a memento of our deep appreciation and our heart is collectively and individually filled with great admiration for you and for your works."

"Thank you. It will have a place of honor in my residence."

"I take my leave."

"Wait, one moment. Before you leave, would you speak with Sananda about some of the work that I have learned that would, perhaps, help you in your joyful releasing and regaining the memory and full experience of your true nature? Sananda, would you explain to him the Serenity work?"

Sananda informs us that he transmitted information about SVH and that he would be happy to make a pilgrimage to their world. "Please allow all to know that we are ever grateful for your humble service to this world."

I clarify, "There's nothing humble about it. It was magnificent and I honor you from every part of my heart. Thank you so much." I have been trying to think of words that would be adequate to thank this man and his people for their service and I can find none. I hope he can feel the gratitude I have in my heart.

Tonas, "He knew of us all before ever undertaking the experience."

"I can take a pleasant surprise like that any day. Let me speak with Woonfred. That will help bring me back to this reality."

During my conversation with my dragon friend, I glean more information about his species. Even though gold is a rare color for dragons, Joyous has remained that color. Woonfred doesn't know if a dragon could change their color if they desired to do so. (Perhaps they all are content with the color they are born with and none have ever tried?)

People could only train a dragon if they captured it when it was a baby; the way they were able to do that was to steal the egg. When I ask Woonfred why didn't the parents just take their egg or their baby back, he says when they tried they were always killed. It could take as many as forty arrows to kill them, but they were big targets to hit.

Hoping that didn't happen too often, I ask him if eggs were stolen frequently. He answers it happened often enough and sometimes there would be only one egg every forty years. This information is so disturbing to me I stop to remind myself that the dragons and their eggs are safe now.

The other bits of dragon lore I learn are: dragons like music, they all look similar to Woonfred—he's one of the biggest—except their sizes and colors vary. Claws on their feet are standard equipment.

"What are dragons eating now?"

"We are eating from the buffet table that Liponie has created for *all* of us."

"What kind of things are on the buffet?"

"Not people."

Laughing, I ask if they are perhaps enjoying cakes and broccoli.

"Liponie thought it would be better to eat ostrich than to eat twenty chickens. It is important to mention that the food he provides us is an illusion. It is made of energy; there are no deaths in order for us to live except for the deaths of the sprinkles on my ice cream." (Ice cream bars with sprinkles and cupcakes are also offered on the buffet.)

"Thank you, Woonfred. I'm still in awe of what Oongarrah told us, and perhaps they will be open to Sananda using SVH to assist them in cleaning up their 100,000+ years on Earth. That is a long time."

"My dear, it was a beautiful day. It is a day to remember."

Privately with Tonas:

After he confirms we are alone, I bombard him with, "OK, snookums, poopsie, booty woo." I'll teach him to "precious baby heart" me!

"You are of comical! I must find a name for you, cuddles."

"How is Helena doing?"

"She is much better; she was singing with Cory earlier. Today they were into the Italian food; it was smelling to the heavens of delight. Cory is cooking away her concerns."

I remark to Tonas that a buffet for dragons is an incredible idea. Tonas says he was surprised also, but he has seen Woonfred eat cupcakes from our buffet. "He is very much an addict, I think. He eats them paper and all, and he smacks his lips and he moves his head back and forth and says, 'Mmm, mmm, mmm.' He is quite comical."

"I think Liponie has things under control, don't you?"

"I am much relieved by the explanation of what is happening. I would not like to say how Changkolar is doing himself to death, but I believe this is his choice. It seems as if to make peace from love or the making of love."

I wouldn't call what Changkolar is doing making love, but at least he will only kill himself. After thanking Tonas for his assistance today, I return home.

I have a few questions for Esthra, because yesterday I felt the energy of my guide Yarnick, leave. He assures me that Yarnick was in presence with me at the council, and he only left the council, not me.

Esthra continues by mentioning that Metatron called all of my guides into physical presence at the council yesterday. Now someone must advise him to keep quiet because I hear him say, "Oh, it is secret."

"Oh, no, do I have to talk to Metatron?"

"He will not tell you. It is a great surprise. There is a mum in the word."

I tell him I'm willing to wait to see what happens, but before even two seconds pass, I hear Esthra admit there will be a very fine celebration on Valentine's Day. All my guides are going to be singing and they will be physically embodied at the council rather than in energy form.

"Did you just tell me the surprise?"

"Of course. We are all coming in costume with halos and we will be shooting arrows at you and Tonas. You must act surprised."

I wonder if their arrows will have the same effect that Cupid's are supposed to have. Hmm…

CHAPTER SEVEN

January 24, 2015

With Sananda in the SBT, I mention that last night I recorded, "It feels like 1967."

"You were discussing this with Kennedy. Everything was out of control then because there were people with agendas who were finding ways to make money out of war. He believes that someone is benefitting from this war we are dealing with. We are considering that Changkolar was being spurred by someone. We hope that Liponie will know who this person is."

"I also got the name of someone called Bahgwah and was told he will be in my future as well. Who is he?"

"He's an important monk/teacher that you will be able to use as a negotiator. He's from a star in our universe named Joelee; Ashtar can go pick him up. For whatever reason, he's communicating with you. This is only a day in the future."

At the Joy Council, I'm really disappointed to learn that Liponie has not returned. I was sure he was back because last night I heard his laughter. Tonas asks me to wait while the full council joins us so they can translate what I heard. I was so excited to hear him laugh that I didn't even consider it could be a transmission. After I transmit to the group what I heard, Tonas says Liponie believes he only has another day of what he calls "mop up."

Tonas remarks that it will be unfortunate if there is another insurgence and asks me if there is a way I can do the magical thing I do. As soon as I intend to open up to communication from my genie, a bunch of funny Liponie-like noises and laughter spout from my mouth.

Tonas says, "Ah, this is almost as if triple cloaked. It is definitely encoded. He also believes that the head of the snake has not been identified."

(Although this next part has been completely rewritten so that it *no longer exists*, I'm including a small piece of that story as an explanation for the return of Liponie.)

Now some sounds come out of me that are so repulsive I feel like covering my ears. Chilling laughter follows and I shudder before I can say, "I didn't like that. Who *was* that?"

"It was a transmission through Liponie. He is in danger; we must intervene now."

More terrifying noises come from my mouth and I manage to say, "Get him out of there!"

Tonas very calmly says, "He is being extracted, my dear. Yes, that was a transmission through him from the head of the snake, I believe."

Then I hear Liponie laugh and say, "I am back, my dear!"

"Hold on, I have to hug you!"

"I have been away at the secret camp."

"I am so glad you are back!"

"It is lovely to be in my own clothing."

"Who was the nasty man speaking through me?"

"I felt it coming through me, my dear. I am not aware of who it was; I have been trying to search him out for several days. This is a well-guarded secret."

"I don't think I could duplicate his voice and I really don't want to. Are you able to read something from what I gave you?"

Tonas reminds me that Liponie would not have heard the transmission and asks me to make a silent transmission of the voice.

"Good, I didn't want to have to voice it again. Here it is … It gives me the shivers even that way. Yuck."

Liponie comments that it is evil upon evil. Tonas suggests that he go back through his consciousness and review all that was brought into his presence. "The others who were in league with this dark one are lost to the cause, correct?"

"They are lost even to themselves."

"Liponie, do you have any clues as to who this person might be?"

"I believe it is in my mental recording of what I have experienced. I put my energy out throughout all Fantrah. Most luckily, Changkolar is no longer interested in Sharinah."

"Is he still alive?"

"He is on his short breaths, my dear. He is about four quados away from the final beat of his heart."

"Four what?"

"Quados is what they call the orgasm. He was desiring extended quados."

"I almost felt sorry for him. I know there are much worse ways to die, but it seems so sad he has chosen something like that. I'm having a tough time with this kind of thing."

"He is having the time of his life, my dear, living out all of his fantasies. And at the end of his final quados, he will be enjoying himself with the party planner, your mother. He will be in full measure of his true awareness of self."

"What is going to happen with his harem?"

"Immediately the 'women' will evaporate except for the ones he originally had for himself. Those women do not know how to think. If there was a fire and another place with no fire, they could not even make the choice to come to the place with no fire. They are mindless."

"I want to help them."

"We can extract them and they can be educated. Sharinah was exactly the same until the moment she was not; something happened to change her in an instant."

"She reached out to me, Liponie."

"She reached out to you because something happened which opened up a gate for her to do so. Do not imagine that she decided one day to make an escape. I believe it was something in SVH that moved through time and activated something within her."

"All right. Let's get back to what we were doing with Mr. Snake."

"He is very well hidden. What do you suggest we do the moment we are aware? I believe it is a situation for the Ashtar Command."

"I agree. Whoever is behind this, they are gaining something from the chaos."

At this point in our investigation, Liponie pinpointed an individual that the Ashtar Command was able to capture. They managed to hold him for a short time by surrounding him with an energy field of love, but I always felt he was on the verge of escaping. After I was given a glimpse of his future escape, we instituted a desperate intervention in the future just before his ascension—yes, even the bad guys eventually become enlightened enough to ascend—by offering him a chance to experience a life that would be the complete opposite of his previous existence. He decided that would be even more interesting than being the baddest of the bad and agreed to release and remove all memories of his experience as evil personified. He chose to move into a new life experience where he would always be and do good.

In order to honor that choice and keep his identity secret, I have removed any further details about him from the chronicles. His old story no longer exists, in fact it never even happened; however, I have retained in this chronicle some information about a few of the safety measures we put in place as a result of this experience.

"Liponie, before we enter the council, I want to tell you that I am *so* glad you're back. It was like trying to get along without my right arm and it's not just the things you do for all of us. I missed you and your bubbliness. I think you might find a little cupcake brochure—I picked it up during a recent trip—somewhere among your things. Welcome back."

"Hmm, it is very good to be back and it is also exciting for me to slip away just for a moment and give my little kisses to Cory."

"She's been cooking up a storm while you were gone."

He sounds astonished when he asks, "She has been cooking?"

"Sharinah's name is Helena now and she's been cooking along with Cory."

When I mention Changkolar's harem, Ashtar volunteers to pick them up but wants to know where to bring them. Tonas suggests Inishimora, but then I hear Charlie say, "Mommy, we can bring them to the Wizard of Oz and he will give them a brain!"

I explain to Charlie that although the Wizard of Oz seems very powerful, I believe Sananda would make a better wizard. Sananda says he plans to give them an activation of some areas of their consciousness and offer education to them. Tonas adds that it will be part of the mission for the instructors on Inishimora to guide the academy students there in assisting the women. I suggest they be kept together in a separate room and gradually introduced to other parts of the ship. Ashtar agrees to extract them in a day or so.

After moving into the full council, I ask the two delegates who wish to join our Joy Council to speak.

"I am here to speak for the Keylonas Universe. I am Champignon Defratross." Speaking with what sounds like a French accent, he tells me his council is anxious to join and bring peace to their world.

Next, I hear a man announce that he is Pronestos Optheos, the councilman from Hellipicore. After several repetitions of these names, I think I may have them close to correct. We both are able to laugh about the difficulties I am having. Some of these names just don't seem to fit into English, even with Osiris doing the translating.

"Charlie, do you want to go with me for the inaugurations?"

"Oh, Mommy, yes! Can we bring my train?"

"No, I don't think so."

"They might like to ride on it."

"Maybe some other time, Charlie. Today we're just going to do business."

I hold Tonas's and Charlie's hands and gate with them to the Keylonas Universe. I don't feel so bad about the pronunciation difficulties I had after Tonas mispronounces Champignon's name and is corrected. I move through our usual procedure but almost forget to have Sananda offer them the Badges of Honor. After explaining the badge, he guides them through activating it.

When we are through with the inauguration for the Hellipicore Universe, I ask Charlie if he has something he would like to toast. I should have been more specific, because he says, "I do, because I like jam on my toast. If you have not had jam, you are missing out on the best things in life. I would like to toast to jam."

"I will add to that toast by saying that I'm toasting to the unjamming of the chaos that has been present in some of our universes and also joy and love to all of you. Thank you for joining us."

Charlie whispers, "That was really good, Mommy. I think they need to have jam."

"Liponie, can you leave a big pot of jam on the table?"

"And toast, for you, Charlie." Liponie laughs and says, "Everyone, you must enjoy the jam!"

Back at the Joy Council, I ask to speak with Liponie for a moment. After he announces he is present, I explain that I have been learning about genies and he is exceptionally different. "I already knew that, but I didn't realize the extent of what genies can experience. Somehow, I want us to do a genie extraction."

"From where?"

"On dual worlds they are usually mistreated and they don't know that it should be different. They are somewhat like Changkolar's harem women. Maybe not to that extreme, but they think of themselves as just toys and abuse is just part of their life. I don't want that to be true for them. We know your master died, but we don't know, and maybe you can't tell us about the spark within you that said, 'I've had enough of that. I'm going to make a life for myself.' These genies don't have any concept of doing anything like that. What do you think happened? Could it have been SVH from your future?"

"I believe it might. Hmm, I have a thought. What if you move into the future and do that magic thing you do in the Fifth Realm—get something from the genies to give to themselves?"

That's the perfect idea! Sananda joins me and we step into the Fifth Realm. Although I can't ask the genies for anything specific, I can tell them what I've learned and ask them to give me something for themselves. After I call forth every genie in all the different universes, Sananda informs me that Liponie is one of the genies who stepped forward.

I explain to the group that we are happy to bring any gifts they would like to give themselves to any and all positions they would like to receive assistance from themselves. Sananda asks me if I would like to hug Liponie since he's got his arms out for a hug. I love the idea of giving him a big squeeze! When our embrace feels complete, Sananda and I take the genies' gifts, step into the SBT and hand them over.

In order to avoid repetition, you may assume that unless I specify otherwise, Sananda and I always step into the SBT to hand over the gifts people gave us for themselves. In addition, Charlie usually makes a template of the gifts to send out as a transmission.

After more questions for Woonfred at the council, here's what I learn: although Joyous's egg was golden, most dragon eggs are off white, like the color of chicken eggs and they are about as big as my head. The baby's skin must be tough because the parents breathe fire on the egg as soon as it starts to open.

"Once the baby is completely out of the egg, I hope they stop the fire and say something like, 'Hello, baby.'"

"It is common for the mother to nuzzle into the baby and for the father to sit up proudly."

"What do dragons eat when they are babies?"

"The first meal of most little dragons in the old days was usually a little mouse. I do not think your readers will wish to hear this."

"You are correct. Even though that is not true anymore, that old story is not something to tell little kids. I'll be back in a couple of days. I love you."

"You are loved by all, my dear, and I am part of that all."

CHAPTER EIGHT

January 26, 2015

I have been thinking about people who would benefit from having an education or who would benefit from seeing the biggest picture that is possible for them. I've also considered people who are "mindless" or have been so subjugated, enslaved, closeted, hidden away or abused in some way so that they have no idea of freedom. People who have been asleep their whole life and don't know it's possible to wake up and have a wonderful life.

In the Fifth Realm with Sananda, I show people the categories I've been thinking about and ask all those who would fit into any of them to step forward. "We just did some work with the genies because they were created as toys; a toy is something you play with and then you can put it on the shelf or throw it away when you're through with it. We would like to get gifts from you to give to yourself at any point in your life if you had any of those or other kinds of issues. Amazing things can happen when people receive something from themselves at the most ideal time. Give us what you want for yourselves and we'll carry it to you."

Today is my mom's birthday, and I ask Sananda to join me in the Fifth Realm so that he can report on what Mom and Dad are up to. There is a barn dance going on in, of course, a huge barn. People are dancing to fiddle music, women are wearing big skirts, everyone is wearing cowboy boots and they are square dancing. It seems Dad is doing the calling for the dance; that sounds like something he'd like to do. Mom is wearing a full red skirt, a white frilly blouse, and clapping her hands to the music while standing below the stage where Dad is calling the dance steps. There is a big cake and also some punch.

We roll forward in time to where Dad has finished calling the dances, and now he and Mom are slow dancing. This is great to know because I don't believe they ever did anything like that when they were alive; at least I never saw them. I decide I'll talk with them some other time.

Moving into the SBT, I ask King Solomon to join me and hear him say, "How exciting for me." That should have been *my* line, but since he beat me to it, I transition into asking him if I'm interrupting anything he's doing; if he's in the middle of some important project, I don't want to delay him. He casually remarks, "What could be interrupted?"

"I don't know what you do in ascended master temples."

"We are always doing something. Ah, I see you are still wearing your necklace. This is a compliment to me."

I'm glad that I'm wearing it there. In my Earth reality, I'm wearing flannel lined jeans and two sweaters with not a speck of jewelry on.

With the pleasantries out of the way, I bring up my plan to find ways to assist the genies. Legend has it that the jinn helped Solomon build his temple, although some sources claim he used demons. There's a being labeled the king of demons that I believe Solomon knows. After I explain that I'd like information about the work he did with the genies, and specifically, ________, Solomon asks me what I know about that individual.

"I know that he was supposed to have assisted you and that he has been called a demon or a genie."

"He is not a demon or a genie."

"Did he assist you with the temple work?"

"Indeed. He is from another universe and he does have great powers."

"Good guy powerful or not so good?"

"There were conflicts on his world and he developed his powers there. When he came to Earth he was very pleased to assist me."

"Do you know what he is currently doing?"

"He is more now assisting the reptilian race. In my time, he was not someone I mistrusted; I was simply careful in giving him the directive for what I wished him to do and he was most compliant."

I had thought that this individual might be able to assist us, but now I realize he is someone to leave strictly alone.

"Did you get a chance to see the culmative?"

Since he says he doesn't know what that is, I explain that it is a vision of what happens when we all reach our highest state of evolution and everything moves into the Fifth Realm. He sounds excited when he says that is what we are all working towards and it would be a worthy vision for him to witness. When I offer to show it to him at the council, he surprises me by asking if he could bring his beloved.

"You must know that the Queen of Sheba and I have found our way to be together forever at last."

This news thrills me to the core and I ask him how it came about. He explains that Sananda spirited her away from her position of being "dead" in the Fifth Realm and brought her to be with him. It seems Sananda is as much of a romantic as I am. I ask if I may speak with her and hear her say, "Of course, you can."

"I'm so glad you are together."

"It is, to me, the right. We left one another in the hope that we would end, one day, together. If we could not come together in life, then we would in death."

"I'm inviting you to a Valentine's Day party on the Moon on February 14th. So put on your dancing shoes and come and dance with us."

I hear her sigh and then she tells me it will be a great celebration for them to come. I add that she can see what the culmative looks like. Since she also doesn't know what I'm referring to, I start to explain about the vision and then decide it would be easier to just show them. They agree to meet me at the Joy Council inside the Earth.

Once I am there, I hear her comment that the building is classically beautifully. After introducing Jedidiah to Tonas, I ask the queen if she prefers me to introduce her using another name besides the Queen of Sheba. I doubt that anyone has ever asked her that question, because she says, "You can call me queen, or you may call me…queen." Then she giggles. As usual, as soon as I speak Liponie's name he is present, and as soon as I ask him to show Solomon and Sheba the vision of the culmative, it is ready to view. Genie speed is as fast as angel speed; I love it!

With Tonas and Osiris: "Today I heard something about unified fields of harmony with consciousness in the Inseanahrah Universe. I believe this means that the next step in their evolution is to become a stream of individuals who are like a collective. They seem to think that this will assist the Nordahnee Universe because they border it. My understanding is that their universe will be sending a frequency in all directions that could assist others; if they do that, nothing can cross their borders unless it is harmonious."

Osiris says they are unaware of this evolutionary choice but he will contact their emissary, Yarah Homma.

I mention that I hope the instruction Charlie gets in diplomacy will open his eyes without making him afraid. (This is one of the safety measures we put in place since Charlie actually spoke with that individual we recently captured.) Tonas says that is why he gave Charlie the title of diplomat. He adds that when Charlie is part of his collective he comprehends, but when he is singular Charlie, he lacks understanding of the ways of duality. Tonas informs me he has communicated with their collective and they said it is through experience that Charlie is to learn.

I suggest it be a top priority to educate Charlie in who is safe and who might not be. I mention that here we're just told not to talk to strangers, but that won't work in this situation.

"I don't know how much longer Charlie and I will be in duality, but I did get some things from my future self about safety and sovereignty for me and mine. Maybe that will help me with insights about future events. I love that Charlie is innocent, but I don't want him to be so innocent that we lose him."

Tonas reminds me that we have heightened security at the council. When I ask, I learn that Changkolar has had his final quados and he is in the Fifth Realm.

Speaking to Zeezzz, "Yesterday, I heard someone say that food helped them turn into a beautiful woman. Then I saw that person sitting and waving at me. Was that you?"

I hear her chuckle and then she admits she is convinced. "How can anyone turn down an existence, even in particle form, of a physical body? I am an organic being now."

"I'm excited for you. What are your favorite things to do?"

"I have been gifted with a key to your garden and I love to walk; it is a joy for me. I can make my way anywhere I wish! Nothing can stop me from moving, bending, touching things and eating!"

"I think you would be the perfect person to speak to the planets, stars, suns, other crystals and anyone who might want to embody or thinks they don't want to embody."

"Especially if they are resistant, for I think there was no one more resistant than I."

I remind her that Cory put up a really good fight. Zeezzz calls her a "chip off her mother's self." She also says she would be pleased to assist with the Valentine's Day party and that she is taking dancing lessons! I ask her if she has a partner and she asks what a partner is. Maybe I won't need to do any matchmaking at all, so I simply tell her it is someone to dance with. It seems that although many men are lining up to dance with her, Sananda is her current favorite partner.

I make a suggestion that perhaps some of King Arthur's knights might be of interest to her, but she informs me she has an idea of someone. "Perhaps at the gala I might catch his eye and dance him into my heart or me into his heart. I am following the theme of my daughter—find a man. I wish to have the sex you see. I have been promised a book that will help me to experience it to the utmost."

I wonder how many people have a copy of that book; it could be that I'm the only living, organic person on the council without a partner who doesn't have a copy.

"Is it a secret about who you have your eye on?"

She asks to whisper the name into my ear and I hear her admit that she very much fancies the handsome star captain, Ashtar. I act surprised and agree that he would be a really good match for her.

There's no way I can be wrong about that. When Jill Marie was talking to her future self to try to find out what Liponie would want for his birthday, that part of her told her that Zeezzz and Ashtar would become partners. It's not that our future selves normally tell us something we don't ask about; she told me that information was offered to her because other questions she asked were not answered.

Zeezzz lets me know that through the assistance of Sananda, Liponie and some others, she soon will have blood running in her veins. Doing impossible things is almost a daily occurrence at our council, but, still, what is being done for Zeezzz seems miraculous.

I ask Tonas to join us and suggest that it would be nice if there was a place for the genies who want to change to be able to receive instruction. He agrees this is a good idea and I bid them both farewell.

CHAPTER NINE

January 30, 2015

I step into the Fifth Realm to see what Mom and Dad are up to. Sananda has accompanied me in order to report what they say, since telepathy is the only form of communication used in this realm.

He says they are sitting on the front porch in interesting chairs, (I bet they are lawn chairs that look like they came from Kmart. Sananda confirms that when I share a mental picture with him.) drinking something that appears to be lemonade, and chatting with my Grandmother Crystal. I'm glad they are communicating; Crystal died several years ago and Mom missed her very much. It seems that my parents are stirring things up in the Fifth Realm, because Liponie was supposed to meet with them this morning.

Addressing my mother, I wish her a happy birthday and remark that I'm glad she can finally dance with Dad. She says he can kick up his heels.

"Dad, are you going to learn to play the fiddle?"

"He already knows how. In this realm you can learn how to do all kinds of things very quickly. When they were reviewing their lives, they experienced everything they didn't do. That means he would have learned to play the fiddle. They're now making plans for the next event."

I've been seeing my Great Grandmother Permelia during my morning reveries. Since I know she must have something for me, I ask her to join our little group. She was in her nineties when I knew her and had very few, if any, teeth. She doesn't look like that now because Sananda comments that she is a pretty lady who has a whole new story for me.

"The story is about prosperity. Instead of having the mentality of struggle and survival, this story reflects a continuous flow of everything you needed. I have the file for you in what looks like a CD."

I'm definitely ready for a continuous flow of prosperity! After thanking Permelia, I use SVH to put the file in place for myself.

At the Joy Council with Tonas and the core group, I ask if Charlie is here. I hear his little boy voice say, "I am here, Mommy." I love to hear him call me that. It's been a long time since I heard that word from my sons.

"Last night I was working on some kind of gift to give to people; it is called the 'One Tribe Automated File.' The students at the Academy of Enrichment have been here long enough to have the privilege of transmitting it from Inishimora. Not exactly the same as we do in the Joy Council, but similar, in that they will hold a thought and then focus their consciousness to transmit it. I'm going to open up and give you the file."

Charlie sounds excited when he says it is very good and it could affect the collective. When he asks how the students would transmit it, Tonas says that if I give the students the concept of assisting us in this way, they would be glad to do it.

We discuss the incursion. The core group are hoping, with the acceptance of all involved, to rewrite the history of it so that the one tribe evolution will be more expansive and graceful. Osiris remarks that Changkolar wishes to have never jeopardized that which is now so dear to his heart.

Osiris also informs me that there are representatives from two universes who wish to join our council. He shares with me that he believes, even though it sounds ridiculous, that Bizzarah Nahcoomeuh is embarrassed since he has not been to our council. During our investigation, we learned that the conspirators had managed to feed Bizzarah, and some members of his council, false information about what was actually going on. It seems important to assure him in privacy that we don't blame him for his hesitancy in joining our council. The plan is that I will gate Tonas, Osiris, Sananda and myself to Bizzarah's office, but at first only Tonas and I will speak with him. When we arrive, Tonas tells me there is a woman who will lead us into his office.

Tonas speaks, "Joy feels, as I, that this has been a tremendous circumstance for you to have experienced."

Bizzarah replies that he is grateful that we have spoken to him. I ask permission to offer him assistance via SVH. With his agreement, I ask Creator to assist both of us to open to the joy of our relationship and to the learning and adventure that we have been experiencing with the role that the instigators in this universe played. I suggest Bizzarah adds anything else to our clearing that he feels would be of assistance, and then guide him in viewing his screen.

He says he is grateful for our kindness, and if they had known what was really going on, their council would have asked for acceptance much sooner. He asks if we will accept them now.

"Certainly, there is no pressure for you to make a decision today; we will gladly inaugurate your council at any time you wish."

"I am stepping forward; it is our choice to be a part of this council. We have been very impressed."

Bizzarah says their council members are ready, I call Liponie into action and instantly their council building is ready. After I gate all of us to it, I hear Bizzarah laugh and comment that the trip was quite magical.

He briefly addresses his council to say that although they have experienced some embarrassments, Tonas and I have assured him that they are honored and that it is acceptable for them to be part of the Joy Council. The inauguration, with the addition of the Badges of Honor, goes smoothly.

In the Astrenoid Universe, we are greeted by councilman Kemper Findarian. Their inauguration also goes smoothly and quickly.

At the Joy Council in privacy with Tonas, I inform him that we have an anniversary coming up. Just as I suspected, he has no notion of what an anniversary is. He is surprised that I remembered February 3rd was the first time I consciously met him. I have to admit to him that the date is recorded in my book. That's a good thing because I'm terrible at remembering dates.

I suggest that we need to celebrate by doing something special. He makes some flustered sounds and then admits he is "whelmed" by this news.

"This is the only time I'm going to mention it to you. With your phenomenal memory, you should be able to remember this date throughout eternity."

"Ah, I must do my research on anniversaries."

"Right, an anniversary of our first meeting is important. Women are into those kinds of things. I also think we should invite Saint Valentine for the Valentine's Day party."

"If we can have Father Christmas, why not?"

I ask for Liponie to join us and remark that very often little boys on Earth want to have a dog for a pet. "I thought about something like that for Charlie and the gang, but I'm wondering about dog poop."

We have quite a discussion about this including: tell the dog telepathically where to poop; train it to poop in a certain spot or put a bag under its bottom—Liponie's idea. Then he says, "I have the answer, my dear. We will pick a dead one. It won't poop at all."

After more discussion, we realize that each of the Swizzlers would want an animal and ninety-four of any kind of animal would be a lot in our current situation. Liponie suggests a zoo; I veto that even though he assures me the animals wouldn't eat anyone. Finally, he says he can create a dog that does not poop or pee and asks me what species I would like. I wonder if he can tune into what animal each of the children would like.

He reminds me that this is Charlie and he will love whatever we give him. I persist by explaining that all dogs are different and suggest we have a class on the different kinds so the Swizzlers can understand what each is like. Liponie agrees this idea is exciting and says to leave it with him.

Two days ago, I became aware that Changkolar would be able to assist us and that he wished to speak with me. Since I promised Helena never to bring him to our council, I have decided to meet with him, along with the core group, on Ashtar's ship. Sananda explained to me that Changkolar spent over four thousand years in Master Academy studying and learning all that any being could possibly ever know about truth, love and honor. He is not the same as he was. (My thought is that this man doesn't do *anything* by half-measures.) Once we are assembled, I address Changkolar, thank him for coming to speak with us and ask him how he can assist us.

He says, "I would like to see the joy that I have experienced since my transition, become a part of my world. I believe it is important for the world of my making, that which I created, to be restored into a higher harmony than perhaps ever known. I am from a world that is filled with conflict; there is constant struggle and there is no true peace. If I am allowed, I would have the honor of creating an academy on that world where I would be a teacher, as Sananda has been a teacher to Earth. I could show the way to those who have no vision of seeing what is possible. The opening of the heart is a gift that I experienced. For others to experience this during life would create a glorious ripple through our collective. Our universe awaits this."

"We inaugurated your council before we came here."

"I am greatly appreciative."

"After I leave, will you speak with Osiris, Tonas and some of the others that I work with most closely about specific people who might need further assistance?"

"It is my desire to reach out to each of these. They respected me in life. They will be somewhat shaken by who I have become, and yet, I believe it will inspire them to see that same spark of lightness within themselves. I have dedicated my heart to this."

Before Changkolar leaves, he asks if he may have a group of counselors to assist him in his universe. Sananda volunteers that he believes Jesus would be the one to assist, then adds that it would be good for the masters in the Fantrah Universe who are in the ascended temples there to also assist. Sananda offers to go along and I agree that's a good idea.

Tonas and I move into privacy so I can hear what he wants to tell me about Zeezzz. In a confiding voice, I hear him say, "All right, let me give you the scoop." He's starting to sound like me! "Ashtar attended a feast in his honor—this was the matchmaking of Liponie—and Zeezzz was there. Their eyes met, it was like lightning in the sky. I am telling you, I think it was love at first sight! He has witnessed her before, and yet, in that setting of cinnamon rolls and pies it was *more* than he could take. He looked upon her sweetness. She has learned from someone how to make her eyes (I'm sure he means eyelashes.) go up and down. I think it was Marilyn."

"I sort of knew about this already."

"Oh, I am sorry. Am I to be included in the meeting with Ashtar and Zeezzz?"

"I'm sure she is interested in him."

"I believe they are interested in each other, my dear. I have never in all of my years in the command seen him look at anyone like that."

"Let's introduce them like we did Gaia and Aton."

"How can we? They know each other; they have shared cinnamon rolls!"

Tonas makes this sound so important—maybe it's really true what they say about the way to a man's heart!

"They haven't had a formal introduction. Let's go."

"We must summon them. Should we have cinnamon rolls?"

"No."

Ashtar greets me; when his voice falters as he asks how he may assist me, I know he's seen Zeezzz.

"I'm introducing you formally to someone who is becoming a wonderful representative for speaking to the planets and stars about embodying. Commander Ashtar, may I introduce to you the lovely Zeezzz. Zeezzz, may I introduce to you the magnificent Commander Ashtar. Ashtar, you may kiss her hand if you wish." I hear her giggle, then I add, "I heard a rumor that she is turning into a wonderful dancer, and it would thrill me to have the two of you lead the first dance at our Valentine's Day party. You might want to practice with her a little bit."

"You do not wish me to step on her feet?"

"Right."

We both chuckle and he adds, "Or her tail, at that."

"Dancing lessons are not obligatory but recommended."

Zeezzz, sounding very sultry, says, "I would *love* to have dancing lessons with you if you would agree."

"It would be my pleasure. Joy, may I show Zeezzz your garden?"

Immediately, following my agreement to his request, Zeezzz admits she has already seen it, but she has not seen it with *him*. Ashtar sounds flustered, maybe for the first time in his adult life, as he says, "I would love to show it to you."

I wait until I'm sure they are gone and then do a little happy dance. At least I managed not to jump up and down with glee while they were speaking to each other.

Tonas remarks that they are like children. "She does this thing with her eyelashes going up and down and he melts in front of her. He is like a little puddle on the ground."

I briefly consider trying that tactic, but no, that is just not me. Tonas would probably think I had something in my eye.

Tonas and I are strategizing with Liponie about how to help the genies that would like to be assisted. I learn there are over a thousand of them and Liponie feels he's the best person to help them. I know that's true, but I mention that I'm also worried I might be giving him too many things to do.

"Please, you must not ever take away a single thing. I am capable, although perhaps not on my wedding night."

"Is there a place they can be to go to school?"

"I think no better place than this. I can create a section for them and we could show them what I have been doing for you."

That's exactly what I hoped he would say. I ask Liponie if he can somehow involve Comahlee in this plan; anyone who insists on being called "The Great" needs help. We decide to see if he will accept working with and being trained by Liponie.

The last item Liponie brings up is that people are lining up for the Joy Club, and he wants to know if it's all right for him to call it that. This is another surprise, but I agree to the name. We also agree that the invitation to this club is open to all stars, worlds, planets and suns. Liponie assures me he is working on all this and that satisfies me that all will be well.

CHAPTER TEN

February 3, 2015

I've been fascinated by the activities my parents have embarked on and decide to make another quick visit. Sananda comes with me, and after some telepathic discussion with them, here is what he reports.

"Your mother is harvesting corn and weeding and making the garden perfect. Your father plowed some land next to their place and they're going to put it in clover. Your mother decided that everybody who doesn't have a task can be cooking. She is providing people there with food and this gives them a tactile sensation of the energy that is formed into whatever she makes. As balanced and wonderful as the Fifth Realm is, this seems to be helping some of the individuals there to integrate."

I just don't understand what they are doing. Planting clover and weeding? I would have thought Mom had enough of weeds when she was alive, but then I remember this is an activity that they are allowing *other* people to experience.

Speaking with Esthra, I explain that two days ago two of the Native Americans were speaking very strongly through me, but I don't know what they were saying.

"They were saying, 'Do not leave us behind.'"

"Why do they think I'm leaving them?"

"You have not been doing as much with that connection. You have been so much focused on the other universes and everything else that's going on. It's not that Earth has left your focus, but evidently those who are sensitive can feel you are not as connected as you always have been. I suggest you use your SVH to put some things in place so they will always feel your constant presence."

After some discussion, I go to my MAPS self and get a file that reflects I have been a constant conduit through all times for all indigenous tribes of Earth in order to assist them with sovereignty, personal empowerment, seeing the vision of their birthright of ascension and rising to meet their soul's purpose. My intent is to inspire them with the knowledge that they are enough; they don't need to worship anyone else because they are the "I Am That." I step into the SBT and offer this gift to members of all the tribes.

Sananda and I then step into the Fifth Realm at the near completion and I ask for all sentient beings on all timelines, dimensions, worlds and universes to give us a file containing the pieces and steps that would benefit their sovereignty, personal evolution and empowerment. This will be transmitted through the Joy Arrows.

With Liponie at the Joy Council:

As I've been cleaning out my parent's home, I've also been bringing all the things I want to keep to Liponie so that he can restore and store them away for me: books, pictures, my little girl clothes and even a 1964 set of World Book Encyclopedias. The only reason I can come up with for keeping an outdated set of encyclopedias, is that my brother and I spent a lot of time reading them when we were kids. I knew they would just be thrown away if I gave them to someone on Earth.

Today, I brought to the council a bunch of valentine candy, Little Golden Books that Mom and Dad read to me as a child and some books from the Bloomington library. I've decided I need to spend time with Charlie and the other Swizzlers and I'm going to begin reading books to them. I hand Liponie the assignment of creating a library for us loaded with Caldecott and Newberry Award-winning books.

Then I show him Mom and Dad's forty-year-old toaster and ask him to wrap it up for me as a present for Tonas.

He makes an uncertain sounding, "hmm," and then comments, "retro?"

"It's very symbolic." Even though he doesn't understand, he agrees to wrap it for me.

Privately with Tonas:

He begins, "Greetings to you, my precious. Before you say a word, may I shower you with flowers of great beauty? Happy anniversary, my dear, and may I offer you this beautiful necklace of diamonds, and the bracelet and the ring for your hand?"

I've been giggling all through his greeting, but mention of a ring brings me to full attention. Instead of gasping, screaming or saying, "Oh, no!" I cover my surprise by complimenting him on the great job he did with his research.

"I did, indeed. I could have bought the underwear. Victoria had a secret that I was wishing to understand, but I could not get past their secret code."

"Their advertising is to appeal to a man's visual nature concerning sexuality."

"Oh, I am not interested in that. I wish to look into your eyes, my dear."

"Tell me about the flowers."

"Everyone suggested roses. I was not sure about that, so, instead of going to a florist, I went to Liponie. Your rooms are filled to the roof with fragrant flowers that are the colors of roses; however, they are very large. The flowers resemble a cross between a rose and a peony and they are placed in beautiful, crystal vases."

"I'm very impressed; you really know how to woo a girl. So I have a diamond necklace, a diamond bracelet and a diamond ring?"

"Yes, my dear. The necklace is as if the cosmos; it will cover your neck and chest. It is as if Egyptian, only it is a spray of diamonds from Solomon's mines. He was kind enough to allow us."

What do you say to a description like that? "Jeepers" is laughably inadequate, but that's all I can manage to come up with, followed by, "Oh, Lordy."

"All the diamonds match and there are many colors deep within them; they are flawless, of course."

"I'm more than whelmed, I'm overwhelmed."

"The ring is quite simple. If you will allow me to place it on your left finger, I would wish to bend my knee for you."

"Oh…"

"It is our anniversary, my dear. I pledge my love to you, and I wish to spend the rest of my life and all of eternity, all of my forevers, with you. And when we have reached the end of our time, I wish to move backward in time and spend the very beginning and forward into the now. It is at our discretion to spend forever. I promise you will never find me to be boresome. I promise to always bring a smile to your face, and, of course, to always, as we have experienced before, to be of service to you. I will always wear my underwear, and if I do not wear them, I will surprise you."

"Oh, Tonas, I love you so."

"You will love me ever more so. It is now just the very budding of our love for one another. Imagine what it will be when your heart is able to feel the fullest measure of it. What you will feel for me will be as if an explosion of the fireworks in the sky that we have seen for some of our celebrations. It will open up to be so very bright and colorful like your necklace, like your eyes, like your lips, like your heart. You are everything to me. You are not required to accept my proposal, but please do take the ring."

"I will. I want that love to manifest however it manifests for me, in whatever timing it manifests. I'm learning to be patient."

"The proposal is now, and the timing for the action upon it is when you are ready."

"Let me wear the ring until I'm sure because I love the way you described the future fireworks I might feel. Thank you, and now I'd like a kiss, please… Here is my gift to you; please open it."

"Yes, I am a little confused."

"It's a toaster."

"Yes, I could tell. We have them in the kitchen, only this one is quite unique. I believe it is an antique."

Maybe I should be embarrassed about my gift after the magnificence of the presents he gave me, but I'm not. My explanation is that, in toaster years, this one is approaching Liponie's age because it's one my mom and dad had for over forty years. "This toaster is more than just a toaster; it represents what a toaster stands for. I've seen a couple of things in my future that I can't tell you about, but I think this might come in handy for us."

"Explain this more, my dear."

"A toaster is something you would have in a home."

"This is hopefulness for me."

"That's how I intended it to be. We'll tuck it away somewhere and one of these days we'll be using it."

"Of course. I will tuck it away."

"Thank you for my wonderful presents."

"I promise that you will always have many roses, and that will not be the only species of flower. There will always be flowers in our life, my dear."

"Good, I love them so."

Liponie joins us and I thank him for the wonderful flowers he created.

"Even before Tonas described them for me, I knew they were big and beautiful. I appreciate all you do for me."

Changing the subject to one of a much earthier nature, I ask Liponie if he's thought any more about the dogs.

"I think we should switch to a pony that does not poop. It would be less work."

That's agreeable to me. I've picked up enough dog poop during my life to want not to have to do that anymore.

After a little discussion, we decide to have a dude ranch where the kids can go to learn how to care for, saddle and ride a horse. That sounds like fun for me, too, and I decide that will be a valentine's present for all of us.

Charlie joins us and I hear his, "Hello, Mommy."

"Charlie, I have to tell you something. I have not been spending enough time with you."

I hear him gasp and then say, "Oh, Mommy, I can have *more*?"

My heart drops when I hear the excitement in his voice, because no matter how much time I've been spending with him, I instantly realize it has not been nearly enough. That's going to change *starting right now*.

"Yes, I got so busy with other things and I forgot that you and the other kids are the most important. Well, Tonas is important, and Liponie's important and the work is important, but I'm really sorry I haven't spent more time with you. I'm going to change that; I'm going to start reading books with you."

"Oh...can I sit on your lap, like in the movies?"

"Yes, and I want to read to the other Swizzlers, too. They can sit around on the floor and listen. I brought a lot of books, but we can do other things, too."

He's giggling and telling me that everyone will be excited. I let him know we're going to start reading today right after I do the work with the council.

With the core group:

"How are we inviting the stars, planets and suns to embody?"

Liponie says he has a full program and they are lining up in the dozens. The Joy Council in each universe is transmitting a welcome and Cory has been explaining the process. Stars, planets and suns will be embodying in their own universe. That's a relief to me; ours would be terribly crowded if they all came here.

Liponie also tells me that since each universe has different species, they are showing options for embodying. He adds, "Yet we feel that the humanoid attributes, the two legs, the breasts and the penis, are very comely, you see. I look upon my little Cory and she is such a beauty. I think it would not have been such an attraction for me," Here he pauses before saying, "had she looked like a frog."

I'm still trying to convey that we need to be able to show, not only what their body could look like, but the benefits of embodying. Liponie says they are planning to offer individuals a computerized system where they could pick out eyes, nose, ears and body type. I agree that is a good idea, at least I think it is. I hope we don't end up with beings with four eyes, two noses and three legs.

"Maybe Zeezzz or Cory could make a recording that would explain the things about their bodies they are enjoying. Do you see what I'm saying?"

"Indeed, I think that it is the consummation of food and sex that are the biggest draws."

"I'm sure you are correct. At the party, we want to have gifts that beings can exchange. Here, we send cards that say 'I Love You' or 'Let's be Friends' or we give flowers or candy for Valentine's Day."

Liponie counters that the first step is teaching them how to walk. I agree he's right and suggest that maybe we need to have pre-party events. We discuss dancing and eating lessons. I learn Ashtar has offered the benefit of his fleet. It seems that Liponie has everything well in hand, as usual, so I decide just to turn this over to him and check in once in a while to find out how things are progressing.

The update that Liponie gives me about the genies is that they are not as accepting of assistance as we hoped they would be. His explanation is that they seem to consider an education program as something that might entrap them. Liponie is going to continue speaking with any that show interest. I remark that I hope they might eventually be open to learning SVH. He reports that Helena will begin her studies of it very soon and feels that it will help her a great deal.

"Charlie, I got something the other day that looked like a rolled up scroll of aluminum foil. I think it's something important; I'm going to intend to show it to you." (I've heard that people sometimes wrap money in aluminum foil before mailing it in a letter because then it doesn't show up on a scan. Whatever I received in the foil package was energetically cloaked.)

"Mommy, it is a contract of heart from a large number of beings that are wishing to leave their former association with the old regime of Changkolar. They wish to have sanctuary."

I ask Osiris if he can take care of this; he agrees to do so and I also show the contract to him.

"The last thing on my meeting before the meeting list is that I became aware that the average person cannot feel a gate between the 5th and the 6th dimension."

Sananda replies that it was believed there was a large enough collective of individuals to hold that bridge. He feels that the waffling energies of 4th dimension (Third dimensional principles are leaking into it.) are perhaps causing individuals to feel somewhat torn. "They are being drawn into a reverie of old experiences which is hindering the elevation of their current reality."

"I have a file that will help people with personal empowerment, sovereignty and knowing that they are enough."

I intend to show it to the group. It's interesting that I don't really feel anything happening when I do this, but it seems to work because I hear Charlie's collective voice ask to be able to add to it. He also suggests we take it into the full council. I agree to both ideas.

Then I mention that I have another thing for the CEV, but again, I'm not sure what it is. Charlie explains that it is, "A vision of the world in its readiness; every part of itself becoming ready to involve its energy in the harmonic of our collective elevation. Our world is learning how to be in the harmonic of the higher energies because of you and the other AMS initiates that are feeling themselves in the different dimensions."

The CEV are going to put all of this into one transmission for us to send out.

Now Charlie begins speaking in a very hesitant manner to ask if one of the stories I will be reading is about the pigs.

"The three little pigs?"

"I think there are three. I'm always concerned about the wolf, Mommy."

I attempt to explain that some stories are made up and some are true. As I continue to try to explain, I realize I'm making a mess of it. How do you explain real and not real with all the things that Liponie and others can do here and that soon we will also be able to do? I end up by concluding that was an old story.

"But they have wolves in other children's stories and they always want to eat somebody. I think this is not a good story for little boys. I don't want to be afraid."

I agree that Charlie is absolutely right, and if it's a story that's not good, we just won't read it. That statement brings back the cheery tone to Charlie's voice and he asks if we can have cookies too.

"Cookies and hot chocolate."

"OK, let's finish all our work now!"

Before we join the main council, Tonas whispers, "My dear, isn't he just charming? I agree with him about the wolf." I ask Tonas to help me choose good books. He replies that he can feel the energy of them, and we'll get rid of ones that don't pass his test.

Meeting privately with Marilyn, Cory and Guinevere to discuss Zeezzz's tail: Cory asks me if I dislike the tail. I explain that the idea of a human having a tail is strange to me, and ask her to please don't say anything to Zeezzz. "I don't want anyone to think they have to look a certain way to please me." When I ask, I'm told that since her tail is very large and lizard-like, she waddles when she walks. With such an appendage, I can't imagine how she's going to dance with Ashtar. Marilyn has no advice for me; she thinks the tail is beautiful. I ask Cory if she can find out anything about her mother's choice to have a tail. She replies that she thinks the tail will be in the way when Zeezzz begins having sex. I'm sure that fact will be a strong selling point for losing the tail and I hand Cory the task of communicating with her mother.

With the full council:

"Two days ago I heard a member of the Choshehoe tribe ask me who I was and why I was listening to their stories. I answered that I am a conduit for the Great Spirit. Then I heard, 'Then listen carefully and you shall hear the truth about us.' I believe this is a tribe in South America that might have become cannibalistic."

Ashtar knows about this tribe; they are from a star named Elipta. We can't leave them the way they are—they will be lost in the 4th dimension when it releases—and they cannot evolve to higher dimensions with their current eating habits. The answer to the situation is to do some work in the past to assist them to remember who they are. Ashtar volunteers to periodically bring emissaries from their star to teach them.

With that situation taken care of, I'm ready to send out the transmission that will assist people with self-empowerment and sovereignty. Charlie informs me there is another transmission that will go out in sequence with it. "It is a message of heart to all worlds, all sentient beings. It is the vision of the culmative; the vision of how each individual plays their role in that journey."

They believe this will also help with the gateway between the 5th and the 6th dimensions and we send the transmission out.

Tonas says, "My dear, before you depart, I wish to announce to the council that today is the anniversary of our meeting. Joy and I have been together for many years, and yet the beginning of that experience was one year ago today. I wish to invite each of you to hold up the glass that has appeared in your hand. Thank you, Liponie. We also have Liponie to thank for the new champagne we have from our winery. He is calling it 'Joy Juice.'" At that revelation, I burst out laughing. "Its true name is Joyous Champagne. We have collected the grapes from the lower valley so that it can legally be called champagne. It is a law of Earth that we wished to follow.

All of you please raise your glass to the most glorious goddess ever born on Earth. Joy, we raise our glass to you; you are the queen of our hearts, and you are the queen of transformation. We drink to you, my dear. And, of course, I am drinking to the forever of my association with you, with love."

"Thank you, Tonas."

"Now you must drink all of your glass, please. Every grape gave its life for this. We are in gratitude." Said in a lowered voice, "Liponie brought a vintner from the Fifth Realm. He has stolen him from the Dom Perignon."

I need to study up on champagne; I've only had it a few times in my life and that was years and years ago.

"Thank you all for your assistance today. Tonas, let's meet in private. I'll be back later to read to you, Charlie. I love you."

"Thank you, Mommy, I love you!"

Privately with Tonas:

"Thank you for such a special day, Tonas."

"And I love my toaster, my dear."

"You gave me such magnificent gifts. I hope…"

"The toaster is a hope for the future. It is a more powerful gift than roses and jewels, although I may say the jewels are exquisite. You are coming right back?"

"Yes, I want to spend some time with Charlie. Please tell me what we do next time I'm here."

"Happy, happy anniversary, my dear. It is our first; I'm grateful for your presence in my life."

"I'm glad to be here, there, wherever I am."

"You are everywhere, my dear."

"It seems that way! Bye-bye."

Speaking privately with Ashtar since he asked, earlier, to speak with me before I left. First, he first shares with me that he is excited about the people who are asking for asylum and asks me to alert him about any future transmissions. Then he gets down to the real reason he wanted to speak with me, which, he believes, is a delicate matter. He starts out by saying, "You are notorious for your assisting individuals to come into partnership. I have an interest, and I thought you would be the only one I could possibly speak to. Do I have your discretion?"

"Yes."

"I am of great interest in Zeezzz, and I do not know how to bring this to her attention. She is much older than I and so wise and so beauteous in her heart. Her energy is so lively and I feel as though I have no sense about me when I'm around her. I cannot speak!" He laughs then, and it is the first time I've ever heard him do so. I've also never heard him speak hesitantly or uncertainly, as he is doing now.

"I think she knows how you feel. She's very interested in you."

"I realize we are both aware of our interest; it is simply that I do not know how to make the next step."

"You went for a walk. Did you hold her hand?"

"Yes, I've danced with her and we have consumed food together."

"Have you told her anything like what you just told me about how you feel?"

"Of course not!"

"Are you afraid she won't reciprocate your feelings?"

"I feel that she might, and that is my fear as well, for I do not know what my next step would be. The passion for my work has taken me over for a long time."

"Here is an Earth saying: Nothing ventured, nothing gained. You need to tell her how you feel."

"There is also the issue of Pelthia; we are estranged, but not officially. I think two million years is enough to say that the waters have changed. Do you not?"

I agree that two million years is a sufficient amount of time to consider a relationship finished.

"I was a failure at our relationship. This is my great concern; my passion destroyed our relationship. Now is an important time; my concern is that she will reciprocate and also my fear is that she will not. I do feel that she is very much interested. How serious, I am not sure. What is your council?"

"Ask Zeezzz for a time when you can speak with her in privacy and share these issues with her. If you can't share with her everything you feel, then maybe she's not for you. I think she is, though."

"She is a delight."

"Tell her that. Explain that you got lost in your work during your last relationship, and you don't want that to happen again. Don't you think she'll understand that you are involved in important work?"

"Hmm, well, I will venture this."

"That's my advice; open your heart and tell her your feelings."

"I will do so. Thank you for your assistance."

"You're magnificent and that's how she feels about you."

"You have this information?"

"Yep, I believe she's quite taken with you, but you want to confirm that for yourself."

"I am grateful to you. Thank you from my heart to yours, Joy."

"You're welcome."

CHAPTER ELEVEN

February 6, 2015

Yesterday, I experienced a connection with a collective of Native Americans. Today, I heard them identify themselves as the collective voice of the elders of their tribe. This connection wasn't as easy to understand as the one I experienced five days ago with a Native American named Napurra, so I set it up that only one of them would speak to me for the others. His name is Tonkra and he says his face is very friendly.

Here are the words the collective spoke to me through him: "We are messengers of spirit and heart. Hear us now. To change the path, simply move your feet to another. When you listen, we speak; when you speak, we listen. Let us speak of what we hope for the future. Let us speak of our hearts and love with life. We look upon the Earth and we see that she is becoming new. We carry this message of newness to all tribes. Long have we dreamed and prayed and hoped for this time, and it is now."

I ask to speak with Napurra again and hear him chuckle. He speaks in a very rusty-sounding voice, "I am Shoshone. Napurra."

"What does your name mean?"

"Blue, my eyes are blue. You are Father?"

"Yes, Mother, also."

"We are curious about you."

"What do you want to know?"

"We are watching you from the skies."

"Tell me about that."

"We are no more in the physical. We have, in our choice to remain, a wish to assist you."

"Are you in an ascended master temple?"

"We have not accepted. We wish to remain spirit until the energy of the Earth is new. We wish to help you; there are many of us that sit around the fires in the sky."

"How can you help me?"

"We can whisper. The message on the wind can be heard by our people."

"Help me to tell what you want to be told."

"The world is different now; the wolf no longer cries in the night. There are only buffalo made for meat or held in recreation. The horses no longer fly across the plains, free. There is no way to smell what is to come; there are too many smells in the air. The people have forgotten how to talk to the land, and the animals no longer speak to them. They cannot understand the language of the animal. We can whisper; what would you have us whisper?"

"That all of that is coming back."

"We have seen great change. What is it that you do in the Earth?"

"I do many things in and above the Earth. There is a wonderful council called the Council for Earth Vigilance that I work with very closely. They are incarnated on Earth in the form of a crystal, but they also exist on the 10th dimension of our Moon."

"Are they like us?"

"They were a consciousness from the beginning of the beginning until a year ago. They now have physical forms that do not look human. They look like sticks."

"Sticks are good."

"As individuals they are like children, but when they are together in their collective awareness, they are very wise. If you wish to speak with the one I work with all the time, his name is Charlie."

"I would wish to speak with this Charlie."

"Let me see if I can get him to join us. Charlie, I have someone I'd like for you to meet."

Charlie's collective voice says, "My greetings to you from all of us. We are in witness to you. Great Napurra, are you the speaker for your group?"

"I am."

"We are aware."

Charlie's singular voice says, "Mommy, he is dead."

"I know he is, but he's been speaking to me. I wanted you to meet him because I think he'll get in touch with you if he wants to tell you something. I'll be with you at the council in a little bit. Thank you for coming."

"OK, Mommy."

Napurra says, "This is a pure soul."

"I love him very much; he's like a son to me."

"We are attempting to understand you."

"I'm a conduit for the Great Spirit."

"This makes more sense. It is a worthy endeavor."

"I didn't know about it until recently."

"I heard you as a child, and through my life. It was you that guided us to remain. You told us that it was important for us to have our hearts glued to the Earth in order to show the way when the times are coming. I believe that the times are here now, and that is why we are speaking to you. There is a good thought that there can be this transition without conflict. We wish to help the Shoshone and other tribes. They are lost, they are forgotten and they are in pieces within themselves trying to be white; trying to fit in."

"I believe the work that we're doing is assisting that to change."

"We are here; we will follow what you have spoken. We will whisper into the wind."

"Thank you for speaking with me. I'll listen for your voice in the morning when I first wake up or during the day if you wish to speak with me then."

"We are listening to you; you speak to us. We will speak to you."

Speaking privately with Zeezzz, she asks me how I am.

"More to the point, how are *you*?"

"I am in heaven."

"I had a talk with Ashtar the other day. Was he able to speak to you about his feelings?"

"He is as cumbersome as I; I think it makes it more interesting that we are bunglesome."

"I think it does too! You could almost be a separate story for me to write about."

"I believe it would be a compelling one."

"Thank you for your assistance with those who will be embodying."

"I am spread very thinly; it is a cause for me. What would I have done had I not had this opportunity to have legs, and a tail?" That last is said with a very sensual tone.

"What do you like about your tail? Is it for balance?"

"I believe it accentuates my ass."

I am startled by her remark and burst into laughter before I ask if her tail is a problem when she dances. Since she says it's not a problem when she dances cheek to cheek, I ask her if it makes her feel less graceful.

"That is an interesting question. I have observed other individuals walking with more grace. Do you think it is the tail?"

"I imagine it is."

"I will try it without. I *do* wish to appear graceful."

"You can always have it back, but I think it would be easier for you to move and dance without a tail."

"Yes, and I have been speaking to Gaia about the sex. She is thinking that there are many wonderful positions that will be enjoyable for me. We were trying to consider how to work with the tail, and so, perhaps this is something for my consideration. It is so beautiful, and yet I could do without it."

"Give it a try and see what you think."

"Did I say the wrong word? Your energy changed when I said, 'ass.'"

My answer is that I was surprised by her use of the word. She explains that she watched a movie where someone made mention of a fine ass, and they were speaking of that part of a woman's body.

I explain that is a word not often used in polite conversation; it is more likely something a man might say to another man when commenting on a woman's body.

"This is exactly what I heard."

"Women don't usually talk that way, but I don't care if you use it."

"I wish to be appropriate. After all, I have my designs. I am studying physiology. I believe that the most beautiful bodies are humanoid. I have selected quite carefully. You do not have the tail; I think it would be a nice addition for all of you, and yet I am now very concerned that I made an error. I wish to walk like Marilyn."

"Then you're going to have to lose the tail. I suggest you speak with Liponie."

"That is exactly what I will do."

Meeting with Liponie, I ask him to move into the past and put a children's library in place two months ago. Having that available will support the rewrite of my life that I did to make it so that I began reading to Charlie and the gang then.

"Jill Marie came over yesterday to talk with Osiris and stopped to look at the library. She told me it is lovely and it is packed with books. How did you get all of them?"

"I went to the Barn and Noble."

"Did you just copy them?"

"Indeed, and then created them again. Tonas has critiqued every book to make sure there is nothing frightening."

Next, I suggest that he make the valentine boxes of candy I brought for the kids bigger. There's only three pieces of chocolate in each box! He is also going to put each of their pictures on their box of candy. My next assignment is to ask him to make some more underwear for Tonas. Liponie tells me Tonas is quite "excitable" about them.

"I know. I want them to be a pretty, off-white color with big red hearts all over them."

There is a bit of silence and then he asks in a very uncertain voice, "Are you sure?"

"Yes, like big valentine hearts that you see for Valentine's Day."

"Ah!"

"Not *real* hearts! Were you thinking I wanted real hearts? Oh, icky!"

"I was concerned, but I feel sure now."

With the core group:

"Charlie, guess what!"

"What?"

"I have a time capsule for you that will make it so that I've been reading to you and the Swizzlers for the last two months."

Charlie says I'm wonderful. I answer that I need to be a better mom because a mom reads to her kids, plays games, does puzzles and other kinds of fun things with her children. "What books do we read?"

"We did a *Mother Goose*. I didn't understand it, but I'm still very happy about *Pickles the Pony*, and there was *The Cat in the Hat*, and the *Twelve Dancing Princesses* was very nice."

"Even though I wasn't very good at games when I was a kid, I'm willing to play games with you as long as you promise that you won't let me win all the time."

"What if you are winning?"

"Then let me win, but don't pretend you can't do something so that I can win."

Now I am required to explain why anybody would do that. Charlie labels the explanation I furnish as not being honest. I verbally agree with him, but I still think that action is sometimes best when dealing with little children. Charlie doesn't really understand the concept of winning because he says the stories are very nice, and, "if there's ever anything that you want to do to win with them…"

"You don't win with stories." I have gotten myself into another predicament of trying to explain an unexplainable idea, at least to Charlie. I start to use running as an example and he wants to know if we are running away from something. I tell him no and change subjects by asking him if he's ever played Hide and Seek. As soon as I ask that question, I feel like kicking myself. Of course, he's never played Hide and Seek and if we ever did play it, I'd never find him. He's a stick! Think of the places he could hide. Then I ask him to think of things he'd like to do and I'll try to do what he likes. He says he will learn about this and wants to know if it is OK for us to play together.

"Yes, that's what kids do!"

"Even if we should be working?"

"You gotta have time for play, because you work better after you play."

There is a hushed tone of excitement in Charlie's voice as he says, "Oh…I think you're *right.*" More emphatically then, "I *know* you're right! It is so true. *Yes.*"

"We need to take time out from work to play, and that means all the Swizzlers, not just you and me."

I offer him the time capsule that I put together so that we will have been doing more things together in the past and start to guide him in viewing his screen. He sounds just a little bit indignant when he interrupts me to remind me that he is a Level Two Practitioner. In a few moments, I hear him utter a very enthusiastic, "Yes!"

"Tell me the things that you like to do most and we'll do more of those."

"We can do everything! OK, Mommy, if I was more to sleep, this would be a good dream."

I ask Charlie if he sleeps and he says it's not his favorite. I explain that is usually the case for all kids and ask if he needs to sleep. He says that so far he hasn't needed to, but wants to know if I would like for him to try.

"Not if you don't need it. Do you need to tell me anything else?"

"I just love you, Mommy, and I'm very excited. This is wonderful."

"I'm excited to be able to play with you. I haven't done things kids like to do in a long time."

Charlie says he thinks we're going to be the perfect family. I realize that he might be right!

I ask if anyone has something to report. Ashtar answers that things are shaping up. "I have been spending a great deal of time with Zeezzz since she is our intermediary with the inanimates (crystals). There has been a very positive response. This could help in the evolution of the beings of all the stars, moons and suns. I wish to say I believe this is a very good project."

"I think so too. What about the Choshehoe? Do we have emissaries going to them now?"

Ashtar says that the emissaries are still conversing with the hopes of reintegrating the Choshehoe properly. They can't go back to their star if they still want to eat people, and it seems they are enjoying the taste of the people they eat. He promises to keep me posted on what happens.

"When the tribes are ready to go, they just let you know. Is that right?"

"We are watching."

"You took the Lowmah back to their star recently?"

"Of course, it is a very satisfying part of the job."

It occurs to me to ask Tonas if he could learn to read English, that way he could also read books to the children. He says that perhaps he could but wonders if it's necessary.

"I realize that maybe reading will be outdated one of these days, but I'm somewhat prejudiced about people who can't read. I've been read to or I've been holding books and reading them myself for nearly seventy years and I enjoy that."

Tonas laughs and comments that seventy years is one blink of his eye.

"Not old for there, but it's old for here!"

"You'll never be old, my dear."

I drop this subject for now, but I'm not ready to give up yet. While telepathy seems to be a great way to communicate and I've occasionally done it at the council, I can't imagine ever giving up reading.

My next question is if our work with the genies is progressing. Tonas believes that if we could recruit the female genie—Liponie's sister—she might make a difference. I wonder if she's lonely since she's the only one. Tonas says he doesn't believe their brain is wired to understand many things that are normal to individuals such as us. The genies are happy to be as they are.

"They weren't really happy as they were or they wouldn't be here, right?"

"What do you mean by this?"

"We went into the Fifth Realm and I asked them for gifts for themselves along the lines of being more empowered and seeing new options. Now we have a bunch of genies, but they're still maintaining their status quo. If they leave I assume they'll just be captured again."

"This is the situation."

"If something is not working, you have to change something."

"You are one that likes to have things happen very swiftly."

"Yes, I do; I admit that I'd like to see at least a small step towards improvement. Somebody needs to tell them if they keep doing the same thing, they're going to keep getting the same results."

"That is a truth."

"Here on Earth a lot of us keep doing the same things (including, in the past, me) until we finally get so sick and tired of the results that we do something new. That kinda sounds like where the genies are. Liponie, I'm going to sic you on your sister. Give her a little taste of how magical a genie's life can really be."

"This will be quite interesting."

The next item on my agenda is to find out how the Equinox people are coming along. Osiris's humorous answer is that we could not pull them out of that place with a pickup truck and a chain. "They are settling in beautifully and they are moving through a full range of feelings and emotions in an illusion of the physical. They are also moving, I think, very quickly out of the energies that are not as supportive of their original role of non-dual. I think their Las Vegas gambling will be short lived. It is becoming 'old hat.'"

"I know I'd get tired of something like that very quickly."

Next, I mention that there is something that the men on Galna can do. "Two days ago I heard, 'Intend for men to create a book in which their Gods are mutual friends with them.' Can the men on that star write books that will be shared with the other universes?"

Osiris agrees that would be helpful. We decide to involve Charlie and the gang in this. After I transmit the information to him, he says it will be easy for him to find a means to transmit this to each of the men.

"I'll be back on Monday and I want birthday kisses from a lot of people."

"Mommy, I have a present for you and you will love it."

"I'm looking forward to that, Charlie. I think birthdays are going to be fun again for me."

"They *have* to be fun, Mommy."

"Sometimes they haven't been very much fun for me, but they are now."

Speaking with Solomon:

He asks me if I like my sparkles of the sky.

"I do and thank you. I was very surprised when Tonas told me they were from your mines. Diamonds from that location are one of the most magical presents I can imagine."

"It is only a tiny fragment, let us say, of what is due you."

"I'm not used to such extravagant presents. I got so tongue-tied I didn't really even know what to say when Tonas gave me the necklace. I gave him a toaster and I got diamonds from your mines."

"I believe a toaster would be a delight."

"Are you able to tell me anything about the seal you wear?"

Tonas whispers to me that there is eye contact between Osiris and Solomon. He thinks they are communing and suggests I give them a moment.

"It is acceptable to allow you the understanding that it was brought to me from Isis and Osiris."

"Can you tell me what it stands for?"

"It is a field of energy that elevates anything it touches by bringing it into a higher harmonic. It is very easy to direct energy when you have such a gift as this."

"With that kind of ring I imagine it would be easy to direct the genies you worked with."

"It would be very easy to direct, and yet, they were compliant because of the power of the director."

I remark that one of these days I hope to be balanced enough to direct energy in a similar fashion and thank him for speaking with me today.

Since I'm ready to leave, Tonas asks if I will be back for reading hour. I confirm that I will and ask him to help me with my schedule so that I balance work and play. He says that Charlie has been sitting on my lap while the others are sitting around me on the floor. I've been reading stories that are short and the kids seem to enjoy them.

I've never heard of *Pickles the Pony*. Maybe I should brush up on children's books that are popular now. It will be interesting to find out what kind of stories Charlie likes. I'm relieved at the idea of not reading 3rd dimension stories like *Hansel and Gretel*, *Little Red Riding Hood* and especially not *Bambi.*

CHAPTER TWELVE

February 9, 2015

I learned recently from Sananda that my guide, Esthra, assisted me with writing a piece of prose, "The Barn Down the Road." Although this was at least two decades ago, today, since it is my birthday, seems like a good day to thank Esthra for his help.

After I do so, he says I am very kind and that he is celebrating my birth today.

"I'm very proud of that prose and I would like to do more of those kinds of things."

"May I be your muse?"

"Yes, and I think Charlie can be, too. The other day I heard myself ask him how to talk to a star. He told me, 'You just say hello and watch it sparkle back to you.' I would like to bring forth fun yet elegant insights like that."

"There are deep waters within you, and also some very shallow ones; each of those are very sweet. You are finding your own way. It cannot be fast enough for you, I know."

As soon as I step into the Joy Council, Charlie exclaims, "Mommy! Happy to your birth! Happy birthday."

Tonas also wishes me happy birthday and I thank both of them. He adds that all of them are waiting for a chance to honor me but he first wants to know what I have planned.

"Charlie, the first important thing is…"

Before I can finish, he says, "This is important, too, Mommy! We worked very hard for your party. I have a big present for you; you will cry and cry and cry."

"Can I tell you a really important mom thing?"

He reluctantly agrees to listen. I start out by mentioning that since he's young, and everything is new, he likes everything. Then I explain that as he gets older, he might find that he starts liking some things more than he likes other things; we call that having preferences. Now comes the part where I casually mention that he and I might have preferences that differ and if he likes something that I'm not really fond of, that is OK with me.

"I want you to be so happy, Mommy."

"And I want *you* to be happy. Charlie, we'll work it out."

I've been concerned that some of the books I enjoyed as a child are not going to be appealing to Charlie because there are quite a few elements of duality in some of them. After I make the point that he should tell me if he doesn't like any of the activities or books that I select, he admits that he didn't like the puzzles. He thinks they're really dumb because he can figure them out in two seconds.

"You mean the one with the nails?" It's called the Twisted Nail Puzzle and I haven't been able to solve it. There is a solution on the internet but I haven't been desperate enough to admit defeat and look…yet.

"It's so silly!"

"But I haven't figured it out yet, Charlie." I start laughing because, apparently, Tonas and I have a genius child on our hands.

"Oh, we will keep them for you, Mommy, but we just look at them and we know how to do them."

It turns out that he thinks jigsaw puzzles are dumb, too. I say that I'm glad he told me and add that I don't want to spend time on things he doesn't enjoy. I also explain that the only benefit of *Mother Goose* stories is that the pictures are interesting and the words rhyme. He wants to know if they really lived in the shoe. I answer that they didn't and wonder out loud why we even read those rhymes to our kids. Charlie's explanation is that people don't know their children are very smart. I suppose many people might think that way.

Charlie wants to know if I am aware he has a sister. I explain that yesterday I heard myself trying to tell her it's easier to be in an individual body than it is to be in a collective; I got that her name was Nicky. He agrees she likes that name and that she has boobs.

"She's very cute. I like her very much and as a girl she's more fun. She wants to learn how to talk and I'm going to teach her. She has made her hair pink. We told her it was OK; it matches her boobs exactly."

This is certainly an interesting conversation, and, so far, I'm managing to roll with whatever comes out of his mouth.

"We've been working very hard on your birthday present, Mommy. Do we have to do work first?"

I remind him that the transmissions are important. He's OK with doing them first, and says, "Let's go to work, Mommy! We can make really important work on your birthday!"

With the full council:

"Yesterday, I was talking with a spirit man named Napurra. He told me it is time for individuals to feel the story of their ancestors and to take into themselves their own personality in their own timing that is, and will be, supported by the stories of their ancestors. He also said it's important for individuals to be themselves, but their heritage can give them strength. He and I put together a transmission to be sent out. He called it 'The Wisdom of the Ancestors.'"

I let them know about the other two transmissions: overlays for the 5th through the 10th dimensions of Earth that I recently received from some of the galactic councils, (Charlie calibrates these to assist the other universes.) and a map for the dual worlds. After I show these telepathically to the council, Tonas explains that the map is a view of the culmative and suggests we also offer it to non-dual worlds. Gaia agrees it would be good for them also to see the steps leading to the culmative; not all council members have seen what we saw at Liponie's party. Charlie and the gang have combined these three into one transmission, which we send out.

Before we party, I ask Liponie if he can send a box of candy to all the members of the Ashtar Command; Ashtar agrees that this would be a message of heart. I want to send something special to the fairies and Osiris suggests we give them marshmallow candies. Gaia says they don't eat solid things; they only eat energy. I suggest "energy candy" and Gaia agrees to work with Liponie to send something.

"Tonas, what language did you learn to speak when you were little?"

"Lyran, and it was important to my father that I have the major languages. I have many hundreds of languages, of course."

Oh, well, another genius.

"How do you say, 'I love you,' in one of those languages?"

"It would, perhaps, please my father if I was to use his native language. In Eshera, it is Ooqwa. Andromedan, though, is the major language that is spoken, so in that language it is Ohsherah.

"Those two are enough for right now."

He wants me to say them to him. I've already forgotten the exact way to pronounce them and make an excuse that I'm language challenged.

He says, "Please, my dear, you must."

I attempt the Ohsherah version and I must have gotten it close to correct because I hear him sigh.

It's finally party time, but first Tonas wants a private word with me. He states that they believe my idea of an ideal party must have chocolate. He is correct, of course. He advises me to be patient because it might take as much as fifteen minutes for Charlie to bring the surprise fully before me. I promise to be the epitome of patience.

On our way to the party, Tonas explains that there will be a candle lit dinner party with orchids on the tables and starlight above. There will be Puccini with *La Boheme* and *Madame Butterfly*; Heifetz will be playing the Mendelssohn Violin Concerto and later the Folgors will be dancing. "It is an opportunity for Charlie to show how much he wishes to do for you. All of the council members with their partners from all forty-six universes are here, so it is quite a large party.

There is another section of tables that you will experience as your surprise. Working with Liponie, Charlie has put this all together. The only food being served is every kind of chocolate dessert imaginable along with ice cream. There is a soda drink with chocolate and whipping cream. Charlie is proud to be your little one and he has lit every candle himself."

"Oh, Tonas, I don't want to let him down."

"Believe me, he is the star of your show today. I will tell you in advance, he is wearing a majordomo costume. He is your great creation of heart; you gifted all of us with them. It has been such a joy for them to be in our life. For me, he is our first baby. We love all of them but he is the one who takes our hearts. Before you enter, may I give my gift to you?"

"Yes."

"I have the female version of the underpants, my dear. I have done my research. I cannot imagine these would be comfortable, so please do not feel that you must wear them. Believe me they are the exact replica."

I'm giggling as I ask Tonas to describe them. He says there is a full drawer of them in my room. The one he is showing me is paisley and very tiny. He adds that if I ever decide to wear them he would like to be my audience. "I do not understand the little strip in the back. It seems like it would be very uncomfortable; please never buy me anything like this."

He must be holding a thong. I say that I've tried them and he is correct that they are supremely uncomfortable. He then asks if he may place a flower between my toes, and, of course, I agree. He promises to offer me a million kisses later.

As we enter the party, I hear Charlie say, "Mommy, you will be so proud of me."

"Tonas only told me a little bit about the work you've done and I'm already crying, Charlie."

"You will cry and cry. If you will please sit beside Daddy Tonas and Daddy Tonas, will you please sit beside Mommy? We have here what is called a stage; there is going to be a procession. There will be much telepathy for you from those who walk across the stage. This is just a small token of the great wonders that are in the beginning. There are many others but we picked the prettiest of all the new love birds for you, Mommy, and for everyone here to witness from the first time ever in all universes." This is said in an announcer's voice and then more softly, "Including the universe that's not yet part of our council." Back to announcing, "They are here to show you their bodies, and they are what you call dating and wanting to be partners. There is one couple from every universe. I will go in order because that makes my brain not hurt."

Charlie's voice sounds very business-like but also very happy as he begins to call people forward. There's no danger of me being impatient; my heart began melting well before his show started.

"May I please have the beautiful goddess, Trowah. She is a star and she has a partner named Gramad who is a moon; they want to get married. They are bowing to you and they will send to your mind their gratitude because they have legs and arms and everything. They each have a whole body. There are many from each universe but we are only going to announce one couple from each universe today."

For a moment, I entertain the idea of trying to write all the names down, but I quickly abandon it. There are just too many names and only a couple of them sound even vaguely English.

Charlie continues announcing names and whether they are a star, sun or moon as well as the universe they are from. Then he explains in a matter-of-fact voice that Gaia has given all of them the book. "For everybody's interest, they all have quarters here and they will probably all be having sex later. (I hope he doesn't really understand what he's talking about. He's too young!) They are all wishing you happy birthday."

He continues with more names and then says, "I wish for you all to know that my mommy wants everybody to be in love. Everybody loves you, Mommy, and they love their legs. There are all kinds of combinations of suns (which are always male), moons (always female) and stars (can be either) and combinations of two females, two males or a male and a female." Charlie stops announcing for a moment to thank all who assisted them to have their pick of bodies. (They were shown pictures of options for bodies; they pointed to the body they wanted and then got it.)

Charlie continues reciting names and then says, "They want to thank you because you have given them legs and bodies and they would never have had that experience, not ever, ever, ever!" After more names I hear that the word that describes the love of the next couple is, "madly." He announces the names of two suns that are very excited to have legs and penises, too. I agree that those are important body parts.

Charlie explains that he has not seen the book, (Good!) but everyone keeps saying it is very important. After a few more couples, he announces that the next couple is in love and it is again the "madly" kind of love. He mentions that the girls with the girls and the boys with the boys have different books than the ones for the boy and girl partners. "Gaia knows things and she is very vigilant." The next thing he suggests is that I start crying more because that means I'm happy. My answer is that even though my tears have dried, I'm still happy.

After he announces the last couple, Charlie says, "Mommy, this is a tribute to you. I wish for you to know that there are many others that have come forward. We have a special dating game that everybody gets to play."

"Charlie, this is wonderful."

In a loud announcer's voice he asks everybody to please stand and hold up their chocolate. "Thank you. Mama, I know you will want to say something to these beautifuls that are in love because of you. Maybe they were in love before. They will have told you stories in their telepathy, but before we can do that we must all hold up our chocolate ice cream sodas. To *you*, Mommy! To the most important person in all the universes. You are the one that makes our hearts fill with joy. You are the one who makes the story real. You are the one that opens the way for all of us to find the unity of the tribe of one. I know there are others that are assisting, but without you none of us could do this and we love you. Happy, happy, happy birthday, Mommy. Now everybody drink from the straw, and you have to drink it all down and you have to make the noise. OK."

"Charlie, come here a minute. I want to hug you." Now I'm really crying and it's very difficult to speak.

"Do you feel my forever love for you, Mommy? I did not even know you for all my life until I did and from that moment my life began."

"I don't want to ever let you down, Charlie. You're so special to me."

"Well, you have to or my legs won't be able to walk on the ground."

At last I am able to laugh. He wants to know if I like my surprise. I say that I love it. He tells me they have all been taking lessons from a guy who is really famous and they are all going to come to the valentine's party and dance. Of course, I ask who their teacher was.

"We thought we wanted to get this guy who makes juice. His name is Jack LaLanne but he couldn't dance good so we had to get somebody else. We got a man who is very famous and makes movies. We've seen all his movies; his name is Frederick Astaire. He is dancing with Ginger Rogers for you tonight. We stole them from the Fifth Realm! Well, only borrowed them."

"I'm so glad you have them; they're my dancing heroes."

"This dance is going to be to a special song about tomatoes and tomatoes. (Those words are pronounced "toomaytoes" and "toomahtoes" in a song that Fred and Ginger danced to called, "Let's Call the Whole Thing Off.") We thought you would like that very much. Papa Tonas, can you please take Mommy down to the table. We will clear everything off the stage and we will start with the tomatoes song. When they are done with the dancing we have a big surprise for you! All night long there will be songs. You will want to listen to all the people you love, so, Mommy, you can't leave. You have to stay here because there's going to be a lady butterfly song; Heifetz will play you songs and everyone here is going to come and kiss your hand. Mommy, I have this other present for you and it's a picture of me; I painted it myself. It's a very good likeness of me, I think."

"Charlie, that's one of the best presents."

"Well, I thought it would be the best one because you love me so *much*!"

"I *know*. I wish I could put it up on my refrigerator."

"We're going to put it in your house here. You don't need it in your house there; you have me there."

"I know, but here you look like a green rock."

"Ah, only if you see me that way, Mommy."

"I'll try seeing you a different way."

"I'm going to sit with you because the show is about to begin." Announcing, "And now, the show begins and everybody has to eat the whole time. Don't stop!" I hear him humming the tomato song. "They're so good; she has feathers on the bottom of her skirt." More humming and, "I just love this song, Mommy. No more jigsaws and puzzles, OK? We have to watch the show now. *No talking!*"

I whisper, "I love you, Charlie."

Whispering back, "I love you, too, Mommy. No talking."

"OK."

Tonas whispers to ask if he can spirit me away. It seems he can also leave me with Charlie so I agree to leave.

"My dear, was it not wonderful? He was so proud; he is your son for sure. He was in *every* universe; he put all of us to task to find the individuals who wished to become partnered. It was his goal to have one from every universe in presence to honor you. He would not stop until he did."

"Will couples have a place for themselves?"

"It is all handled. In every universe, Liponie has prepared a special ship for each couple. There are hundreds upon hundreds of couples in each universe. Did you take notice that we have several couples from the Mystos Universe? It will be a short time before they join our council."

"I tried to tell him I don't ever want to disappoint him. Please help me."

"He has that same concern for you, my dear. He wishes only to make you happy; we *all* are in that same ship, you see."

"There's nothing he could do that would ever make me not love him. You know that."

"Yes, of course. It was to be a secret, and so we pretended to be on task for the valentine project without giving much away. It was the best kept secret; even when you were here, not as you are now, there was much whispering."

"I'm glad that now I can quit worrying about nobody showing up for the party. What kind of books does he like?"

"He likes books about animals, he loves the pictures and he especially loves being on your lap."

"I love the idea of him sitting there. I'm going to cry again."

Tonas reassures me that he can hold my presence beside Charlie so that he won't notice I'm not actually there. It's not that I would be impatient; it's just that I have another commitment I must attend to.

I mention that I might be back on Thursday. Tonas is bold enough to suggest that perhaps we will both be wearing our new underpants then. He's going to ask Liponie to redesign mine. I laugh but don't make any commitment. Let him guess.

Before I leave, I ask Tonas if he thinks all those stars, suns and moons really love each other. He says he believes that the ones Charlie selected have been carrying a torch for each other for a long time, like Gaia and Aton. He also lets me know that Charlie could feel their deep commitment for each other and that they all would like to be partnered forever. I do *not* offer to do any marrying.

"I love you, Tonas."

"Ah, is it true? Is it quite true, my dear? Ohsherah? Ooqwa?"

"Ohsherah."

CHAPTER THIRTEEN

February 12, 2015

At the council, I learn that the Porneeseesee Universe has gone completely non-dual in the last few days. When Sananda describes an object that Oniuh Comb wishes to give me which contains the path her universe traversed, I realize that I saw it this morning. (It was small, rectangular shaped with holes down the right side of it that I somehow knew keys would fit into.) She has requested that I come to her council on their moon, Hahkah. I gate there, greet her and congratulate her. She says her world of Eeshenarrah, as well as everything in her universe, is blossoming. Even the stars shine more brightly.

I thank her for the gift of the template and remark that I'm looking forward to seeing the stars in my universe shine more brightly also.

"My world is now a world of flowers and I have received reports from many places in our universe that everyone is instantly manifesting their heart's desire. Everything is beautiful. Perhaps we can set up something that will assist others to come here and see this beauty for themselves. In order to honor you, we are calling this a template for 'The Path of Sweetness.' Everything now smells sweet so it really is a path of sweetness."

"Thank you so much. I plan to put this to great use."

In the Fifth Realm with Sananda, I call forth from every dual world all sentient beings currently in existence and ask them to examine this template from the newly non-dual universe of Porneeseesee. "See how sweet it looks, feels and even smells. It is the history of their evolution from duality to non-duality. Your path may be different from the path on this template, but if there's anything on it that you would like to use for yourself or share with others, help yourself. Now please give us any gifts that might assist you with your path."

Back at the council privately with Tonas, I ask him to help me with activities and other things to do with Charlie. He says that the Swizzlers are very focused on the work that we are doing. He adds that he believes the reading I am doing with Charlie, as well as spending more time with him, is fulfilling him. His idea is that Charlie's constant need to be entertained and to entertain himself was because he had something missing—a mommy. Tonas says that I'm doing a magnificent job; this really gladdens my heart. Although I know I'm doing much work at the council, I don't yet have a sense of the things I'm doing with Charlie and the other kids.

At my request, Liponie joins us. He wants to know if I have an afterglow from my birthday surprise. I'm still trying to wrap my brain around all that happened. Couples of embodied stars, suns and moons marching across the stage, thanking me telepathically and bowing to me fits into that category of being *way* beyond anything I ever thought I might experience.

"Can both of you help me set up a time to speak with these newly embodied beings? Many of them still want to talk with me. I'd like to make it so they can speak with me for as long as they want, but compress it into a shorter time for me. Liponie, there are going to be more than even a googolplexian number of them. I don't know how we can do this, but help me!"

Liponie is going to arrange a way for me to do this when I sleep. After I show him the little present I brought for Charlie—a statue of Mickey and Minnie Mouse dancing—he offers to create more statues for all the kids. He'll wrap them and put them in a grab bag. He adds that he will assure our little dear one receives exactly what we like. Laughing, I agree that he has a way of stacking the deck for things like this.

Liponie reports that the dude ranch is done and for the faint of heart there is a horse merry-go-round. Hearing the word merry-go-round makes me realize we should have a playground, too, with swings, monkey bars, slides, good trees for climbing, a tree house and a zip line. After I explain what that is, he suggests doors at each end of the line so that the kids can zip from one house to another. We decide to have a circle of tree houses connected with zip lines and also rope bridges. Liponie tells me he saw a wonderful tree house in a movie called *Swiss Family Robinson* and he'd already been thinking of creating something like that for the kids. We decide this new creation is a kismet thing, but once Liponie and I start exchanging ideas, *anything* can happen!

When I ask Liponie what his sister's name is, his tone of voice takes a definite downswing. He wants to know why I ask and I explain that she is going to help us with all the genies hanging around here.

"She is very much bossy. I am maintaining my neutrality."

I can't help but chuckle as I ask him if he prefers not to work with her. His reply is that if he had the choice, he would not. This is the first time Liponie has balked at anything I've suggested; she must be quite a challenge.

Tonas speaks to inform me that Commander Ashtar has been kind enough to create a ship for the genies and many of them have begun to learn SVH. He also says that sooner or later we know they all will have elevated because we have seen the culmative. I agree that is correct, but remind him that the sooner an individual becomes aware of and embraces their sovereignty, the more fun their life becomes.

Calling the core group and Aton to join us, I ask him what the seeds he sent me were about.

"We activated more in your energies which made your foot able to be more firmly planted in your 7th dimension. Never again tell me that you are not aware."

"I'm still struggling with that issue. Even though I'm carrying things back and forth, much of the time I only have a vague idea of what they are. I certainly would like to know more. Two days ago I saw something coming out of my mouth. What was it?"

Aton asks me to show them what it was. I telepathically show them what it looked like and make a noise that sounds like "Blaah."

"What is this 'blaah?' Your mind showed us without that sound."

"I stuck my tongue out."

"My dear, as you might know, the ankh represents eternal life. It is the key to the spiritual as well as the physical perpetual expansion. This is an important gift."

"Why was it coming out of my mouth?"

Charlie's collective voice answers that they have the knowledge. "This key which comes from the words you speak, transmitted through the arrow, is the gift of seeds of eternal life as if in the ankh. This is the transmission point that we shall use in the offerings for individuals in all of the universes from the template from Oniuh that you handed us most sweetly, Mommy."

Aton says that he believes things are coming quickly to me because of their work on my cranium and energy bodies. "All the little packages are coming together to support the universal consciousness elevation."

Before he can continue, I let him know that something or someone who calls themselves the "culmative presence" wants to embody in a crystal. I don't know who the being is. Aton wants me to show them, and once again I show the group via telepathy the information I received.

Osiris explains that he knows of this one. He laughs and says this is a masculine energy and it is considered incorruptible. "We have many names for it but I call it Toshi. It was an important incarnation in my lineage. He wishes to be embodied in a crystal to transmit the culmative vision. If we could encourage forty-six others to do the same, they would have the privilege of incarnation and all could resonate the vision of the culmative. Toshi is energy and has never before embodied."

Osiris calls Toshi into our presence. I hear Toshi say that he believes this is the answer for Earth and that Earth is his priority. Osiris introduces Toshi to me, calling me Queen Joy. That name still feels strange to me; perhaps after three hundred years I'll get used to it. We decide to look for forty-six more incorruptibles who would be interested in resonating the culmative energy in the other universes. Osiris wants to know if I have a crystal that Toshi can embody in right now. I gate back to my house and bring several back. Toshi asks for the simplest one, then asks me to hold it in my hand while also picturing the design of the culmative.

"Open to the presence as if the crystal becomes a vessel for me. Yes, now I am equally present with all of you from this crystal. I am quite pleased with the energy of this space. I am grateful to you, Osiris, for expanding it and making it so delightful within. Queen Joy, I am honored to be of service to you."

"I'm glad to have you in my home."

"I have had my eyes on Earth for nearly seventy years. This day was in my destiny." Then he asks me to, using the Joy Arrows, transmit the vision of the culmative from him to Earth.

Before we can transmit this to the other universes, Tonas reminds me that Charlie has to contact them and find an incorruptible energy in each universe willing to embody. We move into the full council so that I can brief them on what we're going to do with the culmative vision with Toshi's assistance. Then I address Mr. Lincoln to wish him a happy birthday with many happy returns. His reply is that this work is the greatest gift for him.

After we send the vision out through the arrows, I ask Gaia how it felt.

"Mmm, I witnessed a beauteous stream of keys flowing onto the Earth. Yes, onto us from your mouth!"

Charlie says, "Yes, Mommy. This is the key that we talked about. When you speak, it comes through your words."

"Isn't it interesting, Charlie, that I don't really have any idea what I'm saying? I'm sure it comes out exactly as it's supposed to, but I'd like to know more about it."

Osiris explains it is a language that is brought through me and it is associated with the Joy Arrow. "It is our expectation that it is something flowing from the Council of Origin that is activated within you."

That explanation feels right to me and it is very exciting. I've felt for some time that whatever I was speaking wasn't one of the languages of the other worlds nor was it Language of Light. The sounds that sometimes come out of my mouth are almost always playful. It's great fun to just jabber and let seemingly meaningless syllables roll off my tongue.

Charlie says that now we can send out the template from the Porneeseesee Universe that I gave them earlier. "We added a lot to it. We gave it to all the places that have duality so that when we send it out here, they will all send it out simultaneously."

When I'm ready to send out the transmission, Charlie reminds me, "More keys, Mommy."

It's interesting to be multi-lingual in this way. When I learn what I'm saying, it'll be even more wonderful.

It's time to inaugurate the council for the Mystos Universe. They stepped forward a few days ago but Tonas forgot to mention it to me. I ask Charlie if he wants to come along and he says he wants a tickle—that's how gating feels to him. Then he asks if all of them can come. I gather all the kids along with Liponie, Tonas, Sananda and Osiris and gate to the Joy Council in the Mystos Universe.

Hehtarnew Johnrah says, "Greetings to you, Joy. We are the last, and yet we are told we are not the least."

"You are correct! Mystos is the only universe that sounds even vaguely like it could be an English word. You don't have to spell it for me!"

"I wish for you to know that it was not anything of lesser that held us from committing sooner. It was a bit difficult because we wished to involve everyone within our universe and for it to be a collective agreement. This was quite an endeavor and took us almost a full year of your days."

This information solves my puzzlement about why it has taken them so long to throw their hat in the ring. It's hard to believe that it only took them a year to get everyone in their universe to agree on joining. On Earth it's hard to get even…well, you know how it is on Earth.

Addressing Hehtarnew, I say that we honor him for his commitment and marvelous work in securing this agreement.

"We are upholding the vision of unity and fellowship that you have created and the integrity that you have shown in all of the universes. Your patience with us also gave us an even greater gratitude, for if you had rushed us, I believe we would have bolted."

With the pleasantries accomplished, we move rapidly through the inauguration of their council and transmission of our work. Sananda offers the Badges of Honor and Tonas offers the support of the Ashtar

Command. Along with the champagne, it seems Liponie has designed a cake for everyone to eat in honor of Lincoln's birthday.

He explains that, "This birth celebration is part of Earth's history of freedom, the freedom that begins in the heart and grows. There is sometimes controversy and even struggle that accompanies this desire to be free. It was Abraham Lincoln who had a vision for freedom; let us raise our glasses to your same freedom. Let us drink to that freedom and to that opening of hearts to find the element of love that brings us all together."

I bid them goodbye, gather the kids around and gate back to our council. Upon our arrival, I hear an ear-splitting "Wheeeeeeeee!" from Charlie and then he says, "That was fun, Mommy!"

"Can I ask you something?"

"Yes, always, I'm open to all questions."

"Do you think you might like to have a room of your own?"

I didn't anticipate that he would ask me why, but he does. I explain that if he has special things that are just for him, he can put them up so he can see them. He could also have quiet time all by himself.

Almost before I finish he blurts out that the others don't mind! I add that if any of the others would like their own room they can have it. I suggest that maybe Nicky and Pinky would like to share a room and then list several possible alternatives for rooming.

Charlie says this is a new idea because they have always been together, always, always, always. I say it's OK if they want to stay that way and he comes right back with, "Yes, but Mommy, don't we grow from change?"

"We do, but you don't have to change right now. This is something you could do later if you want."

"Can I make it so that it's my own?"

I agree that's the idea and he lets me know he's going to talk to Liponie. He wants his room to look like the North Pole. I quickly find out that this is because he wants to have Santa's workshop in his room. "If I could have the elves they could make me toys day and night."

"I'm not sure about that. What do you think, Liponie?"

"Working day and night is not pleasurable, because we know that when we keep beings constantly in service, there is no opportunity to play."

Charlie's rebuttal to Liponie is that he thinks the elves like to make toys. Liponie admits that Charlie has a point. The compromise we make is that Charlie can have the North Pole workshop in his room, but the elves only need to work one day out of seven. Charlie giggles and wants to know when he can have it. Liponie says it is already made. I don't think I'll ever get over how he does things like that. Since we're on a creating roll, I ask for a big, comfortable rocking chair so more than one of the kids can sit with me. Charlie whispers that this is the bestest idea ever.

Now I say something that does not meet with his approval. I suggest that maybe Charlie needs to give the other kids a turn at sitting on my lap.

I hear a very downcast, "OK," and I regret ever mentioning this. I immediately try to remedy the situation by explaining that this would not be all the time, only occasionally.

"I thought maybe Nicky might want to sit with me a little bit sometime."

Another downcast, "OK."

"You don't sound very happy."

"I'm happy, Mommy."

"No, you're not. I can hear it in your voice."

"But I always want to sit with you."

"What about if there's room enough for two? Then you can always sit with me and someone else can too."

"But you only just became my mommy and I don't want to share you very much."

"You'll still be sitting with me. I'm Nicky's mommy, too."

"I don't think you should tell her that, because then she'll want to sit with you all the time like I do."

Boy, have I gotten myself into a fix here. I'm still trying to remedy it and say, "You know how it makes you so happy when I'm happy?"

"Always, Mommy."

"One of the things you will learn is that it makes you happy when other people are happy too, not just me."

"OK."

"Let's try it; it will be an experiment."

"OK." This time he sounds like he really is OK with sharing me.

"Did you find a book you like?"

"My favorite, and thank you for reading it to me every day, is *Robin Hood.* He steals from the rich and he gives to the poor. He is a hero."

"You know who else is a big hero?"

"Me?"

"Yes, you did much important work with the stars, suns and moons and I really appreciate it."

"I did that. I had help, of course, but not from the council."

"Tonas told me you kept everyone on track and got it all done."

"I got the prettiest ones, too, Mommy."

"You did really big boy work."

Then Charlie volunteers information that surprises me—he's learning how to sleep. I ask him if it is so he can dream.

"I'm still practicing that, Mommy. What I do is I lie down and close my eyes and then I let my body relax. Then I make a little noise." Here he volunteers snoring sounds that would put a champion snorer to shame. "Then I sit up and I stretch. That's how far I am now, but I will be sleeping more and more, *at least* three minutes."

"You don't have to sleep for me." I know that's something a mom would probably never say to a regular kid, but I'm pretty sure Charlie doesn't need any sleep.

"I want to understand it; that's why I'm doing it. I see you sleep a *lot.*"

"My body is different than your body; it gets tired and I don't think yours does."

He agrees that he doesn't get tired.

"Don't worry about trying to sleep. If you want to play all the time, I don't care. I have to sleep and I do a lot of work when I sleep."

"You come here sometimes; you work all the time, Mommy."

"I hope I'm playing, too."

Charlie changes the subject and asks for a horse. Liponie asks me for a private meeting and then explains that Charlie wants to be a cowboy. He's concerned that Charlie is reading our minds. I hope not but there's nothing to do now but try to keep the secret for just a couple more days. Liponie says we have cowboy and Indian outfits for all the kids, and the dude ranch is ready with smells and all—there are even pretend steaming poops. (This is something I could have done without, having stepped in enough real cow poop—much squishier than horse—as I was growing up.) His last suggestion is that we add a tunnel of love to our party. I agree that sounds like a good idea.

The other news he shares is that Zeezzz is becoming closer and closer to Ashtar. When I ask, he tells me that she has no tail now. "She looks beautiful. I think she is reading his mind for what he would enjoy."

I rejoin the full council in order to say goodbye, but first, Mr. Lincoln wants to thank me for his cake. I apologize for not spending any time with him and wish him a happy birthday.

"It was a beautiful Christmas, birthday and every other holiday rolled into one that all this should happen on my day. And the angel food cake, mmm!"

As I tell Tonas goodbye, I finish by whispering, "Ooqwa."

"Ooh, I have bumps of gooses. Farewell, my dear, until a moment from tomorrow."

CHAPTER FOURTEEN

February 14, 2015

Speaking with Sananda, I share that yesterday I saw a section of a garage that was full of lots of stuff and I heard myself say that there are many pieces. "Then I saw several women and one asked me if I would like a map."

Since the place to find out about this map is in the Fifth Realm, we both step into that location and I ask the women who spoke to me yesterday to step forward. Sananda reports that there are nine of them and they are sisters and cousins of people from my genetic lineage.

I had hopes that I might recognize some of their names, because in his later years, Dad spent a lot of time compiling information about his side of our family tree; unfortunately, no matter how many times he explained how so and so was related to this person—and on and on—as soon as he began to relate the names, my eyes would glaze over and my comprehension would immediately drop to zero. Since even cousin is a relationship I just never got the hang of, I drop all hope of knowing any of these women. It's more important to focus on what they want to share with me—how their gifts began and how they developed and expanded them. I learn that the map they are offering me is a road map to help me move past dogma to inspiration and guidance. Put another way, they want to help me circumnavigate future pitfalls so that I can come into my own. I ask them to tell me about their abilities, and, through Sananda, this is what they share.

Martha explains that one of the pieces to my perceived inability to communicate comes from her timeline (five hundred years ago). It was not good then for women to show their gifts or abilities. Her gift was midwifery as well as understanding how the body works in order to heal it.

Another woman named Sarah (accent on "rah") tells me she was a healer who used herbal remedies. Her mother taught her how to find things in the forest as well as how to prepare them. Part of her instruction included knowledge about the Moon, Sun and stars. This was not what we call astrology; it involved tuning into the Earth and knowing how everything interconnects.

Another Sarah (pronounced as usual) had psychic abilities and clairvoyance. She adds that she really had to walk a fine line when she was alive.

Magda's gifts included potions and spells which she used to help people. The example she gives is that if someone wanted to find a mate, she would make a spell to attract a mate to them. There were spells to help people get well and ones to clear attractions to devils and similar energies. She remarks that some of her potions and spells could help me with my orchids. She learned from a woman named Sondra who was a very powerful Italian woman Adept. Sondra was considered a white witch and she lived in France and also Spain about three hundred and fifty years ago.

A woman named Karone tells me her gift was also with plants. She lived about six hundred and fifty years ago, and was also very much in tune with the animal kingdom.

Mary's gift was hearing the whispers. She was clairvoyant and "knew things." She was held in high regard and was not hunted. She lived in England almost five hundred years ago.

I address the group to say that I consider their gifts to be precious treasures, and that I've always enjoyed reading about people, especially women, with their kinds of abilities. I check with Sananda to see if there are individuals in addition to these women who could assist me with abilities similar to the ones they've described. He suggests that these women are very valuable because they are not in my direct genetic lineage; normally, I would not have received anything from them because of that fact.

As they continue to share information with me, I learn that Hortensia was like a druid and has a lot of things to offer. She tells me that I am like the women in the group she worked with and she is excited to assist me.

Another of the women, named Posadra, was considered to be an incredible knower and she was also known for bringing people back from the dead, if they hadn't been dead for a long time. She says she knows that I also have the ability to bring people back from the dead.

Tamara was an Irish girl whose gift was healing. She was also a midwife.

Sananda runs all the files they give me through a filtering system that will boost their abilities for me in my childhood and through my life; it will also clear anything linked to what might be considered bad witchcraft. I use SVH to put those cleared files in place for myself. Before I leave them, I split myself into nine energy bodies and give them each a hug along with my thanks for their gifts.

With Liponie and Tonas at the Joy Council:

"At last, at last you are here; the children are so excited. We are raining little heart candies on them."

I brought a chocolate-covered, marshmallow valentine heart for Osiris and Liponie is going to replicate it for everyone. I also brought my little "Bee Mine" pin; Liponie obliges me by making another one to put on a necklace as a gift for Charlie. He informs me that everything is ready: the tunnel of love, the tree houses, a park, the dude ranch with horses, cowboy/cowgirl outfits for everyone and even paddle boats on the lake. He also warns me to be cautious because my angels and guides have bows and arrows.

"I hope they are rubber-tipped."

"They are made of beautiful light and they are planning to shoot you and Tonas."

I'm relieved they are made of light; I had pictured that perhaps Tonas and I would be walking around with suction cup arrows sticking all over us.

Tonas asks if he may give me his gift. After I say yes, he asks me to close my eyes—funny man. Then he relents and explains that he is placing something around my neck. "The closest stone you could have here would be a ruby; this is in the shape of a heart. It is about the size of the nail upon your thumb."

"Oh, that sounds so pretty, Tonas."

"Happy Valentine's Day."

"I have a card for you; let me read it to you. On the outside it says, 'I'm not interested in a nice normal relationship.' Inside it says, 'I like ours better.' At the bottom I wrote 'Ooqwa, Tonas.'"

I hear him sigh and he says, "My dear, you have no concept of what is to come. I took a little peek. There is a glorious, glorious journey ahead, and, believe me, you will find within your heart a space for this sweet one before you."

"I know I must; however, there's still a little distance between that place and this place."

"In our future there is so much dance, music, flowers, joyfulness, open thoughts and lots of traveling, my dear."

"I want those things, too, and I want to be able to travel and not have my orchids die."

"We will simply bring them with us."

That will work for me!

"Let's have Charlie join us."

"Mommy, you took forever!"

"I'll tell you about what I did later, but now, see this little bee?"

"Yes."

"It says on it 'Bee Mine.' It's for you to wear and it means you have access to do anything with me you want to do whenever you want to do it. It could be, 'Mommy, it's time for me to sit on your lap now, it's time to play now, it's time to read, it's time to ride bikes, or take a walk in the park, or just sit with you.'"

"How is this possible, Mommy?"

"Because I'm giving you permission."

"I can be with the bee!"

"With this bee you can be with me whenever you want."

"I'm going to give Tonas one, too, but your bee is the first bee. So, even before Tonas, if you want to do something, I'm for you, Charlie."

"I have my new room that is perfect or me. I have a special bed and I can lie on it and think. I can be myself; I don't have to be anybody else. I have rows and rows and rows of shelves that I can put things on. The bee is on a string; should I put it around my neck?"

"You can wear it that way or you can put it on your shelf. All you have to do is say, "Mommy, it's my bee time."

"Bee, bee, bee, hee, hee, hee and no one else gets one but Papa Tonas?"

"Just Papa Tonas and you. I want you to know you can sit on my lap anytime you want, Charlie."

"Are you going to be here forever?"

"Sometime I might be there forever but right now I know I've been there a lot."

"Yes, you have; you've been very busy. You've been spending a lot of time with the crying lady."

It seems Helena is having a hard time. Charlie says he's tried to make her happy. Tonas explains that Helena is moving through a great deal in her SVH class; she is having trouble learning how to be sovereign. He tells Charlie not to worry because Helena is in good hands and I know how to talk to her. Charlie says he knows she will be OK because she is here with us and we will help her.

"She does not want to ride on my train anymore; I think she is making a mistake. What does 'OK' mean? Everybody says it in all the shows."

"It's just a word that we use that means it's all right."

"I am OK."

"You are even more than OK, you're perfect."

"I know, and also Liponie has big surprises for us and there is a ribbon across a door! We can't go in there until you come! We've been so waiting."

"Let's go! Hold my hand."

"We can skip, Mommy."

At the entrance to the secret room, Liponie begins speaking about what to expect: there are gifts, candies and everyone has a valentine, a special gift that speaks of the heart. "We have the Saint Valentine. When you step through the door, no matter your status here, you will have either a cowboy or a cowgirl outfit. We have a ranch for dudes. Dudes are individuals who are, somehow, associated with riding horses. There will be saddles that you will learn how to put on your horse; each of you will have a horse and there is a trail you may follow. We have a big barbecue. There is also something I learned from Joy's parents; it is called a barn dance. There is a park with rides for the children; however, one of them, a rolling coaster, is quite frightening. You will have to hang onto your hats! For all of you who are in love, there is a boat ride through the tunnel of love. In it you are required to spend some time kissing."

Liponie calls the children to come and pick a gift out of the grab bag. Charlie gets, of course, the little statue that I wanted him to have of Mickey and Minnie Mouse dancing.

I hear him say, "Oh, Mommy, they are dancing! I have a shelf that I can put this on in my room. All of my brothers and sisters want their rooms, and," whispering, he says, "I think they want to be people now because if you have your own room you are a big boy. I have shown them my room and they love it, yes. I have a valentine for you now." He continues in his regular Charlie voice, "It says in hearts. I don't know the English, Mommy. The heart says, 'I love you forever and ever and ever and ever and you're the best mommy there ever was.' Can I kiss you now?"

"Oh, please do."

Giggling, "I kissed your lips, Mommy! I kissed your lips. Can we cut the ribbon? Can we cut it? Can we cut it? Can we cut it? We have to go in there because there is a dude and I'm gonna become a dude, too." After clearing his throat, he announces, "If everyone is ready, please let the children go first. I will cut it. It's cut! It's like a big barn door is opening. Oh! It's so big; it's so beautiful. Mommy, can I go, can I go, can I go? Ooh! Look at me! I'm a cowboy. Mommy, can you hold my figurine? Thank you, Mommy. Can I go, can I go, can I go?"

"Yes! Go play!"

"Eeeeeee!"

This big little boy is such a joy to me. My heart opens wide when I'm with him.

Tonas tells me there is corn on the cob and many cakes, of course. Helena has been working with Cory to make them and that has been a good distraction for her. He says I look beautiful in my cowgirl outfit and he feels he is quite "dapper." One our way to the tunnel of love, I ask to speak with Saint Valentine before we take our boat ride through it.

Tonas explains that the man is wearing his robe underneath his cowboy outfit and comments that it is quite a unique look.

Valentine says he admires me greatly.

"Thank you, very much. I bet you never thought you would ever be experiencing anything like this."

"I have not viewed everything, and yet, I think I have a belief that there is something here that is so very, very playful. I believe that the history of my bringing special little notes to individuals has become something quite admirable. Certainly, this commemoration is very special."

"It is a special day and we love celebrating it. I especially love celebrating it with all the people I am around now. I'm glad you could join us."

"I'm enjoying the children most of all. They are like nothing I have ever seen."

"They're older than time but they are also brand new."

"They truly are great wisdom bringers to all of us and a reminder that it is not, nor should it ever be, a serious world. It is easy to raise the heart when there is laughter and joy and the sweetness of spirit."

"Yes, have a good time today."

"I will be consuming foods."

"All right and have some candy for me."

"Tonas, what are the kids doing now?"

"They are already on the horses. It took them seconds to learn how to put on the saddles."

"Charlie is a genius. Did you figure out how to do the nail puzzle?" (I still haven't figured out how to separate them.) I don't feel quite so inept when Tonas says he doesn't understand it either.

Tonas says, "I wish for you to know that you are my valentine. The saint spoke of love and how even those who persecute know not what they are doing. They have forgotten their truth of self and so the greatest gift is to love those who are lost to the truth. This is part of his history and why the valentines are handed to individuals who are connected by heart."

He tells me that the plan is for us to share our pieces of cake; he has strawberries with angel food and mine is triple chocolate—perfect choice. We have a special boat with a very large, curved clamshell behind our seat and pedals that we will push with our feet. There is a bottle of champagne to open when we are inside the tunnel. He adds, "You will feel my lips upon your lips most readily within the tunnel. Let us begin pedaling so that we will get to the tunnel very quickly."

Eating chocolate, drinking champagne and being kissed by him while we pedal our little boat through the tunnel of love sounds like a perfect Valentine's Day itinerary.

CHAPTER FIFTEEN

February 17, 2015

There seem to be so many gifted children now and I've been thinking about ways to assist them. This was brought to the forefront of my mind when a friend sent me an internet link to a three-year-old boy pretending to conduct a Beethoven symphony. He was at home listening to a recording that he was very familiar with because his directing was fairly close to what a real conductor would have done. What was most important though was how thrilled he was with the music; his joy, his excitement and happiness to be doing exactly what he was doing was delightful for me to watch.

Assisting children to develop their gifts or abilities and/or be able to do whatever brings them joy is Fifth Realm work. In that realm with Sananda, I call forth from all timelines, children and their parents and describe to them my experience of watching that three-year-old conductor. I add that I would love to play in any future orchestra he might conduct. "Even if he chooses not to continue with developing that gift, I would like to assist him with any gifts that will give him the most joy in developing and practicing. I'd like to help *all* of you develop your gifts, anything and everything that would bring you the most joy in your life."

I offer to the children, their parents and anyone who would wish to exploit the children, SVH processes such as infusions of divine light and love and sacred rays which are non-manipulative. I also ask the angels to put in place a buffer to play down the brightness of the energies of the children to those who would exploit or harm them. I ask for the parents and their children to give us the gifts they would like to receive that will assist them and also to specify all the places they would like to receive their gifts. I also ask for the angels to light up the graceful paths that will assist all of them to be most fulfilled in their lives. Finally, I advise them, "Don't hold back! Bless yourself!"

Handing over these gifts felt so good to do that I decide to call forth all beings in the Fifth Realm at the near completion and ask them to give us gifts they would like to receive on a *continuous* basis through their *whole* lives that would help spur insights and awareness for themselves. I tell them they can give themselves millions of gifts per day or just one, anything that they believe will assist them.

Sananda mentions that Mom has stepped forward to offer me some heart-shaped cookies—she says they are snickerdoodles—as a belated Valentine's Day present. She rarely made cookies when she was alive, but it seems like she's become an expert cookie baker now that she's dead.

(At this point in the story that no longer exists about the bad guy who changed sides, Ashtar and the experts he called in had identified that he had occult protections, but they hadn't been able to break through them. They took the precaution of separating the man's consciousness from his body and only communicated with his consciousness. His body was moved to a different location in another dimension and placed in stasis. Ashtar believed that there was no way his consciousness could communicate with his physical form, and yet, his consciousness was so strong it might have been able to create another body for itself. In addition to those precautions, the fields that surrounded the man were constantly changing so that the moment there was a possibility he could crack the code, it had already changed. Ashtar admitted to me that he had never seen their devices be so useless.

I included this information in order to give you an idea of how I'm not looking forward to finding his *teacher*.)

At the council privately with Tonas and Ashtar:

We have continued trying to track down the occultist. It now occurs to me that a series of numbers I heard this morning might be important. I remember the coordinates we got for getting the first Joy Arrow from the Corena Universe and these numbers seem to also be coordinates. Speaking to Ashtar, I say, "Here are some numbers I heard today that might help—2060284937."

Ashtar confirms they are coordinates and after a few moments I hear Tonas say, "My dear, I think you have found the location we have been seeking. This position is in Fantrah." Ashtar says he will send someone adept in stealth to this place.

With the full Joy Council, I greet everyone and then jump right into business because I'm nervous about what I heard myself ask Woonfred this morning. It's important to repeat my question for him now since this is the time I heard myself ask it. (I know; this kind of thing confuses me too, but better to ask twice than not at all.)

"Woonfred, can you seal the passage into your realm?"

He asks me why he would do such a thing.

"There are some beings who want a dragon egg."

"*What! They wish to have one of our eggs?*"

"Yes, unless someone can think of something better, that's the solution I came up with."

He asks if he may leave and I grant his request. Tonas says everyone is concerned, because if an egg is taken before the 4th dimension drops off it could be held there.

The next topic for discussion concerns something I heard last night. There is a woman who is dressing like a man. As I investigated, I realized that the woman is actually a moon named Shareelah who is conflicted about being a woman. Her partner is a sun named Nobee. It didn't occur to me that we might encounter a situation like this. After I share my discovery with the council, Osiris laughs and says, "Oh, my dear, we accept this, of course, and yet since this is their first time for embodying, perhaps we should set counseling in place in each universe."

I agree with his suggestion and add that although I've been in my body for several years there were challenges along the way. We decide to have Liponie do a bit of schooling in each universe; I know he'll make it fun. I voice my concern that we are spreading him very thin and Osiris suggests we enlist some of the other genies. "They are lining up to enter into the new life program. (I haven't heard that name used before but is sounds like a good choice to explain what we hope to offer them.) We can give them an opportunity to assist others, which will be very exciting for them. We will watch over them."

"Two nights ago I heard Joyyahl Kindar, I believe, explain that the Joy Arrows can be calibrated to show the transmissions we send out in layers so that people can more readily absorb and understand the information."

Charlie says they have received that information and that the arrows are ready to be calibrated to do this from the beginning of our transmissions. I roll back to that day, announce to the council that I have a little something to add to the arrow for our inauguration, add it and then roll back to the current time. When I get back, I ask Charlie if it worked and I hear his singular voice say that he checked just now and all of them are fixed. (Yeah SVH!)

We thought Woonfred was going to stay and guard the entrance to the dragon realm, but now Charlie announces in an excited voice that Woonfred is back. Woonfred reports that the entrance is sealed in fire and that he has returned because he felt that he could not step away from his position here. He has put Chiros in charge until Earth itself unveils their realm. I tell him that I'm sorry he had to do that and perhaps we can open it again before the culmative. He says he believes we will be able to open it when we are in the 8th dimension. He adds that perhaps others of Earth who have not reached that dimension will still want to harvest some eggs and that other worlds in our universe or other universes might also see the dragons as a valuable asset. "That is when I will be most vigilant and perhaps call upon the Ashtar Command for our protection."

"Mr. Kennedy, I know you wish to say something about family."

"It is about the unity that is felt within a family. There are many belief systems, and yet, families seem to hold firmly together when there is trouble. We are a family that reaches to all that exists everywhere. It is time, perhaps, that human beings begin to see what lives outside of Earth. I thought there could be something transmitted to all the universes and to Earth that will unify us as that family. These are my private musings."

I explain that we are going to put in place today transmissions based on gifts everyone in the Fifth Realm gave Sananda and me earlier. Kennedy agrees that would help individuals and yet he still hopes we can send out a vision of all that is a part of our bigger family of the one tribe. "What can be better than the vision shown to everyone of Earth that there is more than just people, the earthworms below, the animals above and the birds in the sky? There are stars, the Moon and Sun above, but none can see that there is anything except dead stars blinking in the sky. The human species is so uneducated about the universe."

I ask Charlie if there's something we can do to assist people to open up to the magic of the, currently, unseen.

He suggests that perhaps we can put together pieces from all the things we have, adding that our world is not the only one that thinks it is alone. According to him, there are lots of worlds that do know about other worlds and they travel to them. He feels that the ones that don't know are afraid to know.

I mention our scary movies (I don't watch them but I see them advertised.) about aliens coming to Earth and trying to obliterate us. I know lots of people watch those kinds of movies and it must stick in their memory that there are scary things out there. That, or the idea that Earth is a tiny, unimportant place in a huge, dead universe, seems to me to be what many people believe.

Charlie feels that we can help people without scaring them and suggests we begin with Earth.

"Last night I had a vision of myself throwing out love—in the form of my red pajamas with white hearts on them—to the universes."

Charlie giggles and says that Zeezzz caught them. My mention of pajamas inspires Charlie to ask if he can have some pajamas like mine. He has a bed now. (I suppose he can use it to put things on; a stick-thin body that never sleeps will never wear out a mattress.) Speaking of things to wear reminds me to ask Charlie if he has nice clothes to wear. He answers that he has cowboy boots.

"Do you have other clothes?"

"I have a hat."

This is definitely another area of Charlie's upbringing that needs to be addressed. My suggestion that he should have different clothes for different activities is not met with one shred of enthusiasm. In fact, he says he's wearing his cowboy outfit now, he loves it and he doesn't ever want to change it.

"Remember when you liked the Mickey Mouse ears?"

"Yes, but I got tired of those."

"You might get tired of the cowboy outfit. I'm not saying you will, but you might."

His, "Oh…" lets me know this is something he hadn't considered. He adds, "I am growing up, Mommy. I'm changing. Every day I get bigger inside and it's because my heart is getting so big."

"I know it is, and it was big to start with, Charlie."

"As big as big can be."

I inform the council that I saw there's going to be a new grid today. Charlie says it will pop on after our transmission. He hands me a compilation of pieces of everything we've done that he believes will assist the bigger vision of family that Mr. Kennedy wanted to send out. Charlie also added the continuous transmission of gifts that people gave to themselves. We send out the transmission through the Joy Arrows and I announce, "There are red pajamas for everybody!"

Then I remember I was actually guided to send it out yesterday, so I roll back to yesterday and repeat the "pajama transmission" then. Now here's a little time travel hiccup. I forget to roll back to today and I forget that I forgot. I hear Tonas remark, "That was amazing, my dear. You appeared right before us and began transmitting from the orb. It was very spirited."

"OK, we did that yesterday, right?"

"This is our today. What are you speaking?"

"I rolled back to yesterday and did it."

"I do not remember doing it yesterday, my dear."

"What is today? Is it Tuesday?"

"No, it is Monday."

After I stop and think what day today is supposed to be, I venture that today is supposed to be Tuesday.

Tonas replies, "No, today has to be Monday. You just appeared before us and began transmitting."

"OK, I'm going to roll forward to today. Thank you, Tonas. Bye-bye."

After I'm back, Tonas asks me if it is complete. Just to make sure, I ask him if it's Tuesday; he confirms that it is. I laugh and say that's good because I was stuck in Monday. Now *I* know when I am but he is confused.

I inquire about the genies and am told that Liponie is instructing them about emancipation. Tonas says that this has caused many of them to have a feeling of rebellion towards those who were enslaving them in their minds. They were shown the culmative and also shown that almost everyone in a dual world experiences a degree of enslavement. They were advised that now is their time to evolve and become a person. Liponie is hoping to bring them into service. Tonas remarks that service for the culmative will be a dream come true for those who were held in service because of their gifts.

With Tonas and Charlie in privacy:

I first ask Charlie what the name of his horse is. His interesting and original reply is that he doesn't know because the horse didn't tell him. I suggest he could make up a name and ask if he's read any stories about horses. He tells me he doesn't want to name his horse, which is cream colored with brown spots, after a chicken. (I wonder what story that was.) Then he asks if he should name it Joy. I'm reluctant to have anything else named after me. When he says it's a boy horse because it has a penis, I suggest that he discuss names with Tonas. Tonas agrees to help with selecting a name.

Charlie says, "Papa, I want to have a good name for my horse because Mommy thinks it's a good idea. If I name it something good, then she'll be happy."

Determined to squelch that idea, I advise Charlie to figure out a name that *he* likes.

"Oh, well, I fed it carrots today and somebody told me it wouldn't poop because they weren't real carrots. Is that true? I wanted to see it poop."

"Charlie, I'm not sure about your horse. The ones on Earth eat a lot of food before they poop. When Liponie's not busy you need to talk to him about what your horse needs. Do I ride with you? I like to ride horses."

"You said you would do it with me."

"Tonas, do you want to come with us?"

"Of course, and we will have a picnic, Charlie. Now run along. I wish to talk to Mommy alone."

Tonas says that Charlie is starting to talk about becoming a real boy. It seems I read *Pinocchio* to him. Now I'm upset with myself there. What a perfectly awful book to read to Charlie. What was I thinking? Tonas says he explained to Charlie that he is a real boy and adds that he thinks Charlie wants to have skin like us.

"I don't want to hold him back from what he really wants, but I don't want him to decide to change just because he thinks it would please me."

"Oh, no, I do not believe that is the reality of it. I believe that in the reading of that book he realized that he was very much like *Pinocchio*; that he is not a real boy."

"He's real to me."

"He's very real to all of us. Yet, he wishes to have a heart that beats. He's very interested in poop for some reason."

"That's a stage that kids go through. We want to take this slow, or, at least the speed that Charlie wants to go."

Tonas assures me he will let me know if Charlie brings up this subject again. He adds that he's only bringing this to my attention because Charlie was very touched by that story.

"How far in the future did you peek?"

"I am not allowed to say."

"Can you tell me a little bit more?"

"You are happy; happier than you have ever been in your life. You are *always* joy to us, and yet, in this, I feel you are joy to yourself. And I believe that you have been preparing for a life that is beyond what Earth can offer you. I think that you have had the imagination, the openness and excitement to read and maybe even to watch the programs that are of a galactic version. In doing so, it is as if you were preparing yourself for our life."

I agree that I've read science fiction and fantasy novels since I was in grade school.

"I have not read science fiction. I only know that there is joy and laughter that is coming from a place within you that is as if a well spilling over and it is so very authentic. I feel the joy within you is authentic now, and yet, there is a distance. When you can truly reach out and feel your hand in mine, that will be a freedom for you. I know that you wish to experience him as he is."

"I do, and I hope I let him sit on my lap whenever he wants; I know he won't want to do that forever."

"Oh, he will grow up. Well, we must hurry things for you, my dear, so that he is still our little boy."

"I hope we can."

CHAPTER SIXTEEN

February 18, 2015

At the Joy Councils with Tonas, Charlie, Osiris, Gaia, Aton and Sananda:

"Last night I heard the words, 'in jeopardy,' then later I heard, 'more than one registered closing.'"

Tonas wants to know what I make of it. I was hoping he could tell me.

It has occurred to me that perhaps instead of sealing the entrance to the dragon realm (If the Chu see something like that they will surely attempt to find out what is being protected.) we should have put holograms in place for all the dragons and their eggs. Immediately, Charlie says that he and others on the council made a hologram in the past so it looks like the dragons never came back to life. That feels like the perfect solution.

The next subject to discuss is that for some reason I've been wondering if there might be "moles" that are waiting for a certain point in time to become active and cause chaos. Since I've learned not to ignore hunches like that, I explain to the group what this kind of mole is and how individuals can be activated at key times to assist the group they are working for.

Tonas speaks to say that he has been observing a gathering of energies for more than a year. "It is difficult to understand what would be the end focus for this, and yet, as you are discussing this, I do have a thought that perhaps you might have an insight here. Truly, if something was to be activated to simultaneously stir up inner conflicts this could create a suppression of the vibrations of Earth. Do you agree, Gaia?"

"I believe you have stumbled onto a very diabolical plan, my dear."

"Charlie, can you tap into anything about what 'more than one registered closing' might mean?"

"Yes, Mommy, we will."

I suggest to Tonas that it might be helpful if he took a peek into the future. Charlie (plural voice) advises Tonas that he must not do this because if he does he will not be able to help us. "Mommy, there is more than one registered closing. Rather than moving backward in time, my dear mother, it is perhaps better to make it look like they are winning."

It is interesting that lately Charlie's plural voice has started calling me Mommy, and "my dear mother" is a phrase the CEV have never used before. Even their plural voice is starting to sound and speak in a more human fashion.

Singular Charlie says, "If we make it look as if any change of the wind could be a win for them, perhaps they will not try so hard."

"I think they would immediately act; I don't think they are going to slack off."

"Ah, but if we make it look like everybody who is awake is slacking, they will think they do not have to try so hard." After a few moments, Charlie says it does feel like they have a plan that is waiting for an execution moment. He adds that we haven't quite waited until it is too late, but we are playing it close.

I request suggestions for a course of action. Osiris says it's important for all of us to play by the rules. I'm not too concerned about the rules, and since I don't really know what they are, I'm going to let these non-dual folks attend to that detail. He agrees that all of them have had a feeling that there is something that is very close and can be considered to be a thwarting agent. Tonas has the idea that if the people who are moles did not agree to play that role, perhaps we can do something. I suggest we ask people in the Fifth Realm for gifts that would assist them with sovereignty.

Sananda and I move into the Fifth Realm at the near completion. When we are in position, he suggests I call forth all beings alive on today's date and also on November 17, 2015, (I don't know what that date is about, but, obviously it's going to be important.) and ask those who had anything to do, whether they knew it at the time or not, with thwarting or slowing down the release of the 4th dimension to step forward.

This reminder that I will be speaking with members of the Chu causes me to request a pause. After a moment of reflection, I ask Sananda to speak to them for me.

He begins, "Those of you that are of the reptilian species (I knew it.), please move to the front of the room. We bow to you for your great role that you played in the evolution of Earth. We wish to ask you if now, from this state, there is something you would like to have delivered to yourself that would assist you to create a new reality that will perhaps support those of us who are wishing to experience a swift and graceful release of the 4th dimension on March 16th. We are willing to deliver this to you.

To those of you who have played the role of adversary we say, 'Well done,' and we congratulate you for you certainly assisted in reflecting the conflict. Now I ask you this, would you wish to offer some gift to yourself so that you can experience another reality? I realize you experienced this during your reforming work here, and yet what a wonderful idea to offer yourself something that would change the flavor of your experience. Make your gift available if you are interested.

Now, if you were exploited without your knowing, you have the opportunity to see yourself rising easily into the higher dimensions. There is a means for releasing the controls that were placed upon you; you can put something in place that will attract you to receiving this gift."

Sananda asks them to hand their gifts in the form of orbs to him and then he gives them to me. We all move into the SBT, I call forward all those who wished to receive a gift from themselves, and hand their gifts over.

We move back to the Joy Council where Aton joins the group. After he is brought up to speed, he suggests we all take a moment to feel the energy of the present. Sananda asks me to send out a clearing to assist people to move gracefully into the 5th dimension and I gift this to people via my e-mail list.

Speaking with Tonas and Charlie in privacy:

Tomorrow I'm leaving for an orchid show in California and I'm taking Charlie in his rock with me. Since I plan on taking it with me to the beach and letting the ocean water splash over it, I ask him if he will feel the water when I do that. He says of course he will and wants to know if he can have a surfboard. I have no idea how he thinks he could manage surfing, but rather than discuss it, I just say we're not going to swim. It will simply be an opportunity for him to enjoy the ocean water.

"Mommy," now Charlie's voice sounds a little tentative, "Papa Tonas said that maybe it is better for me to become a real boy when you and I are on the 9th or 10th dimension. Then we can travel together and I can hold your hand. I like being a Swizzler, Mommy, but if I was to look like you and I was to have skin, I think it would be really good."

"I do too, Charlie, but let me tell you something, we've still got plenty of time for you to decide about that. What I want you to know is that right now you are a real boy to me. If you stay this way I will love you just as much as if you change. When you are really sure you want to become something different, that is fine with me, I'll love you no matter what. Except, if you turn into a frog, I might have a little problem."

"You won't love me if I'm a frog, Mommy?"

"Well, they are a little slimy and it wouldn't be much fun to kiss a frog."

Charlie laughs, says he could become a prince and then he'd be a real boy. I remind him that he's a real boy to me now.

"But Mommy, I can't poop."

"You know, that's not all that it's cracked up to be. I don't think that on the 9th or 10th dimension people will poop so you don't want to change just so you can do that."

Tonas agrees I'm probably right about no pooping on those dimensions.

"See, Charlie, pretty soon none of us will be pooping. Yeah! That's been a challenge for me much of my life. When you get plugged up it's not fun."

That seems to settle his mind about poop because he agrees he has plenty of time to think about it.

"Did we ride horses yesterday?"

"Yes, you were good. We put our arms out like they were wings and we rode really fast. You didn't want a saddle, and that was crazy."

Although I did ride horses bareback as I was growing up, I never rode fast. I must be a better rider there; at least I hope so.

"Tonas tried it and he fell off, that's why I didn't do it."

"Tonas, did you really fall off?"

He sounds sheepish as he admits that he did. His excuse is that he didn't want to hurt his horse by pulling on its mane, so he slid off.

Charlie says he asked his horse what it wanted to be called and it said it wanted to be called Blackie. He told it that it couldn't be called that because it wasn't black and then it said it would like to be called Skipper. Both of us agree that's a good name. According to Charlie, my horse is a beautiful gray color with tiny spots and I'm calling her Sable. I wonder why I picked that name.

"What does Tonas's horse look like?"

"Papa Tonas has a golden horse. It is so beautiful and since it is very big he had a long ways to fall. I encouraged him to have a saddle."

I find out that each Swizzler has a horse that they got to choose the color for, and that one of them has a really pretty rainbow-colored horse. Charlie likes that color so much that he's going to have Liponie change his horse to that color. He asked Skipper if that was OK and Skipper said it was.

I want to know if Charlie will be OK just being in my room during our trip and he says he will be very busy. He asks if he can see me eat just one time. "And if I can see you poop, I won't tell anybody."

I have to laugh for a moment before I mention that he can see me eat here. His reply is that he wants to see me eat the foods that are in the special places. I won't even have to take him out of my backpack because he can see through it. After I agree to take him with me for my meals, his comment is, "Wow!" I had no idea that something like that would be appealing to him and plan to lug my backpack with me as much as I can.

"I love you both."

"We love you, don't we, Papa."

Tonas, "Yes, my dear, we love you very much. We are coming with you, of course. I will transfer onto the ship so that I can keep you within range. I am wishing to give extra guardianship to you."

"Thank you, I appreciate that."

CHAPTER SEVENTEEN

February 23, 2015

At the Joy Councils, Tonas's greeting is followed by smooching sounds and he laughs as he says that my kisses are different when I am there like this. I'm glad to know my presence there makes a difference for that sort of activity, but I have information that Ashtar needs to have right now. As soon as he joins us, I report that this morning I heard, "One name, and it's someone that everyone is looking for. The name is Cromfeld."

Ashtar sounds incredulous as he asks, "What are you saying? It can't be."

He says Cromfeld is their most trusted aid and asks me again how this can be. I shrug my shoulders and don't reply. He asks to take his leave and departs immediately. I remark to Tonas that it sounds like we found a spy. He says that if it is indeed Cromfeld that would make a lot of sense.

"Everywhere we have gone we have been just a little bit short; it is as if someone has gotten there before us."

He adds that on the surface, Cromfeld appears quite dedicated and yet he is of mixed character—meaning he has dual and non-dual genetics. This surprises me since I had assumed that all of the Ashtar Command would be from non-dual worlds.

"Are we still trying to locate the occultist?"

"Yes, indeed, and yet the wagon is playing the music constantly since the very beginning."

I'm trying to picture what a wagon playing music has to do with any of this and then he corrects himself by saying, "Oh, excuse me, the band wagon continues, and it is quite concerning."

My laughter prompts Tonas to ask what he said that was so amusing. I explain that I was having trouble figuring out how a wagon was involved. He apologizes and says he is learning more and more English expressions. He continues by saying that Cromfeld's influence could run deeply within their ranks. They have been discriminate about those who would be within the command itself, and yet Cromfeld is high in their organization and has always been most trusted. "If we are careful, it is possible we could net all of them. Ashtar did not appear himself; it was a shock for him. I must take my leave from you as well, for I have the intention that if this is true of Cromfeld, it will be important to keep it quiet."

After Tonas leaves, Charlie and Liponie join me:

"Mommy! I had so much fun. Thank you for my vacation!"

"Tell me what you liked."

"I got to be by you all the time. I wanted to surf but I couldn't. The sand was a little scratchy and the water was cold! Here, Liponie makes the water perfect for surfing."

"What else did you notice?"

"It was so fun to watch you eat. One day, when I'm a real boy, I'm going to eat like that. It will be very fun because we can go to places and I can sit beside you like a real boy when we eat."

"I still want to tell you that you are a real boy."

"I know, Mommy, but I am in a rock." His voice drops as he says that last, then he adds, "But here I can be a real boy! Someday I want to be a real boy outside of these council places."

"I want that for you too."

"I want to sit beside you, Mommy, and I want to hold your hand. Are you going to read *Cinderella* now or is that for later?"

"I will read to you later."

"I have been doing something very important; I have been taking classes and I will be an SVH Level Two Master Practitioner very soon. And then maybe I can do number three. I wish I could be in the same academy you are in, but I'm OK to just be watching you. When you do AMS work you go different colors all over when you sleep.

When I ask about his horse, he says Skipper is still rainbow-colored. "He is a boy and it is OK to have the penis, you know. Skipper loves me and he missed me while I was gone. After we have our story, we can ride on our horses, OK?"

"Yes. Tell me what else you liked about the trip."

"I liked to be on the airplane. It's really fun because if you push your energy outwards, it's like on Papa Tonas's ship—there's nothing beneath holding it up."

"What did the energy in San Francisco feel like? I drove around quite a bit with you in the car."

"It felt like it wants to be happier. I asked it, 'What is your desire to be, San Francisco?' and it said, 'We wish to be gay.'"

I feel obliged to explain to Charlie that an alternate definition for gay is that it describes people who prefer partners who are of the same sex.

"Oh, that makes sense because it was like they had a home where they felt safe, and they want to be gay there. I think it's a special home for people who want to be gay. Are the gay people happy to be gay?"

I answer that people who prefer that kind of relationship are happier about it than they used to be, but then explain that although our societies in general tend to be more accepting now, there are still humans who consider that choice wrong and even shameful.

"Oh, Mommy, the stars and moons and suns don't feel that way. Can we help the people to be gay?"

Charlie and I discuss this issue a little bit more and I resolve to present it to the council.

"Thank you for letting us have fun and special times with you. Someday we're going to have all the time in the world. I want to always be with you, Mommy, for evers and evers."

"I want that too, but when you get older you may want to have other people with you and me. We'll have to see what happens."

He doesn't get that I'm talking about a partner for him in the future, but he says, "OK."

I ask Liponie to join us so that I can tell him I've missed seeing him and that I'm proud of his role as teacher for the genies. He says there are many, many, many that are ready and preparing to be in service. He feels they will be quite instrumental and remarks that it is a shame we can't put them on Earth and send them around with their magic wands. At first,

I love the picture that creates for me. Then I shudder at the total chaos it would create; humans are not ready for anything like that.

He says he and Cory, Ashtar and Zeezzz have been working in the kitchens because there is a special engagement that is coming up.

"What is that?"

"I think I have spoken too soon, my dear. I believe you will know when you see the two of them together. She has lost the tail. They are in love and they cannot be apart from each other, even for a moment. You are a champion again!"

I'm happy for them; Ashtar definitely needed someone like her in his life. I know the non-dual people exist on a completely different time scale than we do, but no matter how busy he was, two million years is *plenty* of time to be alone.

"Did you get the pie I brought for you?" (Every time I go to San Francisco I drive up to Mill Valley to have a piece of S'more Pie. Before I took my first bite, I gated to the council and presented Liponie with a piece of it.)

"It is already on the buffet; Osiris has had nine pieces and is coming back for more."

"I was thinking of him as I savored every delicious bite. It was so good."

"I perfected it."

Even though the pie tastes incredibly good in this dimension, I know Liponie could make it better. Maybe next year when I go I'll have *two* pieces of pie; how can I have been expecting one piece to last me a whole year?

With the core group, I announce that there's a new route that Queen Kahleah can assist us with. "I also got that there are thirteen more keys and there's a code that's ready. Kahleah told me that there is a book that's been written in the future that can help us with what we're going through now.

I also want you to know that we need to somehow help people realize that the 3rd dimension is gone; many people on Earth are not aware of that fact. Can we transmit that so people won't try to hold onto it?"

Gaia says she feels that ordinary people believe we are a part of a continuing evolution of life rather than moving through the dimensions. She explains that even individuals who are quite awakened are uninformed about the release of the 3rd dimension because it feels so much like the 4th dimension.

Sananda suggests that we send through the arrows a transmission on a continuous basis of the energies of the 3rd and 4th dimensions. He believes that would help people to feel that they are separate energies, and then we could show them what the 5th dimension feels like. "A bridge does not exist between the 3rd and the 4th dimension; it exists between the 4th and the 5th dimension. This is a difficult bridge because these two dimensions are melded into each other."

We decide to transmit the energies of the 4th through the 6th dimensions individually to help people discern the differences.

I ask the group if the people in Equinox still love the experience of duality or are they bored with it. Charlie says he is in very close connection with these individuals and Emissary Inoh wishes to accept this as their place forever. "We kept them in a little bubble so that they would not be found, but we were not very good at this. They have been approached and given a better offer. Inoh has not said 'No' to the other offer but they wish for us to make it so that it looks like they are not going to be in trouble if they do say 'No.'"

Oh, drat, another little issue that could become a big issue. I'm so grateful I don't have to figure out solutions to these kinds of situations all by myself—most of the time, anyway.

Charlie continues by saying they really loved their star, Airio, and maybe we could bring them here before it exploded. That way the people who want to exploit them will think they died in the explosion. This sounds like a great idea to me but I want to get the opinion of the others.

Sananda agrees it will be simple if the Ashtar Command will help us relocate them. "These individuals were eager to make the Earth their new home because it is the center point of the action. If we are to move them directly from Airio, we must create a bubble of non-duality for them so that they may move to Earth in the past in an easy shift. This will also make them useless to those who might wish to exploit them since they will be non-dual and therefore incorruptible. I suggest we place them in Canada near the vortex energies of Lake Louise. There is an ascended master temple there and they will love the energies of that region."

Tonas returns and Sananda telepathically transmits to him what we've discussed. Tonas proposes that we place them somewhere between the 5th and the 6th dimensions and that the 5th dimension energies should be non-dual—as they were before the Atlanteans brought duality into that dimension.

I ask why we can't roll back to before the Atlanteans messed up the 5th dimension with their duality. Sananda says they didn't mess it up; they put in a stepping stone for humanity. "If they hadn't put the energy of duality in the 5th dimension, we would still be another 500,000,000 years in the 4th dimension. It would be very difficult for the Earth, from where it is now, to move into a non-dual state."

I let Tonas know that I told this group about Cromfeld and he informs us that the man is indeed involved in something unsavory. He and Ashtar will be investigating all individuals of the Ashtar Command who have mixed genetics.

I ask if there has been any progress with the occultist. Tonas reports that they still haven't found the head of the snake.

"Before we finish this part of the meeting, I want to say that I hope you all enjoyed the S'more Pie."

Osiris, "May I say to you that it is a triumph. I have had fifteen of these pies already."

I am staggered by this admission. *Fifteen pies?* All along I've toyed with the idea that Osiris has been joking with me about his gustatory enthusiasm for marshmallows. I like them too, but…marshmallows? As a final test of his sincerity, I comment that he must really like marshmallows. He says it is his favorite human food and I'm finally convinced he's sincere.

Although experiencing strange happenings has become almost commonplace for me, this morning I experienced a more personal occurrence that felt very odd. Speaking with Aton, I inform him that early today I felt an eyeball moving into my third eye. He replies that soon it will begin to blink. I answer that I think it already does.

"Let me see you. Of course it is. You will also notice an eye on the back of your head. You will experience these in your hands and all of your chakras. This is a part of the whole package."

I remark that this sounds creepy. Aton disagrees and asks me to look at him, saying that he's covered with eyes and so is Osiris. (I still think it sounds creepy.)

"Do they all just wake up gradually?"

"Not gradually at all. They are the eyes of your presence. It is who you are, my dear, the awakened one."

"OK, I'm still waking up, though."

"It is part of the evolution. Please recognize that before anyone is fully awakened they experience a progression to this state. I like your eyes, my dear, and we love you."

At my request, Queen Kahleah joins us. After she announces herself, I ask if she has some information for me and she replies that she has a great deal of it for me.

"It is important for you to recognize that there are quite a large number of writings that exist that are a part of the evolution of our clan (the Atlanteans). I think these would be of interest to you. I believe that Charlie and the rest of his council can disseminate from these volumes and perhaps assist to create a program that could be transmitted to Earth to show the human beings of Earth the grace of their kin. We are all part of human and as such it is very simple for us to be viewed as part of this evolution, we simply took the journey earlier. You are crossing terrain that we have not, for we never experienced the 4th dimension."

She suggests that writers of future books might be able to access the perfected versions of the Atlantean manuscripts. She reveals that there will be more than one hundred books in the near future and over the next hundreds of years many more so. "I think the full compilation of all of these volumes will be easy for you to get in that place you go (Fifth Realm). I cannot access this place." She advises that I get the manuscripts and bring them to Charlie. She also explains that in the Fifth Realm, I have the knowledge of the thirteen keys and I can retrieve it from myself there. I thank her for this information and release her.

Charlie says this is really exciting and asks me to bring this to him in the form of a telepathic transmission. He explains that he doesn't want to learn English but would rather use telepathy since it is more truthful. I mention that I'm used to using words and he counters I won't need to use them much longer because we're really moving fast.

In the Fifth Realm at the near completion, I call forward human beings who, when they were alive in the 7th dimension and upward, wrote books about the Atlanteans. I ask them to transmit the pristine version of their works to me in an orb. Then I move into the SBT, call Charlie to come get the orb and hand it to him to take back to the council to make into a transmission.

Back at the council, I return to the subject of the Equinox people by asking Tonas where the plans for their evacuation stand. He explains that they need the exact coordinates for the dimensional field where they will be placed and adds that Metatron can provide this. I ask him to join us and hear him thank me for inviting him.

I realize he should be part of our core group and ask him to join. He accepts and informs me that the telepathic transmission he just received has brought him up to speed with what we are doing. He has the coordinates and suggests we should do the transfer on a special date in the year 1999. "This will give them extra points for being part of the Earth's population. Gaia, will you approve these coordinates and this dimensional frame?"

She approves and agrees this is the most wonderful plan of all. "Charlie, I give you all the credit. Now they will have an immediate transition in their own energy field. Please scoop a little of the energy of their star, Tonas, so that you can pour it into that space. We will create an energy link that allows that energy to continue to radiate. My beloved,

Aton, will you shine upon them as you did from afar? It was more of the violets, blues and golds."

Aton says he will make the shine upon them match the way they were shown upon on their star. "In fact, we will allow them to understand and experience the beauty of their world and yet to know that they are of Earth. We are not replicating Airio for them, we are offering them a home that reminds them of the place they so loved." He asks if Gaia will allow the energy of their essence of Corea. (She played the same role for Airio that Gaia plays for Earth.)

Gaia agrees that it would be beautiful to have Corea join her and suggests I offer the Five Star Serenity Send-off to Corea since her body died when Airio exploded. She will then be in an ascended temple; Metatron can meet her there and escort her to Lake Louise. Gaia wants to know who will be the negotiator for this.

Charlie replies that it would be his council and asks if that would be acceptable. He adds that they (the Swizzlers) have been doing a lot of the negotiations. I reply that it is acceptable to me and I hear his little boy voice say, "OK, Mommy." Then he giggles and says, "I will do a very good job, and so will we."

Charlie announces that the CEV have the thirteen keys and a file which is the full measure of the stages of 3rd dimension up to the 10th. "Each dimension is clearly identified as separate and we show how each dimension feels and resonates. We believe that this should also be transmitted beginning in 1972 from Inishimora."

"I was twenty-six then. I'd been married three years."

Charlie says, "I wish that I was your baby then."

"I do too, but I've got a lot of time with you still. Did you know that we can have millions of years together? We can have *more* than the three hundred and fifty years until the culmative because we can hit a pause button."

"Pause button?"

"Gaia can tell you about it."

After she telepathically transmits the information to him, I hear him gasp then say, "Oh, Mommy. Oh, boy! And I will be able to sit beside you and we will eat cakes and pies!"

"We'll eat cake and pie (I bet I can eat more S'More Pies than Osiris.) and we'll travel the universes."

"Can Papa Tonas come too?"

"Definitely, and Liponie and all the gang."

"Wow!" This is followed by giggles and an urgent voice that says, "Let's get this started right away. Let's make it happen now!"

Charlie says he put the information in the orb into a diamond and has handed it to me. As we send it out, I hope that humans will finally get that the 3rd dimension is gone and that those who are hanging around in the 4th dimension will be able to feel how sweet the higher dimensions are.

I gate with Tonas onto Inishimora where he confirms that we are now in the year 1972. I wasn't sure I had managed that, but I laugh and comment that I'm grateful I won't need a whole new set of driving skills for this kind of work. We hold hands and send out the transmission to Earth like we used to. Then Tonas asks me, "Now, my dear, send that transmission out as we move forward through time as if a wind has caught hold of us…and here we are. That was what you call a trip down memory lane."

In privacy, Tonas says he thinks we will soon have wedding bells. "Ashtar is most smitten; Zeezzz has completely given up her tail. She wishes only to be fully in the measure of her heart with him. It is one of those love stories that will last through time."

"I'm glad that he has more to his life now."

"I would wish this for him forever; you should see the glint in Zeezzz's eyes. It is a success made in the heavens."

"I had a vision of us in a sailboat. We'd want it to have some kind of motor also, but I can just see us and the kids with the boat sails out as we fly with the wind. That's one fun thing to do since we're going to have millions of years."

"This was the best news of all; we'll have forever. There is no place in all the universes that is out of our range, even now. Imagine what it would be to have the time to experience this. We must have a very large ship since it would be difficult for Charlie to be separated from the other children."

"Yes, maybe even two or three."

"I have been sailing through the stars; to sail through water I think would be very easy."

"Sometimes there are fierce storms."

"These will not be a problem for us; we would simply quell the storm."

"Sometimes it would be fun to just ride through it."

"Oh, how delightful."

"I love you."

"I adore you and I love every inch of you!"

I exit to smooching sounds.

CHAPTER EIGHTEEN

February 24, 2015

At the Joy Council, Tonas says he has a great surprise for me. I reply that I hope it's a good one, because I'm a little leery of surprises these days.

"I have created a beautiful place for you for our very first journey with our ship. It is a great palace near water where the ship is anchored. There will be many horses of the variety with the horn in the front."

"Wait a minute. Where did you create this?"

"It is a little place that I have found that I think is quite beautiful and very green. It is in this universe and it is a non-dual world called Hosemelia. All the floors of the ship are crystalline so that you can see what is beneath at any time. There are mermen and merwomen and many things that were of Earth. Although these have been restored on Earth, they never left this world."

I'm going to ask Tonas more about this later, but right now I need to give Ashtar a number I got this morning. When I ask if he is near, I hear him reply that he is.

"Here's the number, nineteen, space, six, space, then seven, seven, two, four, eight, nine."

Asthar explains they had already investigated that location but found nothing. I offer to escort them back in time and we move onto Ashtar's stealth vehicle. He suggests that if I gate his ship to the location, I can intend to select the most appropriate time. He has all of his officers join us, I gate to the location and he asks me to move them into the correct position in time. As soon as I transfer the ship, Ashtar says they are transporting to the surface and asks Tonas to stay with me on the ship.

Tonas tells me it is now a waiting game. I say I never thought I'd be involved in anything like this, but before we can chat more, Ashtar announces that he is back. It took him only about twenty seconds to return and he says that they now have over nine hundred men who have been delayed in their plans. We wait about another minute for these people to be transmitted to a holding place and put in stasis. In the meantime, I ask Ashtar if these people were part of Cromfeld's group. He answers that the organization is like an octopus and they have been collecting the arms as they move toward the centerpiece. After I gate us and the ship back to our current time and position, Ashtar comments that this was very helpful for them and that this gating tool I have is very sneaky.

"When you're working with sneaky people, you need to be able to be sneaky too."

"Yes, and we are so very up front with our hands out to show that they are empty, you see."

"There's a place for that, but I'm more anxious to do what needs to be done in the most divine way that it can be done."

Before Ashtar takes me back to the council, I inform him that council member Bromeeshna Carote is angry that his wife, Toesheenah, has been incarcerated. This man spoke to me last night as I was lying in bed getting ready to sleep. Talk about direct communication!

Ashtar says he had just cause to do so. I suggest that perhaps Ashtar could speak with the man in private. He says that now that they are aware of this problem they will allow him to visit his wife, but he will have to remain on the interrogation ship. He adds that Bromeeshna can be present as his wife is questioned. "We are lacking in some of these skills. These are things we have not been faced with."

"This is a big mop up operation which is something you've probably never had to do."

"Indeed not. We have been very focused on assisting humanity and holding off all those who would attack Earth. This is not an attack and yet it is offensive."

Discussing the situation with Ashtar, I find out that Cromfeld doesn't suspect anything and that he is connected to the still uncaptured occultist. The command have been covering their tracks so that none of the, for lack of a better word, bad guys are aware they are being rounded up. Ashtar says he feels sure this will be mopped up in time for the big party Liponie is already preparing for March 16th. He is calling it "launch day."

"I hear your romance is going smoothly."

"Oh, my dear Joy, in the midst of all this, she is in my heart every moment. I am so grateful to you."

"I'm happy for you. Perhaps, a part of your life was just waiting to blossom with the love of a woman. Congratulations."

"Of *this* woman, of this one. She is beyond my imagination. She is bigger than life; she will keep me on my tippy-toes, believe me. We are speaking of a family, but please know that I am very committed to this mopping up. In my heart it is important now for my family. Have no concerns."

With Tonas back to the council:

Before anyone can join us, he asks if I would like to have a little kiss from him. I giggle agreeably and he adds, "If you wish to investigate, I am wearing my underpants."

"I got so busy with business I forgot about those. Oh, Tonas."

"I adore you, my dear."

"Can you tell me how far in the future you peeked?"

"There are several openings that appear to be gateways into a speedier entry into a life experience that is to be dreamed of. This is what spurred me to begin preparing a special home for you. I have rooms for all of the children; it is quite a large place."

I ask for more information about the ship he made. Although it has sails, he says it also has a perpetual generating device that uses the principles that Tesla discovered and those principles are used even on Inishimora. "Tesla channeled these; ours are more advanced but they use the same principles."

I mention that those principles never got off the ground here and Tonas says he understands they were stopped. I'd heard that but I don't know any details about Tesla's work.

With the core group:

"Sananda, Kamala Shrow spoke to me the other night and said, 'I have been all forty-seven of the beings you see standing before you. They have not all been of the highest caliber but the line clearing could transform even the darkest ones. Could you bring that tool into these universes?'"

"I did not consider the line clearing tool; it is outdated for Earth and yet it would not be for these individuals. We need to have these updated for all of the other universes. Will you ask Jill Marie to do this, please?"

"I will."

"I'm supposed to get some special shielding from the future."

Osiris volunteers that he can help me and adds that Metatron is also here.

I ask who wants to dive in and get them for me and Charlie says they are all going to put their heads together to get the shields for me. Sananda offers what they have created. After I eagerly accept, he describes me as invulnerable. Even though things are always being updated in the SVH shields, he suggests it would be advisable for me to periodically ask for updates. After I ask the best way to do that, Charlie suggests I ask the Swizzlers, because they know things I can't possibly know yet. Although I'm surprised by this information, I know he's not going to tell me anything about the future. I ask him to remind me occasionally to get updates, and am somewhat encouraged when he says that very soon I will know about these things. I'm even more curious, but resign myself, as usual, to waiting.

"The other thing I want to address is that the essence of the star that exploded did not have the Five Star Serenity Send-off. Since she didn't have it, what did we miss?"

Sananda explains that the process was offered to beings but not to the stars, moons and suns. Although there are not many who have transitioned that way, he thinks it's a good idea to offer it. Using SVH, I add this in the past to the offerings we made to the different universes so that all transitioning stars, moons, suns, asteroids and any field of energy with an essence of presence shall have the Five Star Serenity Send-off. Sananda also informs me that the former residents of Airio are now settled very comfortably in the area of Lake Louise.

"On Friday I want to address the issue of homosexuality because on Earth that has been considered a sin."

I explain that I'm used to the idea of people being gay, but when I started thinking about celestial bodies being gay that was a new concept for me. "Many people have been taught that homosexuality is wrong and it has been considered very shameful in the past."

Gaia says that she feels the reason for this belief is that there are versions of Creator replicated in most species. "Creator is the essence of that which is the spark of all of us, and there is an individuation within the illusion of separateness where the wholeness of Creator becomes as if a masculine or a feminine. Aton and I are embodiments of those two parts of self; perhaps the misconception comes from the idea that to be in perfection, you must have that match."

I share with the council that in earlier times it was important to have children as a result of intercourse, because you had a better chance of survival if you had a large family to assist with the work that needed to be done. I add that pleasure during sex was not considered important, only the production of children.

Gaia sounds excited when she suggests that they must see her book. That might actually help if people were to believe who wrote it…but maybe not even then.

In privacy with Tonas and Charlie, I ask Charlie how he's coming along with his horse. He proudly announces that he is a "bares back" rider.

"Is he still rainbow-colored?"

"Yes, and Liponie is going to make him so that when he poops it will be rainbow-colored; it will be beautiful."

Since Charlie is still hanging onto his fascination with poop, he and I have a brief discussion about it. During our trip, I took him in my backpack into the bathroom stall with me. I mention that I was a little nervous about him watching me poop even though I sat down on the toilet. He comments that there was a big flush and that he needs to know about these kinds of things for when he is a real boy. I suppose so, but pooping has been such an issue for me my whole life that I'll just be glad when I don't have to do it anymore.

I ask him what book we're going to read today and he says it is *Cinderella* again. I learn we also read *Snow White* and Charlie remarks he is really off apples now. I remind him that there's no need to worry about apples on our ship and he agrees that food here is always perfect.

After saying good-bye to Charlie and getting a hug and kiss from Tonas, it occurs to me to ask what the name of our ship is. He says we are going to inaugurate it together. I share the idea of having more than one ship because then we could race each other as well as swim back and forth between them.

"You have such an adventurous mind; it is delightful. You will keep me on my tippy-toes. Zeezzz has captured Ashtar's heart, as you captured mine so long ago. Remember, on Hosemelia, my dear, there is a crystalline palace for you."

CHAPTER NINETEEN

February 27, 2015

At the Joy Council:

I heard some things last night that require immediate attention. As soon as Tonas and I exchange greetings, I request that Commanders Ashtar and Voldan join us. (I haven't consciously worked with that commander, but I did hear myself ask him last night to keep an eye on something.) After Tonas informs me they are present, I greet them and then say, "There are three regions that have some kind of energy reading device which can detect your ships, even your cloaked ships, before you enter. If you would like a jamming code that will cloak your ships, I have it for you."

Ashtar says he doesn't need to ask me how I know this; he simply needs to ask for the code.

"The numbers are: 8632 2147.2."

Tonas laughs and explains that the two commanders left in an instant. When I reiterate that there are three regions, he says he didn't hear me say that because his mind froze. He asks me what the three regions are and for a moment I'm at a loss as to what to tell him. I know the answers are in my levels of consciousness; I just have to be able to relax enough to access the information. After a few deep breaths, I intend to open the levels and let the information we need flow out of my mouth. I find myself explaining that it is not just three regions that have a device, it is three *universes*: Fantrah, Nordahnee and Lowmeesha. These are fully covered and the opposition is preparing to cover all the universes. Uh oh, I knew this was going to be a big deal.

I feel panicked but Tonas calmly replies, "Ah, then we must be cleverer. Let me call the commanders back to us."

After I share this new information with them, Ashtar remarks that a jamming code is important but it is only temporary; when someone is aware they are being blocked they simply work to find another way. He wants to find another way to surprise these people and at the same time let them believe their device is working until he can fish out all of the individuals who are part of this conflict.

My idea is to gate the command to the past, to all the places that they arrived too late to capture anyone. Ashtar recommends doing this first because that might circumvent the problem of the device. In answer to my question about the occultist being behind this new scenario, Tonas says that he feels this being is assisting *anyone* who wishes to thwart our work. I wonder out loud if it is possible to capture him and Tonas says they have been working night and day to do that.

I've been thinking all along that we are going to have to do something extraordinary to capture this individual, and now I'm sure of it. I ask if they could secure him if I took some of the command with me, and gated to where he is. Tonas says he would never forbid me to do anything, but pleads, "We do not wish to throw you to the lions. Please do not test me in such a way; you are everything to me."

"I just feel that we will have to continue putting out these fires as long as the person who is striking the matches and throwing them out is free."

Ashtar wants to deal with the reading devices but agrees that there is a bigger piece of this problem that needs attention. I suggest we do what we can and then regroup for more strategizing to see if we can discern the location of the occultist. Ashtar mentions that perhaps Charlie and the kids can deduce the location of this being, but when I ask if it would be safe for him to do so, Ashtar replies that they are being very careful, even with themselves. That answer makes it easy for me to decide not to involve Charlie—at least until it will be safe to do so or there is absolutely no other choice.

Ashtar puts a ship in each of the two hundred thirty-one places that were empty when the fleet arrived to search them. This could be interesting, because although I know I can split myself into that many parts, I've never attempted gating others on this large of a scale. I think it's a good idea to ask Sananda for guidance and he joins us. Ashtar explains about the energy-detecting device and that since we don't know how long it has been active, we are moving into the past.

Sananda directs me to stay in my current position here. Tonas is to stay with me in every position and he will have his arm on my shoulder. "I am creating a buffer space for you in each of the ships; gate your energy bodies into each and move into the frames of time thirty minutes before these positions had warning of the Asthar presence. Hold the space in each position."

Sixteen seconds after I move every ship to the past, Sananda informs me that they captured the full complement of individuals at these meetings. He advises I leave the ships in position in the past and suggests I move myself back into oneness with my presence here and now. Ashtar rejoins us to say that this system is effective. "We have incarcerated several thousand and I believe we have several 'heads of the snake.'"

I now move into the SBT, since it is the safest place to be, as I try to zero in on the location of the occultist. I open up my levels of consciousness and also intend to work with the Creator, the only safe and undetectable "outside" source I can consult. After a short period of time, I realize that the occultist has split himself into four parts. I also intuit that if the Ashtar Command were to capture one part of him, it would simply melt like an ice cube and that energy would join the other parts; any kind of capture has to be executed simultaneously for each part. Worse yet, I know that he is planning to be in all the universes very soon. I knew this was going to be difficult but I didn't know it was going to be *this* difficult.

I need four sets of coordinates for his locations. I'm given codes that I can feel are connected to numbers; I'm sure this is a security measure to keep me from having the actual numbers rattling around in my head. I call Commanders Asthar, Tonas and Voldan as well as Sananda into the SBT and give them the codes. I explain to them what I've discovered up to this point. Then I add that my concern is that if he is this powerful, we need to make sure that we can safely contain him.

Ashtar says that in order to leave a trail of what is expected, they will have to leave a portion of themselves behind so that they don't appear to be leaving. He then repeats the information I've given him and asks if I am aware of what happens if they are off the mark by even a nanosecond. I reply that I don't know; I only know that the extractions *must* be simultaneous. Ashtar believes there must be something more that will allow them to act at the same precise instant.

After more investigation, I learn that, at this time, three of the parts of this person are actually holograms, although I believe that eventually he will be able to become separate physical beings. There is no way of knowing which one of him is the real one, and even if we do capture that part, he could transfer over to one of his other parts. I ask Sananda if he could help the Ashtar Command position their ships in the SBT and act from it simultaneously. He can, but admits we need Charlie's assistance. I finally realize that the SBT is the safest place for Charlie and release my reluctance to request his assistance. Once he is present, I ask Ashtar to transmit to Charlie everything he needs.

Charlie says he is very good with math, but he needs to have all of the CEV with him. I ask the rest of the kids to join Charlie and hear his plural voice say, "This will become a very tight strategy. What is the extrication?"

Asthar says we must have a means for extricating this individual in an instant and placing him in stasis. Sananda informs us that he has remembered a technique that was used years ago. "It was very swift and particalized an individual directly into the stasis. If we transmit this to the CEV they can put together the foundations for this using mathematics."

After a few seconds, Charlie says this is complete. "I like the set of codes you have given me. These will remain as the inaccurate coordinates. It will only be in the mathematics that the correct numbers will be in presence in the moment that the positions are locked. Then the extrications will come as if a beam of light shooting into time and drawing back into the SBT. Thank you, Mommy, for allowing us to do these works here."

I still want to know if we can keep the occultist once we capture him. Ashtar says it goes against their focus to incarcerate an individual without an opportunity to have rehabilitation. I am relieved when he also says that perhaps they can wait for the rehabilitation until the worlds are immune to his energies.

"I'm OK with rehabilitation, it's just that if he escapes we would never catch him again. Sananda, where would be a safe place to keep him?"

"I am somewhat concerned. I have never experienced anything with such attachment to the energies of evil."

After I make a couple of suggestions, the others put their heads together and design what they feel sure is a safe method of containing this individual until the culmative. I am so light-headed with relief at this news that I begin laughing. The others must be experiencing that same relief because I hear them laughing too.

I am shocked back into instant attention when I suddenly become aware that the occultist is getting ready to become *eight* beings. The command needs to move immediately to where he is still in four parts. We all move in the SBT to where the extraction will be completed. Sananda is working with the Ashtar Command to calibrate their ships to be invisible as they move through the SBT. Charlie says he doesn't want anyone to even think about the codes; he wants them to be part of a plan that, "only the ship knows." They're going to use the extraction method Sananda suggested that will bring the occultist into the SBT in particle form and place each part of him into a crystal. Ashtar says it is necessary for Charlie to accompany them but insists that he will be safe. At this stage of the game I can see no option but to trust Ashtar's assessment.

After they leave, I wait in the SBT for what seems like a long time, but probably is only a minute or two. Now the only thing left to do is to gate into the council and confirm—I hope—that everything went smoothly.

Tonas says, "Congratulations to all of us, my dear."

"Are we all safe now?

"Ah, safety was never an issue. When you have a plan there is never a concern for safety."

That's not true in my dimension, but I don't feel like quibbling about it. I just want to know what happened. Tonas explains they are keeping the four parts of the man separate and in stasis. The four Ashtar Command ships holding him will wait in the locations our group selected until the moment prior to the culmative. The second the last individual steps across the bridge into the Fifth Realm, the pieces of the, hopefully rehabilitated, occultist will be released into the four universes he previously occupied and nothing will be there except the bridge into the

Fifth Realm. Tonas adds that the man will surely have remembered the truth of his inner goodness by then, although in his mind not even a blink of time will have passed.

Tonas is ecstatic and exclaims, "We are a team of heart! Believe me that this stasis will not influence our time with each other in the forever. It will be after all individuals have had their ascension." (He's talking about when he and I, and anyone else who wants to, hit the "pause" button before moving into the Fifth Realm.)

I have been shaken to my core by this experience and for awhile I consider just saying goodbye and returning to my home to try to regain a sense of safety and normalcy. If we had not captured that man or if we had failed in our attempt to restrain him… I stop myself from following that train of thought. Rather than return home, I need to do some regular council work to keep my mind busy and off of what we just accomplished.

I ask Sananda to accompany me into the Fifth Realm. In comparison to what I just went through, speaking with my parents, who have been dead for a couple of months, about items I've found in their home seems utterly mundane. Better yet, it is also completely safe.

I found some arrowheads and a stone ax head in their basement and I want to ask Dad where he found them.

"I miss you guys. I'm still cleaning out the house and I brought some things with me that I want to give to you. I know you can create anything in an instant, but I want to give you your hat, Dad. I haven't been able to throw it away, so here it is. Mom, here are your kitchen canisters that you can use to keep your flour and sugar in for the cookies you're making. Do whatever you want with these things, OK?"

Sananda says my parents are just standing there smiling at me and he has a sense those items have already been recreated. I ask Dad if he found the arrowheads on the farm and learn that he found them on the mound—an area of a pasture we used to own. He also says that there were a lot of tribes that migrated through our area: the Delaware, Kickapoo, Miami, Chickasaw and Dakota Sioux.

I hold the arrowheads I found in my hands and ask the individuals who owned or made them to step forward. Sananda reports that three men and a woman stepped up. I ask if any of them have anything to say. A man who says he is Winnebago and a woman of the Illini tribe say that their hands touched those things. They moved with the animals following the Kishwaukee River because of the fishing. They smoked and dried the fish they caught. Their ancestors are all over on the lands. I thank them for the information.

With Liponie at the Joy Council:

I brought an old mirror and a nice pair of Dad's cufflinks for Liponie to fix up for Tonas. It feels good to hold such ordinary objects and not think about what we just… Instead of continuing that line of thought, I address Liponie, hand him the objects and explain that they are things Dad wore on his uniform when he was in the Army Air Forces. "Can you make a little jacket for Charlie and put these medals, pins and patches on it? Can you also make some of the Disney costumes that are worn in the movies the kids like?"

Liponie says they mostly enjoy cowboy wear and then suggests clothing from the different cultures of the worlds. I agree that's a great idea. I have some trucks for Charlie and I ask Liponie to make some for the other kids, too. He lets me know he has already put Dad's medals and patches on a Levi jacket for Charlie.

I want to know if he got the old Sunbeam mixer that I recently gated to the council. My mom used it for years and when we were kids my brother and I would each get a beater to lick after she'd made a cake. He says that he improved it and they are now using it in the kitchen. I'm delighted that it's being used again. One of these days I'm sure I'll be able to do some of the things Liponie does, although maybe not with the flair he pulls off, but for now I appreciate his help and tell him so. "Thank you for helping me with these silly things I've been bringing to you."

"They are not silly if you love them, my dear."

Charlie joins us and says, "Mommy, we did such good works."

"You did, and I have some things for you."

"For me? There are things for me? Are they presents?"

"Yep, Liponie please show him the jacket." I hear Charlie gasp and I begin to read to him what one of the medals has on it. "This pretty one says, 'Efficiency, Honor and Fidelity.'"

Charlie repeats the words to me and asks what they mean.

"You know what efficiency means, don't you?"

"Efficiency means me; I am always efficient."

"Fidelity means you're true."

"Mommy, it was made for me. Wow!"

I show him a patch that has a radio tower with what look like lightning bolts coming out from it and he gives me his impression of Morse code, I think. Anyway, I hear a lot of "deet, deet, deet, deda, deet, deet, deet," and he explains that they have that in the movies. He looks at some other pieces and says it's like the "olden days," adding, "Mommy, it's the history of our world."

"Charlie, I was trying to explain to you the other day that when kids here grow up they usually want to have a partner and their own place that's away from their mom. You may want to do that in the future, but if you want to stay with me always you are welcome to do that."

"Mommy, I don't ever want to go to anybody else but you."

"Not now and I'm fine with you staying with me forever. You don't have to think about this now; we're still having fun being kids, right?"

"I might want to be a kid forever!"

"That's OK with me!"

I ask Tonas to join us and say, "Hello, sweetie."

"I love this that you call me 'sweetie.'"

I realize I didn't find out about the home he made for us on Hosemelia and begin to talk with him about it. I learn that there is a marble stair case that moves from the front entrance down to the water's edge. When I ask if our home is luxurious and "comfy," he says they are the same thing. Not convinced of that, I specify beautiful, thick rugs on the floors and several other furnishings I think I will enjoy.

"You will enjoy what we have created. Since Liponie has his fingers in it, you know it will be to your exact liking, and if not, he will change it in an instant."

That definitely settles my mind about the furnishings.

With the full council, I announce that, "Here I have the, ta-da, book!" I hold *Path of Sweetness* up and then pass it around telling all of them they can pour more love into it if they wish.

"It is so exciting! It has happened, my dear."

Now I just have to start editing book two. I hope the next ones are simpler to do. This first one had a very steep, almost perpendicular, in fact, learning curve.

"Three days ago I heard, 'There is a possibility of a jump in evolution staged from the past. There can be a special immersion of enhancements using the big picture carried back and flowing forward in all universes at the same time.'"

I ask Charlie if we can do something with that and he says he is already working on it.

While he's doing that, I ask who can talk about the new stages of evolution being revealed. This is something a woman named Nahshee Toombweah, who is on the Joy Council in the Porneeseesee Universe, told me three days ago.

Nahshee announces herself and begins to speak. "The new stages of evolution which are preparing to make themselves known are making a foundation. A great wealth of new wisdom is ready to be birthed onto your world so that when the 4th dimension is released the lid will come off, so to speak, allowing the treasure to be witnessed. The world is ready for this treasure for their heart speaks loudly of its hunger for it. The treasures are the gifts that are within the heart of each individual of this world. Those gifts are the ability to see beyond the illusion and to embrace that which is authentic truth. Another gift is love of the self and recognizing the value of self. What I see as the greatest gift is to be able, in all measure of presence, to recognize the paths leading to the discovery of that destiny that is *always* known by the spark of self and is being unveiled more and more in this new energy. It is the journey of the individual that is the most important for the essence of soul already knows the path leading."

"Thank you for sharing that with us. I'm looking forward to what you have described. Charlie, are we ready with the special immersion?"

He explains that the special immersion is a vision of what was, what will soon be, and also it is every path that ever could be. "I made an interface with every human being on Earth and asked them to show us their paths so we can project all of them. This will be a means for individuals to see that there are many choices."

"Do any of the other universes need anything like this?"

"I would need to connect with everyone in every universe. I am still working in this moment but soon we will have an interface with every sentient being in all the universes. It will be done in a minute."

It is difficult to imagine someone with this capability playing with toy trucks. How awesome he's my little boy!

"While Charlie is doing this, can someone clear up the time travel thing for me? When I get to the point where I can move my physical body to another place when I gate and I move back in time and see myself, what are the consequences of that?"

"Are you speaking of the paradox, my dear?"

"I don't know. The science fiction books I've read postulate that it is not good to come face to face with yourself."

Osiris laughs and says it is possible to stand directly in front of yourself. He adds, "We have stepped through time and witnessed ourselves over and over again in the ancient academies. Every time this occurs it changes everything from that point of connection."

I ask him to repeat that and he says, "To appear before yourself would alter everything from that point forward."

Alarm bells begin ringing loudly in my head as I realize this might not be a good thing. If I do something different in the past I could lose Tonas, Charlie, Liponie, *all* of these people!

Tonas says, "My dear, I have just had a terrible thought. That could be a means to erase all of our good works, would it not?"

Osiris says, "We must guard your past from yourself as well as any other that might influence you in a negative way. If you were to traumatize yourself…"

I feel a sense of urgency to finish our work. I want to concentrate on setting things up so that I don't screw myself up or let anyone else do so in my past. Charlie has finished the transmission and it will be for all individuals. I zip through sending it out, thank everyone and bid them all farewell.

CHAPTER TWENTY

March 3, 2015

I've completed working on making my past immune to outside negative interference as well as interference or visits from my current self that might negatively impact my current life. Part of that work involved asking everyone in the Fifth Realm who might try to negatively influence me to give me an antidote to that as well as anything else that would make me invincible to negative influences.

I've been thinking that there might be some last ditch attempts to screw up the release of the 4th dimension. With that in mind, it seems like a good idea to put something in place to encourage people still hanging out in or holding onto that dimension to get ready to slide into the 5th dimension. Maybe some individuals want to be big frogs in the little pond of the 4th dimension but I hope to show them they can be quite content in a bigger, cleaner pond.

In the Fifth Realm with Sananda, I ask all sentient beings of Earth who had resistance to releasing the 3rd, 4th, 5th, 6th, or 7th dimensions when they were alive to step forward. I show them how things look now, the way they're headed, what the endgame looks like and how it would look if they'd like to have an easy, graceful and fun path. I suggest they give us a file that contains an antidote for their resistance as well as the vision of what their graceful, easy path looks like. The vision should also show them the benefits in each stage of their evolution—what's in it for them.

Then I ask for beings in every universe that had been resistant to the elevation of their world/universe from any point in their dimensional frames leading up to the highest pinnacle to step forward. I ask them to hand their files to the Joy Council person in charge of their universe who then gives the files to Sananda and me. I call Charlie into the SBT and we hand him the files to take back to the council.

With Tonas at the Joy Council:

"We knew you would be coming; we were alerted by our dear one. He has learned to skip so he is skipping everywhere all excited."

"I need a hug and a kiss to start."

"This is the only way to begin, my dear."

"Let's have Aton join us."

After he announces his presence, I inform him that this morning I heard myself say, "Let's hit thirty without breaking a sweat." Then I heard myself say, "Now it's just a matter of picking up time." I know this has something to do with reversing the aging process and I'm excited to ask him about it. He comments that this is very interesting and asks what my thought is about it.

"'Picking up time' gives me an image of just lifting a span of years out of my lifetime; this sounds like a really marvelous idea to me as long as I don't lose the memories of those years. I think it signifies that time doesn't log in with regards to the aging of my cells and that I can speedily move to the appearance of a woman of thirty years of age."

Aton says he believes this is the answer for all individuals of our world that have the vision to continue evolving and releasing the aging factor. He also informs me that aging is a disease. Although this is a fascinating tidbit of information, I'm averse to experiencing any more of this disease. Aton agrees with me that this can be a transmission.

"Hi, Mommy!"

"Hi, lovely!"

"I got it, I got it. It's ready and we added more. And Mommy, I know how to skip now and also I know how to jump the rope."

"I was just going to ask you about that."

"And I know how to climb the rope and there was this other thing that we did that is very, very scary, Mommy."

He begins whispering and repeats that it's very scary, but there's a net underneath to catch him; he's walking on a tightrope!

"Ooh, that is scary."

"It's very scary but Liponie made a net to catch me. I fall all the time."

This admission surprises me because Charlie is normally instantly adept at new activities. The reason for his falling is made clear when he says he thinks he should stop wearing his Mickey shoes. Since he is so thin, as soon as he mentioned tightrope walking, I had a mental picture of him falling headfirst and slipping through the net. The Mickey Mouse shoes are so big I suppose they'd keep him from falling all the way through, but… After stopping that train of thought, I mention that he needs the little slippers that would help his feet feel and grip the tightrope; Mickey shoes are *not* good for walking a tightrope.

He tells me they are cute, though. I agree through my laughter, but repeat that they are not for tightropes.

I let him know what I told Aton about picking up time and ask if he can help me. He says he will take this into the whole piece of him (his collective) and they will put their heads together. I ask him to make it into a transmission and he comments that this will help people forget about getting old.

I answer that I hope the transmission does help because the process of aging is thought of as inevitable here. "Except for a few of us, everybody assumes they're going to get old and die."

Charlie now admits that he saw a very sad movie and that Tonas told him he should not have watched it. "It was with the spiritual lady, so I thought it would be OK. It was called *Terms of Endearment* and it was not endearing at all. I think there were good lessons in it for people who had those kinds of things to learn but I cried and cried and cried. Finally I got some tears."

"Oh..."

"I had to ask for some because nothing was coming out, Mommy. Nothing was coming out at all! It's better to have the water come out."

Although I've never had a problem like that—I've had my full share of soggy pillows—I agree with him that trying to cry without any tears coming out would be terrible!

"Liponie made it so that I had snot and everything. He said you can't have a good cry without snot. He gave me a handkerchief and showed me how to blow."

He adds that he's going to show everybody but he doesn't want to use that show. I mention that I've never seen it and he cautions me not to watch it because it is very sad.

"There was another one that I watched that was very sad. I didn't have any tears then, but I would have cried if I had known that you were my mommy. It was called *Bambi* and it was very sad. It was very, very sad and I don't want you to ever die. We must make you always very safe so that no one will ever shoot you."

"Right. That sounds like a good idea."

"Do you snot when you cry, Mommy?"

"Yes, and my eyes get red and puffy and I don't look very good. I spent a lot of years crying."

"Never again because you have us and we love you. There is no reason ever to cry now."

"It was a challenge for me when my mom and dad died."

"Yes, it was lucky they weren't shot." That Bambi movie has really stayed with him. "You will never get old. You have too many things in place for that to happen." Whispering, he advises me not to ever worry about getting shot or getting old.

"Let's help other people with that, because as I explain to individuals that there's no need to get old and die, I really want them to be able to feel that option."

"This is the best idea ever. I will never die, not ever, ever, ever!"

A note of pleading enters his voice as he asks me if he can come too. (I'm going to another orchid show in Santa Barbara in a few days.) "You're not packing yet but I got my ears on."

I ask him if he's going to be doing work or does he just want to come along for fun. I hear him giggle and then he says, "I can watch you eat all day! I can watch you eat the happy foods all day. You make 'mmm' sounds in your head!"

"I do?"

"Yes, you go 'mmm, mmm, mmm' in your head. I can hear them loud and clear."

I really do enjoy the food in California. There's a little restaurant in Santa Barbara that I love to go to; it has the best French toast I've ever eaten. Even thinking about it now I can feel the mmm mmm's in my head. Charlie's right!

Then he says that he is always working—even when he's playing he's working. I kept him with me all the time on our last trip, but I'm nervous about taking him with me on this one since I lost things and left things behind. After I agree to take him with me, he promptly invites all the other Swizzlers to come along.

I ask him what we've been doing and learn we tried the Hula-Hoop. He adds that I was funny. Then he laughs and says, "You can't do it very good, Mommy." That's not news to me; I never could manage one of those. Then he says we played jacks. I tell him I never learned how to play that. It seems I'm no good at that either, but, of course, Charlie is very good. I mention that I couldn't jump rope very well when I was a kid.

"This is what you did. It was so good because you just looked at me and you held my face and you said, "Let me show you how to do this." You showed me and I could do it immediately because I'm a boy. Boys can do these things. You showed me how to skip and play jacks and do the Hula-Hoop. We didn't read yet."

"I couldn't skip very well when I was a kid."

"You showed me how to do it and I can do it. Mommy, it's really cute when you can't do things."

This statement goes a long ways toward making up for all the times I felt bad as a kid when I was lousy at the games other kids played. I couldn't hit the ball in baseball, I hated dodgeball and kickball, I didn't know how to play jacks, I was no good at Red Rover and forget about trying to skip rope. That thing looked lethal as it was twirling around. I don't repeat all that to Charlie; I just tell him I was not coordinated when I was little. I'm OK with being a cute failure at everything at the council, but thank God I don't have to play any of those games on Earth.

He says, "All I know is you tried and tried and tried with the yo-yo and it would only yo."

I just can't hold back my laughter at my lack of yoing ability; normally, I can make a yo-yo, yo-yo. "I guess I'm showing you how not to do things, huh?"

"You showed me how to do it and I could do it immediately because I'm a boy."

"When I talked about skipping, I actually meant jump rope."

"Sometimes you twist up in the rope and it's very funny. You make us all laugh; you laugh the loudest, Mommy, because you think it's so funny. When you fall down you laugh."

"It wasn't funny when I was little, Charlie; it was really difficult."

I've been starting to get a little teary-eyed regarding my lack of grace when I was little, but before I get too carried away, Charlie interrupts to ask if that was in the past. Oops, I realize I need to do some clearing on that issue with SVH.

"You clap for me, Mommy, because I can yo and yo."

"I bet you're a champion at everything you do, Charlie."

He casually admits that he is.

"Tonas, sweetie, what is 8151228?"

"It is a very important place in your universe. This is the coordinate for a star named Mohltar where there is a forever stream of shallow water that can be ridden on. The stream is like an incredible slide for a children's playground. I was explaining to you that this is a place we could take Charlie and the kids and ride it. It is as long as from one end of your country to the other and it moves through many terrains. It follows a bed of smooth rock and is quite a playground. You can ride along for a great distance and then drop into a shallow pool; there are beautiful shade trees. I was telling you about this place and you were quite interested."

I agree that sounds wonderful and ask if we would also need a little boat to travel in. Tonas says that although it is quite daring in some areas, most people simply ride the wave of it and let the natural flow of water carry them along. It's hard to imagine a stream that long but I let him know I'd like to slide in it.

I want to get an update on how things stand in the universes and ask for Ashtar; Tonas says he is in the kitchen. I have to giggle at the thought of one of the Supreme Commanders of the Ashtar Command working in the kitchen, maybe even licking batter off a spoon. Then Tonas adds that Sananda is teaching Level One Mastery in the kitchen. He agrees with my remark that things must be smoothing out and says that they see resolution to the conflicts in all the universes within a matter of days. This is really good news; I'm looking forward to having Jesus and the others back with us.

When I ask, I'm told that only sixteen of the indigenous tribes from other worlds that have been living here are left. The Ashtar Command has extricated nearly four hundred tribes.

With the full Joy Council:

I begin, "Hello, and welcome to March. We have a lot of snow on the ground here; I got stuck getting out of my driveway and had to shovel my car out of the snow. It's a drizzly day but I'm happy to be with all of you. I've been cleaning out my mom and dad's house and I found some of my grade school papers that Mom had saved. There's a little poem I'd like to read to you, Mr. Lincoln. It's called "A Walk with Lincoln," and it was written by Joseph Auslander.

When Abe had too much on his mind
(His spirit bent beneath the rod)
He left affairs of state behind
And went to walk with God.

He found Him in the lonesome hills,
The tranquil rock, the rooted oak:
He found Him in the faith that fills
The hearts of simple folk.

From wars and wild alarms of wars
Oh, come and have a quiet word
With Abe whose tall hat bumps the stars
Where he walks with the Lord.

Mr. Lincoln replies, "How lovely."

"Thank you for your role in our history, Mr. Lincoln."

"Thank you for *your* role in the history of this journey past, present and future. And thank you for allowing me to be a part of this journey. It extends my magnificent history."

"We have a couple of wonderful transmissions. I'm really excited about the one that we got in the Fifth Realm that shows everyone what's in it for them as we move into the higher dimensions." I share that this seems like the final piece that we needed to assist in releasing the 4th dimension and that perhaps people who have been stuck in 4th dimension challenges will now want to leap into the 5th dimension.

Osiris replies, "I believe that is true, my dear. In the group focus for all, it is known what is in it for everyone. For one to benefit is for all to benefit, and yet in a dual world there is that hunger to never lose an opportunity. This is called fear of loss."

"Charlie, is the aging one a separate transmission?

"We put everything that had to do with aging into a transmission for all the species of the different universes and we also have the other one with the vision of what's in it for you."

"Is it true now that Earth people will start having the awareness that they don't have to get old and die?"

"It is true and there is no profit in it."

"Exactly, those who check out will miss all the good stuff that's going to be coming along?!"

We send the two transmissions out separately and I'm feeling so good about this that I sing them out through the Joy Arrows. Charlie says, "Wowee!" This felt like a wow moment to me, too. Since I'm curious as to how Gaia feels, I ask her to comment on what we just did.

She answers by saying her heart is filled to over-spilling. "Aton is very attentive and he is most glamorous as he shines many colors and lights upon us. My dear, this is a *dream* for me. Have no concerns, the release will happen as if a clock working."

With her assurance, I thank the council and bid them goodbye.

Tonas says that Charlie is with him, and, "It is like nothing else to feel his hand in mine. It is lovely to have children, is it not?"

"It is. I never thought I would be able to experience that again; I'm really tickled that I can."

"Tickled?"

"Yes, that's just an expression about being happy."

"Well, I have a tickle for you. We have created your own ship for you, my dear."

This takes my breath away. A ship of my own! Starship captain, Joy! I must be standing there with my mouth hanging open because that's what I'm doing here. I manage to utter a weak, "Oh."

"Yes, it is true and we have a special name for it. It is Trifreeah. The best description of this word is freedom of heart and freedom of heart equals joy. Thus, Trifreeah is joy. This is a very feminine ship; Charlie has insisted that it be very pink."

I laugh and confirm that pink is one of my favorite colors.

Charlie says it is made out of pink crystal. "There is a hot tub and there is a heart bed in it. I saw it on a TV program and I knew you had to have a heart-shaped bed and a hot tub in your bedroom. It has a bedroom for me and there is a bedroom for Papa Tonas with a heart-shaped bed also. He does not have a hot tub; if he wants to have one he has to come into your room." Then I hear Charlie's giggle.

Tonas comments, "You see what we have here, dear. He is matchmaking just like his mother."

I'm agreeing with Tonas through *my* giggles as he comes up with one of his Tonasian expressions, "There are apples falling from that tree, believe me."

Tonas says that the ship is hovering just above the council. They are going to open up some kind of connection so that everyone can be part of the presentation. Tonas requests that I christen the ship by hitting a bottle of champagne against it. I protest that I don't want to hit the crystal. I hear Liponie laugh and assure me that I could hit it with fifty torpedoes and not harm it. He continues by saying that although my ship is not as big as Inishimora, it does have council chambers and kitchens complete with toasters.

In order to get an idea of how large the ships are, I ask Tonas how many football fields Inishimora would be, since I know about how big one of those is. He says that before we expanded it for the Academy of Enrichment it was fifty or sixty football fields, but now it's about six hundred football fields big. Trifeerah is about the size of three football fields. That sounds like it could be a manageable size as long as Tonas is with me.

"So now we can just zip around in the universes when I am able to do that?"

"Perhaps you would like to go for a ride with Charlie and me. I have a special meal that my dear son inspired. He feels that you must have chocolate pie with a double dip of whipping cream."

"That sounds really good, Charlie."

"I am looking forward to this, Mommy. This is why I got a mouth! Papa Tonas and I are going to sit with you and we are going to eat many pies. I made six, Mommy, with my own fingers."

"I'm looking forward to tasting them and then I'm going to give you a big, smeary, chocolate kiss on your face!"

"I will never wash it off."

Tonas asks Liponie to open the ship so we can transmit into it and then exclaims as Liponie draws the corner of the ship *into the space of our room.* I'm handed the bottle of champagne and Tonas says it's important to break it on the ship to inaugurate it. I'm still feeling reluctant to do this but he says if I strike it he will inaugurate it. I give up and ask for the bottle. I assume I manage to whack the ship because Tonas announces, "This is the inauguration; the beginning point of setting the sail of Trifeerah. It is freedom of heart; it is joy. It is *all* of our gifts to you."

"Thank you so much, all of you. Kisses to you and my love."

Tonas whispers that Charlie is bowing and bowing. In his normal voice he suggests taking "our little sweetie" to Mohltar. I'm all for that! Tonas reminds Charlie to bring his swimming costume. When I ask if I have one, Charlie says that he put everything in my closet, even baby clothes! I'm taken aback by that news; perhaps Charlie has seen something in my future! I relax when he explains that he told Liponie to put everything I love in my closet. Liponie must have included the clothes I had when I was a little girl.

Charlie whispers, "Wait till you see. I have a bed that looks like a flower." Then I hear him sigh and say, "And we are going to have chocolate pie. When we fly we can see everything whizz past. It's going to be so fun. It's going to be better than the airplane, Mommy."

I agree that the airplane was crowded and not much fun. Charlie adds that there were smells. Tonas tells me that I will be in the captain's chair and apologizes as he tells me that Charlie has insisted I wear a helmet. There are no complaints from me; that's a small price to pay for flying my own starship.

CHAPTER TWENTY-ONE

March 9, 2015

Two days ago, before I went to sleep, I went to the Fifth Realm with Sananda and asked people to give us gifts for themselves to help them be inspired. I mentioned inspirations for solutions for pollution and free energy but added that any inspirations they wished to gift themselves, even just to smile at another person or pat someone on the back were fine. To the people who had been opposing solutions to free energy because of a fear of loss of income, I suggested that if they were inspired to support those solutions they could experience doing well by doing good. The next morning, as I was waking up, I heard someone say, "They affected this with good measure."

I've been thinking about the situation we left the occultist in. He's supposed to be rehabilitated by the time all of us have stepped into the Fifth Realm and he's released, but what if he's not? Even with all the universes empty, I don't want to leave someone loose behind us with the capabilities he had when we captured him unless he's had a change of heart. There's no telling what kind of mischief he could come up with in a playing field of forty-seven empty universes. I get the shivers even thinking about that; accordingly, I ask those involved with his capture to join me in the SBT for a powwow.

We toss some ideas around and come up with a non-manipulative strategy that will involve every aspect of his soul and genetic lineages. We're going to pinpoint the moments when those aspects died, received the Five Star Serenity Send-off and stepped onto the bridge, then instill the euphoric energy of all those moments—this will simply be an infusion of divine truth—into him the instant he is released.

Sananda and I step into the Fifth Realm at the near completion to connect with him. The good news is that he's there, which means at least some part of our strategies will work. Sananda reports that he appears to be a handsome seventeen-year-old boy. I feel compelled to speak to him and words flow out of me in a language that I don't consciously know. We show him the package we made for him and ask him, if he has anything additional that might help him to "see the light," to give it to us. I let him know we'll put this in place as a gift for him to assist himself.

We rejoin the core group in the SBT and I show them what we just did. Osiris asks me to leave it with them and they will make the arrangements so that this honors the occultist. It is a step-by-step plan that will be set in place at the time of his release. Osiris adds that, "It will be seamless, my dear. There are no mistakes." This feels, to me, like the final step we needed to put in place so that this scenario has a wonderful ending. I'm relieved to turn this plan over to Osiris and the Ashtar Command.

I've been contemplating ways to address the disease component of aging. I know that problems show up first on a person's energy body and then manifest in their physical body. In other words, the physical body has a response in order to block what is coming from the energy body. So the idea would be to heal my energy body and get rid of anything that would block me from allowing what's healed on my energy body to transmit onto my physical body.

I get a vision for what this looks like as well as an antidote to aging from my MAPS self and from Mom and Dad. I want this to be the most magical thing that I've ever done for myself in the way of restoring the perfect divine version of my human physical body with healing for my energy body so that it sends that healing to my physical body.

I ask for templates including systems and principles that will be continually reflected from my energy body to the new cells of my physical body as they replace the old cells. I also do clearings to release anything that would re-establish within my energy body that might prevent it from seeing a constant vision of a twenty-nine-year-old ideal non-dual version of Joy Elaine.

Then Sananda and I go to the Fifth Realm at the near completion, I tell everyone there about the work I did on my energy body and ask for those who existed on a dual world to give us gifts for themselves that would assist or enhance their bodies to be healthy, vital and disease free.

Yesterday, I saw a piece of paper with a column of names on it and then I saw a bunch of children playing behind a fence. Rather than being a trap, the fence felt like it was something that kept them safe. I think the council can create this place and some children can experience their regular life but also experience when they are asleep being trained by masters like Isis, Osiris, Mary, Jesus or Thoth. I start to get a list of names of Earth kids, but then I realize this would be good to offer to everyone in all the universes.

I move into the Fifth Realm, transmit to everyone a vision of the training space and master instruction they could receive and ask them, if they are interested in participating, to put their names on a list for me. I take the list of names to my future self and ask for a template to build this special place of training and playing for everyone. I take it to Charlie in the Joy Council in the Earth and ask him to work with Osiris on it.

At the Joy Council with Liponie and Charlie in privacy:

Liponie sounds like he's ready to combust; there is a tone of barely repressed excitement in his voice as he reports that many things are happening. Things are always happening here, and although I'm curious as to what's going on, I remind them both that we need to make some plans for Tonas's birthday. Charlie's idea is that we should have a swimming pool party.

"I'm open to doing anything but how about this. Liponie, you and Cory, Ashtar and Zeezzz and Charlie and I surprise Tonas and spirit him away to his parent's house for a birthday party. Do you think that would be possible?"

Liponie says he can make a lovely dinner party. I add that then we can do something more adventuresome that Charlie would enjoy. I ask them to please do some research and we'll talk about it next time I come. Charlie says he thinks scuba would be the way; obviously, he's all for some kind of water experience. I remind Liponie that we need to check with Emmon and Firona to make sure a party would be OK.

Charlie wonders if they even know what a birthday party is and reminds me they're not from our world. I agree that's true but then I inform Charlie that I helped Tonas celebrate his birthday last year.

Granted, I only brought him a cupcake, but we were still newcomers to each other then. Liponie says he'll meet with them before the day is done. I remind Charlie this is a big secret. He says he won't tell anybody but points out that since Liponie knows it will just be us three.

"Mommy, I like my new glass. I do, I do."

"You're right on my finger." I did some work to set up extensive protection and fail-safes so that Charlie can be in one of my rings as I travel this week. The big crystal was too challenging to lug around on my last trip.

"I know. I can feel you. Put your hand near your heart, please."

When I do so, he tells me he can feel it beating. I ask him if it will be uncomfortable for him if I wash my hands in cold water. He says it won't and adds that it doesn't make him dizzy when I move my hands around. I remind him that when I put his rock down on the beach he told me later that the water was cold. He says that he could feel it but it didn't bother him. I mention that he might be immersed in sudsy water if I wear the ring when I'm washing dishes. I hear him laugh and say that will be a new experience; he'll get to go swimming. He suggests that I could wear the ring on a necklace; that way he could hear my heartbeat all the time.

"It goes, bum, pa bum, bum, pa bum. It is a song to my heart. I love you, Mommy. Thank you for giving me this pleasure."

Charlie is so lovable every time I talk with him I feel like a better person; I even feel like a good mom. That was something I attempted to be for my two other children but sometimes I fell short.

We have some work to do on my trip to California this week so I've put the pieces for that in a time capsule for him to look at. We'll be helping the 5th dimension be more balanced as if it was on its own and free of the 4th dimension.

With the core group:

Tonas comments that I look beautiful. I wonder what I'm wearing; he'd say that if I showed up in a gunny sack so I'm not going to ask. There's a lot of work to do but I'm inspired to answer his compliment by saying he looks beautiful, too. Then I ask if he is wearing anything special.

"I thought I would go without today…"

"We call that going commando."

"I am commando today, my dear."

I should not have asked because now I feel so flustered I just want to hide my head and try not to think about what he's *not* wearing. Then, of course, my mind trips down the hallway of wondering what he would look like without clothes on at all. I immediately yank it back from that steamy trail and try to concentrate on business.

Tonas adds, "You have surprised me."

That makes two of us who are surprised. I very quickly change the subject by asking Aton how come I'm still awkward on the 10th dimension.

"What do you mean, you are awkward?"

"Charlie said I can't skip rope and I'm falling down."

Liponie starts laughing and says he's witnessed this, himself. Tonas chides him and says they must laugh with me and not at me.

They still haven't answered my question. I reiterate that I'm disappointed I'm not more coordinated in that dimension and ask Aton if he can help me. He says he has a great deal to offer me today. I ask if we can do it now and he agrees. He wants everyone to watch.

"Come here and sit, my dear. Do you mind if I open your cranium?"

I chuckle nervously at this request because I wonder if he's joking or if he really intends to lift off the top of my head. I ask him, "What am I supposed to answer to that?" No one answers me so, logically, I say, "OK."

I guess that was the right thing to say after all because Aton assures me my brains will not spill out. He adds, "We are instilling some very important elements. Ah! Very good. It is my pleasure to offer you this special new component. It is very well known to individuals of Lyra and other non-dual worlds. It is a swifter processer of information. We are engaging it now if some of you would like to look inside her head. It is very impressive, yes?"

"Did you really open up my head?"

"Yes, indeed."

"Oh, my god! That's so incredible."

"It is not necessary for you to call me a god."

"Well, you are. By the way, all those years that I would drive somewhere, sit in my car and stare at the Sun just before it went below the horizon in the evening, did that do anything? Did you feel my eyes looking at you?" (I'm referring to something called Sun gazing. Look it up on the internet for a description.)

"My dear, I have known you from the beginning of the beginning. I would recognize you in an instant, though I must say that when you came to me well before your incarnation, our first meeting was a surprise to me."

"Tell me about that meeting; I didn't realize I had met you before I incarnated."

"It happened several months ago in your July or August. You were connected to this particular time and yet you were peering at me in the past. I was working to assist an individual who was what you would consider primordial, yet she was an aspect of your soul lineage. She had a genome that was configured to be similar to yours. She was black. The next thing I knew, someone was peering at me. It was you, and then you asked me what I was doing. I explained what I was doing. Then I heard your little voice say, 'I want some of this,' and I wondered who this gangly little thing asking me that question was. You must realize that was 3,000,000 years in the past of the present."

I understand what he's talking about now, but it's still very strange to think of speaking to him in a time before I was even born.

"Before I came to the council I worked to do some healing on my energy body so that it doesn't transmit not good stuff onto my physical body. Can you see any difference in my energy body?"

"I find a great deal of change since the last time you were in my presence here. It seems to be written in your aura that there is change. This is quite advanced. I am impressed, my dear."

"If aging is a disease, as you said, then there have to be components that can be neutralized or eliminated, right?"

"Of course, aging is definitely a disease. There are parasites within the body eating it. There are many different balances that are out of synch with the ideal position of a body functioning correctly. If it is out of synch, this creates disease, disease creates degradation, aging and then ultimately death."

"We did some work with templates about aging the other day. Is there more that we can do?"

Aton suggests we work on this after the 4th dimension has released. I ask Charlie and Tonas to remind me to do that. Charlie says he wants to be this age forever, and asks that we work on no aging for him, too.

This is not something to discuss with him now. There are advantages to growing up, but I'm sure he's not ready to hear about anything like that right now since he only just got to be a kid. And, as I think about it, if he wants to never grow up I'm OK with that decision, too; however, I'm not willing to take that option away from him permanently. This could be a little bit of a sticky situation in the future, but I don't have to deal with it now.

"What happens when the 4th dimension drops off and the green thing around my pineal gland starts working?"

"It sends vibrations outward with a resonance that will assist you to elevate your personage in many different ways. Your consciousness will apply ever so much more and the endocrine glands of your physical body will work more effectively."

I ask for an update on the cannibals. Tonas says they have been re-educated and are eating other things now. They are waiting until the last moment to leave Earth. This prompts me to ask why the tribes from the stars came here in the first place.

He replies, "They came here as instruments to assist humans, just as many of us are in service."

"What do they do to assist us?"

"They were transported to Earth, typically, by ship but also through portals. They took positions away from normal human beings and held positions as guardians for your young species. They watched for asteroids and supported balance on the Earth. Many changes have occurred on Earth in the last 100,000 years and these individuals are capable of balancing the energy. Because they exist on Earth, it is possible for them to make determinations about Earth."

"They were able to divert asteroids?"

"Most assuredly. They can do this even today."

If any of you have had concerns that a big meteor might hit us and annihilate part of our planet, perhaps you will let those go. This information about the capabilities of members of the tribes is astounding to me. I share with Tonas that we think of these hidden tribes that are sometimes brought into our awareness as being very primitive. Tonas matter-of-factly states it is understandable we feel that way because they do not wear clothing and they have dirt upon themselves. He adds that the other piece to why we might think they are primitive is because some of the tribes lost their way and thus, their abilities.

"I want to move quickly today because I still have a lot of work to do. Please forgive me if I rush. I recently got the words Petar Ahneeshtah and the coordinates four, zero, zero, zero. This has something to do with Nokeenosah Shertee and something that can be put in place on June 18th. The part of me there may know what this is about, but I don't. Can someone tell me about it?"

Ashtar replies, "We call him Nokeen. That is his nickers name. He has brought to the council the vision of a recalibration of some of the grids in the different universes, including his universe. It was his idea that there could be a balancing agent put in place so that the cosmic egg of all the universes could feel what the reflection of a more balanced energy might be. There is a concern that this could quicken some individuals faster than they are ready for, so it was thought that if we waited until closer to the middle of June when the 5th dimension is more settled it might not cause a calamity for those who were resisting. In different universes, all of the council members are willing to focus so that their universe will be ready for the new calibrations. Petar is the center point where each of these energies can move outward as a pulse."

"Two days ago, I saw some numbers roll up in my mind; they are related to grids and they might be related to this. Let me show them to you."

I transmit telepathically what I saw and Ashtar confirms that's what we've just been talking about. He comments that the numbers are a little different than the ones they have. I explain that I actually received two sets of numbers; the second set I just showed him came to me after I did some work in the Fifth Realm. He asks me to show him the first set of numbers and I do. That set matches the numbers they have. Ashtar says that since the numbers can change we must be flexible with this plan. He adds that precise calibrations are called for since different positions will have different dates. For Earth this will be mid-June.

With the full Joy Council:

I'm feeling slightly mixed up about what I've done and what I still need to do. It seems Tonas notices that and comments, "It was the lack of underpants, I believe, that has created such mental fluxuation."

"I can't even think about that now; it just sends me completely off the tracks. Hello to all of you. Charlie, please tell them about the work we have today."

"This work is important for everyone who will support the energies of the triangulation codes and prepare the world to make its release of the 4th dimension. We are going to transmit these codes to the people who are willing to support that release."

I make an effort to sit in my chair because my energy feels like it's flying around the room. I assume that I manage to do that since no one says otherwise, and then we zip through sending out the transmission.

I haven't consciously spoken with many of the people sitting around the main table for some time, so I ask if the knights, Lancelot in particular, are still sitting around it. Tonas confirms that Lancelot is present and, since this is a man in history I've been fascinated by for some time, I ask to speak with him.

Lancelot says, "My greetings to you."

"Greetings." As soon as this word leaves my mouth, I realize I should have left this conversation for another day when I had more of my wits about me. Since it's too late now to retreat, I gather my courage and speak. "I'm embarrassed even talking to you about this, but you were, and still are, quite a romantic figure in the hearts and minds of many of us on Earth. Of course, all the knights were, but you had quite a reputation."

I hope that last word doesn't cause him to misconstrue what I'm trying to say, but before I can dig myself in any deeper, he states, "It is because of my beauty."

"Weren't all of the knights handsome?"

"Not really. Sir Gareth was as a toad."

That blunt description startles me, but as Gareth makes no sound of protest, I assume it's correct. I ask Lancelot what he looked like when he was incarnated.

"Hmm, I think if we were to look upon height, I was almost your height (5'6") maybe a little taller, broad shouldered, muscular and a flattened stomach with many ripples. I had a few scars, having taken a few blows in my life. My nose was never broken, and my eyes were searing blue."

Mmm, it does sound like he was quite handsome and I tell him so. Then I ask how he was trained.

"I have to say that I learned the art of chivalry. There was training for such things, you see. Did you not have training?"

"Nothing about chivalry. We are educated but this consists of learning how to read and write and things of that nature. That's going to be different in the world to come. Chivalry sounds like something we *should* have learned in school."

He says he believes it is an important piece and asks me to imagine what it is to "embrace honor in *everything* that you do."

I suppose I should have asked him more questions about this art, but at the time it seemed like too big of a subject to tackle. Instead, I move our discussion to a subject that's frequently on my mind and ask him if he's found a partner. He replies that he has not and then I mention that I'm sure there are some lovely women around. He remarks that he has witnessed a few. Suddenly, I realize I'd better not snoop anymore, if Lancelot prefers men that would dash all of my romantic notions about him. I manage a graceful exit by telling him I like to keep abreast of the romantic happenings on the council, and ask him to let me know if he finds someone of interest. He replies with an awkward-sounding, "OK" and adds that Charlie has told him this is the affirmative.

In privacy with Tonas, Charlie, Liponie and Helena:

I want to know if Charlie enjoyed the water place. He says he did and adds that he always loves the water.

"That's why I made the suggestion that's a big secret from Papa." As soon as he says that, he realizes it was a mistake and goes, "Uh oh, Uh oh, Papa..."

Tonas jumps right in with, "There is a secret from me?"

I begin to try to cover Charlie's tracks, then give up and comment, "Oops. Let's mute that, Charlie"

Tonas is not going to accept that and remarks that there is something afoot. I counter by saying that we're just talking about ordinary things. Since I'm hopeless at lying, I switch the focus by addressing Helena.

"Congratulations, Helena. From the things I've been hearing you've made remarkable strides."

"I am a different person. Do you hear the strength in my voice?"

"I do and I'm thrilled for you."

"I am not wishing to leave, so please, may I stay?"

"You may stay forever."

"This gives me great pleasure; I have found my works."

I ask her what her works are and she says she is efficient in the kitchen. Her description of what she does is that she is a "special mixologist." She just finished mixing asparagus with pearled onions and then creamed some to make a special sauce. "Everyone consumed it with great passion. Asparagus is now my favorite."

I'm glad to know that people are offered some vegetables and not dining completely on desserts, although I know the people from non-dual worlds could live and flourish exclusively on that. I remember Osiris telling me he ate fifteen of the S'more Pies; I'm still imagining trying to eat just one.

I tell Helena that I'm glad she has found something she enjoys and add that it's wonderful when you find something you love to do. She agrees and says that she feels free now. "I am no more carrying the weight of my life experience; it is the past for me and I am leaving it in the forgotten." She continues by saying that she is learning to dance and Charlie is showing her how to dance with the Hula-Hoops.

I remind Charlie we will be leaving early Wednesday morning. He's excited as he says he will be ready and adds, "I don't have to pack a thing, Mommy. I'm just going to take it with me!"

I'm looking forward to the day when I won't need to pack a thing. I had the realization a few days ago that I won't even need to carry a purse when I can manifest instantly!

CHAPTER TWENTY-TWO

March 11, 2015

Yesterday, I heard some numbers that I'm sure were coordinates. This made me a little nervous because usually when I hear something like that it's not good news. I didn't hear anything else though, so I allowed myself to relax just a little bit and continued preparing for my trip to California.

I've been on high alert for several days now because of the proximity of the release of the 4th dimension. It doesn't seem logical to me with all the incentives we've been sending out to encourage folks to let four go and move into the 5th dimension that there would still be strong opposition. But then again, when have humans always made the logical choice. To make matters more interesting, in addition to some humans opposing the release of the 4th dimension, the Chu strongly oppose that release because they will have less influence over others. Many of this species exist on Earth, but they also have a population on some planets in our solar system.

Today, I was up at 3:30 a.m. in order to catch a plane to fly to Santa Barbara with Charlie to attend an orchid show that I've been going to for a few years now. Needless to say, I was very tired when I got on the plane and spent much of the time trying to sleep. I kept dozing off but as soon as I'd fall asleep I'd hear things. Then I heard several things that made me zoom back into complete wakefulness.

As soon as I got to my hotel room, I stepped into the SBT and asked the core group to join me for some serious strategizing. Here are some of the things I heard or saw on the airplane that I share with them:

"The number is 900, those are the heavy hitters."

I saw a file that was ready to be uploaded into a computer.

I saw some words rolling down a screen in my mind.

I heard the words, "in secret" and then saw an oval piece of paper that had marks on it resembling chicken scratches.

I heard "three o six."

Osiris agrees that we have a problem and then reminds me of something I didn't even think to consider. Our Joy Council consists mostly of ascended masters; they can't be considered residents of Earth, or even of our solar system and so they don't have voting privileges. In other words, we are unable to use their names to petition the Andromedan Council—the main council that oversees interactions concerning Earth—to disallow what our opposition is planning. We need "live people" from planets in our solar system. I remind the group we have the people who were in Equinox. Osiris agrees they could help and suggests we add all of them to the Joy Council. He suggests that to be safe we need at least three times nine hundred people to offset the opposition's plan.

I open my levels of consciousness and direct my attention to areas that feel like they contain answers. It sounds silly to describe this activity as rummaging, but after I rummage around in the levels a little bit, I'm able to determine that there are a little over nine hundred humans who have been influenced by the Chu. They are unaware of this manipulation and are indeed the moles we thought we had taken care of. The file that's waiting to be uploaded is the plan the Chu are ready to activate. It seems that somehow I intercepted one of their communications, because Osiris translates the words that I saw rolling down as, "The final moments are the most crucial and the ones that hold the highest vulnerability (for humans). This is the moment of our triumph."

At the Joy Council, Tonas greets me by saying this is a surprise visit. I alert him that this is an emergency meeting and ask for the core group to join us. After he gets updated about what we've discussed so far, he says instead of just a little resistance this appears to be an all-out onslaught.

Since attempting to sleep and then waking up enough to remember and write down what I heard might have caused me to miss some things, I telepathically transmit to the group everything I experienced. When I finish, I speak some language that makes me feel slightly sick—I hate it when that happens. Osiris says this was a great deal of information.

Ashtar asks to speak, and then says, "My consideration is the indigenous. I believe the possibility of them remaining on Earth must be brought to them. Perhaps we can find a way to extricate them."

"You feel that we need them in addition to the individuals from Equinox?"

"Of course, for they are from several different worlds that are part of this system."

"I hate to have them stuck here but I also really don't want whatever the opposition is doing to succeed. From the beginning, the purpose of the tribes has been to be of support to humans. Surely we can find a way to unweave them from the 4th dimension."

"I think I have an answer, my dear. May I have this moment? It is I, your beloved. Ah, they are all raising their hands. They believe they are *all* your beloved. Put your hands down!"

The way he says this is so cute I have to laugh. I needed a momentary break from the seriousness of the work we've been doing. Only six days to go but it feels like I've been on high alert forever.

He goes on to say that those who have left have been reinitiated into their worlds, but perhaps they would return, anchor their energy in the 5th dimension and put their foot in the 4th. He thinks that this way we could extricate those who are nearing their timing to release.

He also suggests asking the ones who would be willing to return to Earth to join our council. It would be necessary to bring them back about thirteen years in the past to establish their voting privileges. We're also going to bring individuals from all the inhabited worlds in our universe and position them on our council a few months in the past. Sananda agrees to work on this in the present and also the past. I give this solution a thumbs-up.

"By the way, today I saw a young man with wavy brown hair that went past his shoulders walking by me in the distance. He glanced at me then continued walking. Let me show you this person."

Tonas explains this was a human hybrid who thought he saw something for a moment. It's not good if anyone like that even *thinks* they see something. Tonas tells me they're going to find what this being thought they saw and make a cloak for it. A few seconds later, Sananda gives the cloak to me.

He's a good multi-tasker because he says that there are over two hundred beings from each world positioned on Earth now, adding, "They are attempting not to use up the resources." That seems like a minor detail right now when I'm concerned about people being stuck in a dimension that is no longer connected to Earth, or, the opposing side triumphing in their bid to hold *onto* the 4th dimension.

Sananda reads my concern because he says there are many of the opposition that have been activated into service all over Earth. He doesn't really know what this service will consist of; it might be doing something that will affect individuals who are on the cusp of making a decision. We just have to try to take all possibilities into account.

I confirm that I don't know any details of their plan; I just saw the file being readied to be loaded. Sananda checks again and says he can't read it either.

We all ponder the 3:06. Osiris says it seems to be a time stamp and wonders if it corresponds with the ripple across Earth as the final moments of March 16th come into play, saying, "The circle closes as the day ends and begins the new 17th. Leave this with us and we will begin working on a plan."

Since this is a very big thing I don't have to try to figure out how to do, I'm glad to turn it over. I speak to my ring and ask Charlie to join us since currently only his essence is here. It seems a little silly to speak to him that way but I hear his voice say, "I have been listening, Mommy. I'm here and I have the full scooper-dooper. I agree that it is a time stamp. I believe that a less than one-hour period becomes a very important piece and that there is something planned for that time.

We must have all of the new consortium in place. I agree with adding the Equinox people and also that having at least two hundred people from every planet and star is necessary. I wish to assist you, Osiris and Sananda, in recruiting these specific individuals. They must be very much screened and all must wear the badge."

Tonas asks for a moment to check something. Then he tells me they just checked to make sure the information I received wasn't planted.

It wasn't. "You are receiving it because you are an open conduit, and receiving is part of what you do." He finds it curious that I was able to receive it, (I do too.) because they must have used great encryption. Our team is going to quadruple their efforts, beginning well before 3:06.

I remind them that our recruiting must be kept secret. Ashtar agrees to contact all those who returned to their homes and ask them for another commitment to return to Earth today and maintain their presence at least until June. They would then be returned if they wished. He says it will be easy to do this because of the cloaks that were placed to make it look as though the people never left.

I ask if it's possible to take the indigenous tribes still in the 4th dimension out in the past and then bring them back now. That way they wouldn't be stuck in 4D. Ashtar confirms that they will begin extricating them in the past, raising them to a connection with the 5th dimension and then replanting them.

By the time we finish with these indigenous tribes they are certainly going to be well traveled. I make a mental note to remember to thank them profusely for their assistance.

I'm ready to leave the council and I tell Charlie that I hope he can enjoy our vacation. He reassures me that he has the program locked up in his mind, and adds, "If you go to sleep, Mommy, before you wake up I will be back with you with all my heart and soul. Right now just my left toe will be there."

My last thought before I fall asleep in my hotel bed is that I'm glad our kid is a genius but I especially appreciate his quirky sense of humor.

CHAPTER TWENTY-THREE

March 15, 2015

Last night I saw a black covering that was part of a tent and heard myself say, "I'll see you guys." I know the covering represented cloaking and so it looks like the other side is going to give up hanging onto the 4th dimension and shift into the 5th dimension. In case you haven't figured it out by now, they have agendas which do not complement anything that the masters of light stand for. Osiris has cautioned me to attempt no contact with them until I am fully in the 7th dimension; this is a suggestion I definitely plan to heed.

With Tonas, Liponie and Charlie at the Joy Council:

"My dear, it is an exciting time. Is it not?"

My plane didn't get in until 1:00 a.m. this morning. I didn't get to sleep in my own bed until about 4:30 a.m. so I'm not able to reply very enthusiastically to his question.

The first item on my list is to check with Liponie to see if all the orchids I attempted to gate to the council arrived. He replies that they have had to expand in order to fit them all in. I got really excited standing in a greenhouse in California with huge specimen orchids that wouldn't fit in my little greenhouse when I realized I could copy them in the SBT for Liponie to take to the Moon.

I also visited a candy store that had lots of chocolate, including chocolate covered marshmallows. I've been on the lookout for things like that to give to Osiris to help feed his marshmallow addiction. Liponie says they have a new buffet featuring the food items I copied in the SBT.

"Hey Charlie, how was the trip?"

"Mommy, it was the best ever. It was just us."

"I had the ring you're in on my finger all the time so you were with me in the shower and when I went to the bathroom. I was a little bit embarrassed at first because I've never taken a shower with one of my kids."

"But, Mommy, I love your body."

"Unless you were a baby here, Charlie, it wouldn't be proper for me to shower with you."

"Ohhh…well, I'm a Swizzler son and it's OK."

I wonder who I could talk to about this arrangement I have with Charlie in my ring. I can't imagine there has ever been a situation like this in any universe, and certainly not on Earth. Charlie is one of a kind, well, one of ninety-four kinds.

Then he asks me if he can always be in my ring. I thought he'd pop out of it and move back into his big crystal once we got home. He says he loves being in it and adds that all the other Swizzlers can still feel him, plus they are together in their minds and in their hearts. I agree that he can stay in it.

With the core group:

Last night, I heard that ascension can take place in 3013. It appears that there can be an extension because that's longer than the 350 years the masters have told us we would experience before ascending. I'm OK with that because I'll have more time in the higher dimensions with Tonas.

Osiris agrees that this is possible. Tonas didn't want to tell me about this because he didn't want me to think there was something wrong. Osiris adds, "You see, once everyone is in that great frame of sweetness, it is perhaps like staying three days in a luxurious resort instead of only one day."

I let the group know that this morning I became aware of a gate in North America that needs to be reactivated. This, I believe is a part of my personal mission to assist the release of the 4th dimension. Osiris confirms that this work is indeed my own sacred piece to do, but also that I have to wait until tomorrow to do it.

I also saw a bag of something for the "house of modern"; in other words, visions of future possibilities. I am told that this also must wait until 4D has released but it will be an excellent transmission after that has occurred.

"I saw a little boy a few days ago and heard, 'my strength will help his artistic ability.' Can any of you tell me about that?"

Aton replies, "Everything that you are becoming is an inspiration to those children who have innate abilities that are being awakened which are similar to that which you are developing. They are not quite able to apply because they are not fully in a non-dual dimension. You are a reminder to them and it is many of their abilities that will be affected and enhanced."

"It is exciting for me to be able to do that."

"It is no less than what you are always focusing on, my dear. Is there anything that you are more passionate about than this council? I cannot imagine it, for you live and breathe it, and that which you breathe from it is quite sweet and perfumed by your own delightful presence."

Now, I ask Aton if he's been able to spend any time with Gaia in their special place. He tells me no and adds that this is an important time to focus on the work we're doing. He does say that maybe later they will take a vacation. That creates a lovely picture in my mind—the Sun and the Earth on vacation walking hand in hand along a beautiful beach. I wonder if Gaia can embody on another planet, maybe not.

I agree with Aton that it's nice to get away. "I had some great food and the air in Santa Barbara is very sweet, right, Charlie?"

"It is, Mommy, and if only Papa Tonas could have been with us when we had the pie. It was a very chocolatey thing." (He's talking about the S'more Pie I had on our last trip to California.) "It was as if we could bathe in it. We could bask in chocolate; I love chocolate, Mommy." This is a kid after my own heart, for sure.

I remind Charlie that, although I didn't find anything really great in the way of chocolate to eat, I had the wonderful French toast they make at Renaud's Patisserie. "There are a couple of great restaurants and a lovely bookstore in that little shopping center. Is that an energy spot?"

I find it interesting when Aton comments that I create an energy site everywhere I go.

I'm ready to leave but Charlie first wants to know if we can always sleep together. He says, "When you and Papa Tonas are together I won't look," whispering, "when you do things."

This request is a surprise to me, plus, since I'm wondering how much he knows about things Tonas and I might do, I don't immediately say no. I tell him I'll have to speak with Tonas about it.

Charlie continues, "Until then, Mommy, can I always sleep with you because I love you so much. And when you have chocolate it makes me happy because I can feel how much you love it because I'm part of the energy that you are emitting from the very essence of yourself. It's like rainbows and hearts and flowers. Chocolate is your favorite!"

"I think you're right. You're welcome to sleep with me all the time until I am in a different kind of relationship with Tonas. Then we will have to re-evaluate that."

"Well, I will not wear my shoes to bed."

CHAPTER TWENTY-FOUR

March 16, 2015

This morning I heard, "Somewhere there's an empty spot; that's where the challenge is. Move that completely into assisted living." Then I saw a chunky-looking man come out of a door and look at me. This vision was followed by seeing a younger man sitting on a chair and looking up at me. As I pondered how these people might be connected to empty spots, I remember that they had a vacant feel to them. I then realized that people whose minds are gone, for example, people with Alzheimer's, could be tagged and used as votes by the opposition. That would allow all kinds of energies to be transmitted through them.

After more reflection, I sense that I am going to also need to assist people who have been on drugs. People who use substances like that often have fissures in their energy field; these allow them to be easily manipulated. I've heard of things coming through, talking to and/or doing strange things to people who have abused drugs.

There's only a window of a few hours to do everything we can to assist the release of the 4th dimension, or at least, prevent the other side from holding it here.

For individuals who can't think for themselves, I go into the Fifth Realm with Sananda to get permission for us to be their guardians for the necessary divine period of time. I ask them for the right to hold them in a space of sovereignty when they were alive so that they were not manipulated by adversarial energies or beings.

I also call forth those who were debilitated by the use of drugs or alcohol and had fissures. I remind them that those openings could allow them to be overtaken or used when they were alive and ask them to give us as many gifts to assist themselves as they would like.

I start thinking about people who are mentally ill and decide to call forth anyone who has a potential to be utilized through any kind of disconnection of focus or consciousness. I ask for anyone who lived during this framework of evolving time who would like to gift themselves with something to assist their smooth evolution or to help them maintain their sovereignty to give us gifts to take to themselves in the SBT.

At the Joy Council, Tonas remarks it is quite a day. I agree with that assessment—lately there have been more "quite a days" than I like—and immediately ask for the core group to join us. When they are present, I tell Commander Ashtar that this morning I heard myself say that there are about seventy-seven crystals that are overdue. I realized that there are a lot of masters incarnated into crystals and positioned on the Earth like the indigenous people have been.

He wants to know their location. I'm not sure I have that information but maybe I do. Here's another of those, "let's see if I have anything" moments as I pretend to show him the locations. After a few moments, he says they will make contact with each of the crystals, extricate them from the 4th dimension and then restore them into the 5th dimension once it has settled in.

"The next thing I saw last night was someone placing a small round object on a table. I think I must have been watching someone place a weight on a map and I bet it's not our map. Let me see if I can show you what I saw."

Ashtar sounds surprised when he says, "Oh, gracious goodness. This is quite an interesting opportunity. Are you all seeing what I am seeing?" Then he gives a delighted sounding chuckle. "This would not have been possible for us to see, my dear."

Charlie says, "Mommy, Mommy, Mommy, this will give me strategy. We will go to work on this right away. We need to strategically apply a transmission so that we allow this map to remain however it wishes to look for these individuals. We can be sneaky!"

The next thing I mention is that this morning I saw a younger man standing sideways to me and facing left with his headset on. He turned his head and looked at me. Ever since the guy who wasn't completely human saw me, it seems like lots of folks are ogling me and I'm rather nervous about it. After I show them what he looked like, I hear Asthar say that the man has no individuated essence of soul within him, adding that, "He is, let us call it, a transmitter as well as a receiver."

"I need a shield for someone like that." Sananda steps forward and tells me they have calibrated some energies to make me invisible to these beings. I immediately take that upgrade for my shields.

I inquire of Sananda if there is anything we can do to assist people like this man, often referred to as "tribals," who have no individuated soul. He replies that this is part of the journey of that species, but adds that he's sure something will come into my mind for them. We can't get anything from the Fifth Realm for them because they are not part of it at this time. He asks Gaia if it is possible for her to offer them something to elevate as a part of her own future in the Fifth Realm. She tells us she will ponder this and that these beings have a right to exist through her essence.

"I had a macabre dream about a withered, dead-looking snake that I stabbed in the head. It bled but it was still alive. Can you help me with this very muddled and upsetting dream?"

Osiris replies that he sees this snake as a rendering of, perhaps, what was and adds, "I am feeling that this will be an inspirational possibility for you to raise yourself as well as others as the world elevates. I believe this is a witness for you of what is occurring on Earth now."

"Is there something to do with fire energy?"

Gaia replies that she is holding a vision in her heart of the inner burning fire, the spark of the new spiritual and the new sensuality and magic of Earth. "I believe this must be initiated on the 17th. What we will focus on transmitting to the Earth is a vision of the old ways of being rising up as if flames and smoke moving into the 5th dimension. It is there that the snake will be reborn, leaving behind it the old story. Oh, it is marvelous, is it not?"

Leaving behind old stories that are not empowering does sound marvelous. I'm also interested in experiencing the new energy of snake, and especially the new energy of magic. I've been reading a great book lately about magic. In this book "real" magicians are pretending to do magic, but they have to mask their abilities. It occurred to me that I could really have some fun standing on a stage and levitating for an audience. I wonder what the reaction to something like that would be… Maybe I'll try something like that in the future.

I share that I heard something about Australia this morning. Ashtar confirms that the aboriginals in a certain section of that country are transmitting codes on a continuous basis. He also lets me know that most of the crystals I mentioned earlier have been extricated, although some are still waiting until the last minute to leave. They will be returned into the 5th dimension at times they choose.

Even though Charlie is in a crystal and I've known for years that crystals frequently contain master beings, it still seems odd to me to have a being living inside a rock.

I have one last set of numbers that Ashtar feels is a time stamp. He asks me to leave it in their hands because he doesn't think it is safe for me to apply. With a caution like that, I'm ready to pitch it to them like it was a hot potato.

Before I can join the full council, Charlie informs me that I need to know that Chuckie has a penis and that now we can enter the council. Oh, boy, another interesting development.

Tonas remarks, "Oh, my goodness, he has been waiting all day to tell you."

"OK, I'll congratulate Chuckie, then."

With the full Joy Council:

I begin by announcing that we have another Swizzler who has chosen a name. "Chuckie, congratulations on your new name and your new physique."

Tonas says that Chuckie is clapping and that all the Swizzlers are learning sign language. Chuckie also signals that right now he wishes to talk with his hands but soon he will be talking with his mouth.

"I'm looking forward to hearing your voice and your words. I know telepathic communication must be really great, but I'm still used to talking. It's nice to hear people's voices."

I continue with addressing the full council and share that soon I hope to be able to get a good night's sleep. Taking a "vacation" in the midst of what has been happening was a really crazy idea. Then I remind myself that if hadn't been so fatigued and trying to sleep on the plane, maybe I wouldn't have tuned in to all the messages I received.

"I have a wonderful gift for Earth today that consists of some codes that are going to go from my heart into the planet. I don't know the details of the work but it's coming from my heart so it has to be some pretty good stuff."

I ask Sananda how to begin the transmission because it is opened by a sequence of eleven numbers which I don't want to say out loud. He suggests just thinking the numbers will be sufficient and then I should intend to open my heart. He adds that Charlie has several things we've been working on throughout the week and he suggests we transmit those first. He lets me know that Charlie has handed me a tray with several orbs to activate.

"Can you give me a heads up about what the orbs contain?"

"Mommy, we've been working on several things for the Earth to help it remember the part of itself that is so clear and true and already loves itself. This is to help the people who have forgotten this or never even knew it. There are also special works for individuals so that when they wake up they get supported. If they are concerned about the elevated feeling they are experiencing it might make them want to go back into their shell. There are nineteen different orbs; do you want to know what each one is?"

That was enough information for me. I open my heart, intend to move that energy through the orbs, then through the crystals, the Joy Arrows and out to the Earth speaking the language from the Council of Origin as I do so. I feel so good after I do this that I give Charlie a kiss—he giggles—and then I blow a kiss to Tonas.

It's time to do my heart transmission now. I think the numbers to begin, then say, "Here are the codes from my heart with all my love, joy and happiness. We send this through the crystals, the Joy Arrows and then to the Earth." I finish this with Council of Origin language which, this time, ends in a series of yips and whoops. This language is, as Charlie would say, way more fun to speak.

Charlie's comment is, "Wow!" Then he adds, "I'm pretty excited, Mommy, because we're going to have a whole new world."

I'm ready for that too.

"This morning I heard Charlie talking about a star in another universe. I believe her name is Vageeuh?"

Tonas confirms that she and her partner, Bowkuh, are moving through their universe assisting in a big way. "They have also made themselves positions where everyone can come to learn and expand; it's similar to what we're doing with Inishimora."

"We want to encourage them. Can we let the other universes know about what they are doing?"

Tonas agrees that's a good idea and reminds me that all the universes are hearing us now. He suggests that perhaps Liponie and Charlie could make these stars the stars of the show.

Before he can continue, I begin laughing at the idea of stars being stars. Tonas doesn't laugh; he just goes on explaining that there could also be planets and suns that might turn out to be stars. I continue laughing—only on the Joy Council could there be a discussion like this.

I ask Tonas if we have representatives of all the indigenous tribes as well as representatives from all the inhabited places in our universe on our council now. He confirms that we do and says it is exciting because they are looking upon Inishimora as an example.

"What's the population of our Joy Council on the Moon now?"

Tonas says it is 40,000,000. This surprises me because we used to have 94,000,000. He explains that many of the indigenous peoples, for example, the Native Americans, are now part of the Earth Joy Council and that the Moon Joy Council is now a true representation of all the worlds in our universe. It's exciting to learn that there are nearly 137,000,000 on the Earth Joy Council.

Private meeting with Tonas and Charlie:

"Charlie, what do you do when I sleep?"

"Lots of things but I give most of my attention to the council."

"Don't worry about trying to sleep because I know you don't need it."

"Sometimes I pretend. I close my eyes and everything."

"Do you have a nice wardrobe in your new home in my ring?"

He giggles and says he has many clothes, but there are certain things he very, very, very much likes. "Right now I think the sailor suit is very cute. Popeye has a nice one so I've been wearing one like his."

I ask him if he has his horse Skipper in the ring with him and he explains he can have anything in there he wants because, "Liponie is magic."

I reply that I want to be magical, too. Charlie tells me I am magic and Tonas agrees, saying, "My dear, you are the essence of magic."

I ask Charlie to let me speak with Tonas in private. This brings a small protest in the form of a question from him about Chuckie. "You don't want to see his penis?"

"No, I congratulated him. You see, here on Earth it would not be proper for me to see his penis."

A small period of silence while he mulls that over is followed by, "Really, Mommy?"

"Yes."

"Well, it was an exciting day when he got his penis, and Liponie made it so that lemonade comes out."

Oh, great. What do you say to a revelation like that? I feel like sticking my tongue out and saying, "Yuck." What was Liponie *thinking*!

"Chuckie thought it was really a good idea to have lemonade."

"Charlie, it's just not appropriate for me to see his penis."

"Oh, OK. I think he wanted to give you some lemonade, so just close your eyes. I had some and it's very good, Mommy."

I'm still spluttering trying to come up with something brilliant to say and no words are coming. I feel myself capitulate and say, "All right. Let's have Chuckie here and I'll just close my eyes."

Charlie tells me Chuckie is moving his hands and reminds me to keep my eyes tightly closed. Then I hear him say, "He made you a snow cone, Mommy."

Oh, this is even worse. I remember being admonished not to eat yellow snow. This cone is not even going to come close to my lips.

Charlie says Chuckie just curtsied to me because he saw that on television. I congratulate him on learning sign language and on his new anatomy. Charlie lets him know he can leave now. Then he says, "I will leave now so that you and Papa can do the kiss. It's OK because I have things I have to do. We're all focusing very much on the Earth and I need to go right now! Bye bye."

Tonas advises me not eat the snow cone and says that was a little much even for him. "Do you think I should have a talk with him?"

"Yes! I'm also going to ask for uploads about higher dimensional sexuality, because I had a challenge with wearing my ring in the shower. When you were growing up did you see your mom and dad naked?"

"I don't believe that I ever did."

"So you didn't all get naked, jump into a big hot tub and talk about your day?"

"There would be no reason for me to see my mother or my father without their adornments. I wouldn't be fearful of it, but there would be no reason for it."

This information is a relief for me to hear. I've been wondering how much different the customs concerning nudity and sex are in the higher dimensions. Maybe I won't be too shocked after all.

CHAPTER TWENTY-FIVE

March 17, 2015

I've been considering what sexuality and sensuality will be like in the higher dimensions and decide to get some assistance from Isis, Osiris and Hathor for those areas, plus any other non-dual systems and principles that would be helpful for me now. Since they can have energy bodies in many locations and Andromeda is where they reside, it seems like a fun idea to drop in on them there for a visit.

After I feel myself in their presence, I telepathically show them my requests and add a request for assistance with raising children in a non-dual setting since my experiences with the Swizzlers are completely unlike what I experienced raising my two sons. Charlie is so unique and my relationship with him is also very unique and precious to me. I realize I may make some mistakes but I don't want to make any major ones. Since he may one day decide to become human, I need to be able to set boundaries that support his learning about Earth life.

I realize I'd also like assistance with relationships of all kinds: intimate, personal and casual relationships with others and my relationship with my evolving body. A vision of what an ideal relationship with Tonas would look like is another jewel I request.

My mind is whirling with ideas, and, while I'm at it, I ask for the vision of me being a successful author, traveling the world, discovering new things to write about, increasing my "clair" abilities and anchoring into the 7th dimension with my foot firmly planted in the 8th dimension. I know those things are coming, but if asking can speed up the process, all the better.

None of the masters I'm addressing have spoken to me, but I can feel their intent focus on my requests and I know they are going to give me all that is possible for them to give. With that in mind, I open up and request a smorgasbord of gifts—whatever they want to give me that I didn't know to ask for is the way I put it. I hold my hands out and know they have given me a file to work with. I take this to my MAPS self to get it boosted and to get systems and principles for what I received.

This morning I heard, "Step into the Fifth Realm and ask for assistance from those who would thwart." I move into that realm with Osiris and ask him to ask those who would thwart the easy, graceful evolution to higher consciousness as well as the work the Joy Councils are doing, to step forward and hand him gifts related to those areas. I'm determined to stay safe and anonymous regarding these individuals. Here, they are in their near perfected state, but they are not that way in the dimensions that they and I currently exist within.

This morning, when I listened to what I recorded in the digital voice recorder I keep under my pillow, I heard, "First thing I knew, I had my little sister." After I said that, I saw a chart that had a spiral on it which was completely full of little boxes with symbols in them. This is something to speak with Sananda about because I never had a little sister.

I learn my mom had a miscarriage; I'm sure Mom didn't even know about it. Sananda explains that the miscarried fetus originally planned to incarnate into my family unit to assist me, but maybe I can assist her to incarnate somewhere else. I love the idea of having a sister! After some discussion, I realize that if I help her incarnate into a crystal, she can be embodied on the Moon until we have the knowledge and the ability on the 8th dimension to safely embody her on Earth. Sananda recommends having her begin in the past so that she will have been at the council and witnessing what's been happening.

I search around my house to find a crystal to use and then step into the SBT with it. She needs a name, and, after a moment, I decide that Jewel would be perfect for her. I address the essence that would have been my sister, speak with her telepathically, show her the crystal that has been prepared for her by the Creator and, with her permission, ask Creator to instill her into it. I call Charlie and ask him to take this crystal containing the essence of my sister to the Joy Council. I know Liponie can create a body for her because he's done that for Cory and Zeezzz.

Moving back to my list of things I heard last night, the next thing I recorded was someone telling me, "The work is based on refute of light." I move into the Fifth Realm with Sananda and call forth all who resided on Earth, especially those who lived in areas that refuted the light. Here is what I ask them, "I would like for you to give us gifts for yourself that will also be made into a transmission. Our theme is one of gifts to promote peace, honoring the differences of others, maintaining your sovereignty, encouraging yourself or any kind of advancement you would like to give yourself. The idea is to become aware of, and, if you choose, assist yourself to embrace the spirit of a new unity consciousness when you were alive. We've been calling this the one tribe; it's an acknowledgement of the magic and wonder of all beings and knowing that we are all connected."

At the Joy Council with Tonas:

He says they have been sweetly anticipating my arrival. I search through my repertoire of appropriate responses to such a delightful greeting…and find nothing. Settling for an inadequate but cheery, "Hello, Tonas," I ask to speak with Charlie. Immediately, he says hello, tells me he has everything ready, and Jewel is happy. "I gave her to Liponie and he made her six years old. She's blonde with blue eyes and she's gorgeous."

Tonas says it will be easy for her to understand what's been going on. She appears to be in a physical body but it is only an energy body at this time. Liponie made a room for her next to Charlie's room.

"Charlie, here's what I'm thinking about you as my son. I don't want to hamper or hinder you in any way, but at some point you may want to look like an Earth boy."

"I *want* to be a real boy."

"My point is that I would like to treat you more like I would if you were my son here on Earth."

"OK, Mommy, but it won't be like on television."

"Right. This is really about the penis situation, and I need to speak with Liponie also. I know you and Chuckie were really excited about it, but here on Earth, unless you were really little, you wouldn't show your penis to other people."

Sounding sheepish, Charlie says, "And they don't give people lemonade."

"No. It just was a really odd experience. I don't want to hurt Chuckie's feelings but he needs to keep his pants on in public and only make lemonade for himself in private."

"I think his penis needs to be not making juice drinks."

"I agree."

"Thank you for teaching me, Mommy."

"I'm trying my best, Charlie. I hope you'll forgive me if something doesn't work, but we'll figure things out together."

"OK, Mommy. Chuckie is new; he's not like us. We talk!"

I ask Liponie to join us and hear him say that he has a sense he is in a little bit of trouble. I reply that although I don't want to stifle the kids, lemonade coming out of a penis was not a good idea.

"I did not know what to say to the boy! He was striking out for something new and I thought I should not thwart him. I did not know he was going to be offering lemonade to others. He does not have urine, you see, and he wanted something to come out."

"From now on, check with Tonas or me if one of the kids wants something that seems way out. There was no harm done but…"

"I am dreadfully sorry, my dear."

"We're told never to eat yellow snow here because that's where something or someone has peed, and he makes me a snow cone!"

Liponie's gasp signifies to me that this issue is settled.

I recently became aware that Helena wished to speak with me. After she thanks me for seeing her, I ask her if I may have a hug. She asks if that means I wish to touch her. After I say yes, she gives me permission to do so. Then I hear her sob and say that she is out of place here. I want to know why she thinks that and she says, "Everyone is in love or partnership. They are all working and I have no duties."

"I thought you were our primary mixologist?"

She replies that it was interesting for awhile, but she doesn't want to be cooking all day. I don't blame her—that doesn't sound like fun to me either. I remind her there are other things she might do and say, "Please don't leave, Helena. I'm so proud of the things you've learned and done."

She says, "I have sovereignty."

I agree that is true and that I don't want to keep her here against her will. Then I'm inspired to ask her if she would like to help my little sister. For the first time since we began talking there is a note of curiosity in her voice when she asks me to tell her about that. I share Jewel's story with her and suggest that she will need someone besides Charlie to be her buddy and help her along.

"Are you suggesting I could be her mentor?"

"Yes, her companion or her mentor. I'm there but I'm really not completely there." That necessitates an explanation which I'm sure Helena doesn't really understand. We continue discussing the issues that have distressed her; besides being bored with cooking she feels out of place because she's not interested in having a relationship. She tells me she does like the idea of being a friend to my sister.

I ask her if it would be all right for Tonas to bring Jewel here. She first wants to tell me that she is not a good mother; she did not teach her children to love and she doesn't want to ruin Jewel. I suggest that she forgive herself because she didn't know how to teach her children to love; then I offer her a quick SVH clearing about this issue which she accepts.

She says she thinks I must have been the most wonderful mother. I interrupt that line of thought immediately by confessing that I fell short of that goal. I share a couple of things I wish I'd done differently but add that I did the best I could. Then I say to her, "And that's what you did too. You survived, which was remarkable considering the circumstances you had to endure."

With relief, I hear her say that she would like to stay and be this little girl's… Since she's searching for a word, I volunteer that she could be Jewel's nanny. Then I have to explain what a nanny might do. She seems to accept that role, but in order to forestall any more scenarios like this in the future, here's what I suggest, "If at some point you feel you *must* leave and you feel strong and *good* about that decision, then, of course, you have my blessing. But until you reach that point, I'm asking you to stay."

She says she will comply. That's not the reply I was hoping for so I reaffirm that I am only making a request and not ordering her to stay.

"My reasoning is, the longer you stay here the stronger you will get and the more you will learn how wonderful you are. You won't worry that you don't have a partner or that you're not contributing because those things are not important. They seem important because other people are doing those things, but that's not where you are now in your evolution. Give yourself a pat on the back for all you've learned, and if you want to learn something besides cooking, go for it!"

"I became quite bored with it."

"Then it's time to learn something else and there's plenty here to learn."

That obviously hadn't occurred to her because her "Ah" sounds like that realization just hit her. I make arrangements with her for Tonas to introduce her to Jewel.

With the core group:

I learned this morning that 799 of the indigenous people who went back to their stars want to recommit to Earth and I ask Gaia to help them. She suggests that several of the council can assist with that and I turn that over to her.

I show the group the page of scribbly marks I saw yesterday. Ashtar asks me to give the full measure of this to him telepathically and I gladly do so. He assures me that they will follow this to "the furthest distance." I ask him if I need to know what it is; he tells me they are aware of what it is and suggests it's best for me to focus on other things.

I describe and mentally show them a chart I saw yesterday that had a spiral on it which was completely full of little boxes with symbols in them. Gaia says it was a designation of a soul essence and it would have been instilled into the crystal that Charlie brought here. That fits because I saw it right after I heard myself mention my little sister. I'm relieved that *I* don't have to do anything with something like that. Gaia adds that they are taking all that they can off of my plate. That sounds good to me, because lately I've been teetering quite frequently on the edge of "over the whelmed."

"Another thing I saw during the night on the 16th was a little ground squirrel racing towards my right across the ground in front of me.

I was told that this is someone our family is not aware of. I'll try to show it to you."

Tonas comments that this was a metaphor.

"Are there people we need to assist that we don't know about?"

Ashtar says he believes there are quite a few individuals wanting to jump the ship they are in. "These are individuals living on Earth. It will be delicate but there are many here who will be able to handle this better than you. We are holding you as our little angel and we will not allow certain things to harm you or know your position. *We* are invincible to them; many are wishing to leave their affiliation."

"The last thing I saw yesterday was a small black part of a machine lift up from the larger part of the machine and I heard, 'That's not part of the programs.' It felt like something similar to a 'black box' in that I believe it contains the history of the 4th dimension. It should have left with that dimension."

As soon as I picture this for them, I hear Tonas say, "Oh, oh, oh! There must be a reason why it's still here." He adds that they will do some research to find out why it has remained.

"Aton, yesterday the lid came off of something."

He explains that was a preparation for what has now occurred. "There is a grand celebration that is occurring all through this universe, other universes and here as well. We have stopped to take a breath; we have been dancing."

I realize with dismay that I've been too tired to even notice the shift that happened when the 4th dimension left. I've just kept my nose to the grindstone and continued to plow my way through things I've been seeing and hearing. I've been so focused on assisting this dimension to release for so long that I haven't even stopped to embrace that it has left. I guess I should celebrate. Maybe I'll go have cake tonight!

I mention that two animals have come into my awareness recently. "Yesterday I saw the word 'albatross,' and today I saw a red fox."

True Heart says the albatross is now one of my totems and is also an important messenger about being newly awakened. He adds that independence, more grace and open-mindedness lay ahead for Earth.

Concerning the fox, he comments that it is always guiding me and it is persistent. He suggests that it is time for me to embrace more of what is pushing me out. "Release the camouflage and instead of being only an observer, allow yourself to be noticed by those who will be interested in the words you write and speak."

I know I've had a tendency to be reclusive for much of my life. He hits a tender spot for me when he advises me to allow myself isolation without being lonely. I agree that I occasionally feel a little lonely, but the good news is that I'm too busy to feel that way for very long.

"This is your time. It is important for you to embrace it."

I ask him if he is still tutoring me about the animals and he tells me it is our "together passion." Then he adds, with a laugh, "It was either the albatross or the possum." (In other words, either wake up or continue to play dead. Oh boy, does he have me pegged.) I agree that I can do a marvelous imitation of a possum, and laugh with him.

I finally feel ready to facilitate the transmissions and so we all step into the full Joy Council meeting:

"Congratulations, and thank you for your assistance. We made it! We just have a few loose ends to take care of today. There are two transmissions we will be offering to the Earth. Perhaps, Charlie, we can send these to the other universes at some point. Is it possible to create a transmission about embracing and balancing the energies of the king and queen within?"

Charlie agrees that we can probably think of something that would work for each of the universes. He says he will talk with all the different universes to create transmissions that will assist them.

We begin to send out the transmissions, then I realize I didn't even say hi to Saint Patrick. Charlie says he already came and gave everyone blue flowers. When I ask Osiris what they were, he admits he is not a flower expert; Gaia volunteers that they were primroses. I ask what the significance of a primrose is. She says that they are important to Saint

Patrick and that he is known for the color blue. "There are individuals who think he is known for the color green. Truly it is his desire always to bring happiness and kindness to the hearts. He is always in enjoyment of blue and his aura is of blue."

Language of the Origin flows from me and I add, "God bless the Irish and everyone of Earth today as we send out these transmissions."

Private meeting with Tonas and Charlie:

My question is, "What can you two tell me that you couldn't tell me before?"

Tonas wants to know if this is a trick question. I don't know why he would ask that, but I say it is not.

"If there's something you couldn't tell me when the 4th dimension was hanging on, tell me now."

Tonas says he will take a look into the future and have an answer for me. I remember that there are 578 days until something happens and ask him if he can tell me about that now.

"It is about the days when you will find yourself in a little different embodiment, a little different awareness and with abilities that will rival anything you have experienced before."

"How many days are left now?"

"You are designing this."

"Could it be like two hundred and something?"

"I will only smile at this."

"Charlie, is there something you couldn't tell me before that you can tell me now?"

"Mommy, we're working on many things, and we are hoping to make things easier for you. You work so hard."

"I'm OK with that for now because I've had an overload of work, but you know I like to know details. I don't mean details that would be better for me not to know. Just don't shut me out completely."

CHAPTER TWENTY-SIX

March 21, 2015

A few nights ago I heard something about the answer being in the past. As I ponder that bit of information, I have a sense that maybe some people are still holding onto 3rd and 4th dimension mindsets. If we can assist people to release any of that old kind of thinking, it should be easier to integrate the energy of the 5th dimension and that would also help to open the gates to the 6th dimension for individuals who are ready for that energy. It seems like a good idea to go into the Fifth Realm with Sananda and ask people if they'd like to give us something new.

Here's what I say: "Earth has released the 4th dimension. I would like for you to give us gifts for yourself, things that perhaps you gave us before or maybe even new things that might assist you to release outdated beliefs and embrace higher dimensional energies. This is an opportunity for you to help yourself and the Earth now that we're playing in a new 'ball park.' In case you didn't play baseball, what I mean is that now we're in a more exciting arena to play and grow."

With Liponie at the Joy Council:

He is usually laughing as he greets me, and this time is no exception. He tells me much is happening. I apologize that I haven't had any time to consciously plan things with him like we used to and ask him how the genies are doing. He says they are very coachable. Some are still deciding whether or not to join us but there are probably four hundred here now.

"What have we planned for Tonas's birthday?"

"Something very similar to what we thought of before—a candlelight dinner in the garden."

"Are we going to do something else that includes Charlie and the kids?"

For the first time since I've known him and maybe the first time *ever*, Liponie goofs and reveals that the kids are planning to put on a play based on one of the books I've read to them, *Annie Oakley*. When he adds that they won't even let him watch, he remembers he was supposed to keep this a secret from me. He groans and admits, "It was to be a surprise for you as well. I have done it, haven't I? You will not say anything?"

I agree to keep this a secret. After I remind him that Charlie wanted to include swimming for the party, Liponie says they are setting up a little park. Charlie's idea is to feature the 60s since he is creating a beach extravaganza.

With the core group:

Over the last few days I've recorded thirty-six bits of information that I need to discuss with the council. Seventeen of them are of a sensitive nature. In other words, they are some kind of code involving cryptic sayings, names and/or numbers. As I was considering trying to find out more information, it occurred to me that Ashtar and Tonas are much more qualified to do that. From now on, I'm just going to hand that kind of information directly to them. If they need my assistance I'm sure they will ask me. I wish I'd thought of this sooner because this way is also safer for me. After all, I've not been trained in cloak and dagger work; well, I've been trained in cloak (through SVH) but not dagger.

I move down my list and telepathically transmit to them what I saw for each of the items. When I ask if there's anything I need to know about any of this, Tonas advises, "Best not."

I add that the news is there are still thousands of people in the 4th dimension. I know this is one reason why I haven't been able to celebrate the release of it.

"Let me tell you and then show you what I saw. I saw my big green garbage container open up and in it there were three stacks of colorful cards with names on them. I was told I only have a one-time pass to get things from the 4th dimension, so I want to make sure we get everyone and everything we can from there."

Tonas says this is sensitive information and asks me to give them the full transmission. I still have a tendency to think that words are enough of an explanation, but telepathy obviously imparts more. As soon as I show them the garbage bin, Tonas says that was what they needed to see.

We spend some time talking about the best approach to make sure we get everything out of that dimension. I plan to leave what I have with

Charlie and move into the Fifth Realm after I ask a few more questions of the group.

"What really happened when the 4th dimension released? You were talking about having enough votes. It wasn't that the galactic councils looked at Earth, counted votes and determined that the 4th dimension could go, was it?"

Gaia replies that she has the answer. "It is a vote, you might say, of energy; are there more votes for moving forward or for remaining where we are? At that point, there were enough works by you and your team, all of us here and all of the other teams and individuals on Earth that were focusing on moving forward. These votes carried forward, the blocks were released and we rose. Did you enjoy it, my dear?"

I'm saddened by the realization that I still haven't stopped to celebrate and enjoy releasing the old and embracing the higher energies on Earth. Gaia asks me if I enjoyed the "spectacle." I'm not sure what she is referring to until she reminds me that many stood outside and stared up at Aton and the Moon. Drat, the solstice slipped right by me. At least I took the time last night to go have Oreo cake and ice cream. Come to think of it, eating cake and ice cream could qualify as my version of taking time to smell the roses.

I'm still wondering who released the blocks to moving people "camping out" in the 4th dimension fully into the 5th. Gaia says it was a collective decision made by the people of Earth. She asks, "Have you not heard how animals talk to each other and make movements that they all understand? It is when a certain number of them agree that they all move together to a place."

"I just wanted to get a little clearer on that. I knew my picture of millions of people moving into voting booths and marking 'yea' or 'nay' didn't fit with what actually happened."

She remarks that that would be a very smart way to do it. She obviously has not seen any of our elections covered on TV.

I ask if Sananda is present. He replies that he is but that Liponie is standing here tapping his toe. (When I first came to the council today I asked Liponie to find out the ages of Helena's children.) Liponie lets me know that Bizzarah told him Helena has five boys. "There would have been six girls but they were extinguished at birth."

This news is a tremendous shock to me. Liponie adds that it was heartsickness for Helena. I'm still trying to comprehend what she must have gone through and I just can't fathom something like this.

I ask how old the boys are since it might be possible to put the SVH work in place for them if they are young enough. Liponie says they are sixteen, fourteen, twelve, eight and six. On Earth, it is possible for a mother, with the assistance of an SVH practitioner, to put all the SVH work in place for her children from conception up until about the age of twelve or maybe even fourteen. At that age, anything the young adult would not consciously choose is released by their Higher Self.

I ask Sananda if Helena is aware of this and he says she is trying not to look there yet. He believes it would help her and adds that the children have been trained to be as their father was.

I don't know how stable she is and I don't want to present anything to her that might set her back. I do believe that at some point it will be very healing for her to be able to assist her children and maybe even to be with them again. Sananda reminds me that although the little one is perhaps not as much like his father, he is still influenced by his older brothers. I remind *him* that they haven't had any SVH work. He agrees to work with Helena, saying he will be "delicate" in approaching her about this.

I don't want her to draw back into her old persona of Sharinah, but I know she regrets not being able to love her children. Sananda is going to approach Changkolar since he wishes to assist in making changes. I leave the group with the assignment of figuring out ways to help the boys, but most importantly, to continue assisting Helena.

"I'd like to have kids here at the council for Jewel to play with, perhaps children of council members from some of the non-dual worlds. They would not be here to work but just to play with Jewel and the Swizzlers. I remember agreeing to have a secondary council of children here, but none of them were to be younger than twelve. "

Tonas says we are working on this council and offers to do some work on bringing other children here just to play. He agrees it would be an asset to have children experience playing here and growing within a council and suggests we could do something like this in all the universes. That idea meets with my approval.

"Aton, a few days ago I saw a fan blade turning in my third eye."

"It is not a fan; it is a vortex like the others. Each of your chakras now has extra energy that is as if many little orbs within them circulating in an anti-clockwise manner within the vortex. This is modeled after our dear Isis; she has offered herself as the template. This is about balance, my dear."

"I'm all for balance. Is there anything else you'd like to tell me?"

"There are more things. As you evolve, we continue to set these positions in place. Just being within the world as it is, is an elevation, even though you are not anchored to the 5th dimension. You only have a wisp of that dimension; we had to put some necessary attachments so that cars would not drive through you."

I laugh and suggest that he is making a joke. He agrees he was.

Addressing Melchizedek, I thank him for the time capsules he and Heifetz gave me in the SBT. A few days ago I had the thought that perhaps it would be possible to uninstall the old ways I've played the violin and I know Mel assisted me somehow.

He says it was a little different than uninstalling. "It was an unwrapping of the old story."

"How will that assist me?"

"It will help to unmake some of the patterns that make it so you are less flexible."

"Speaking of flexibility, I was thinking about how my body would be different as I move more into the 7th and the 8th dimensions. I assume that when I'm fully in the 8th dimension I wouldn't, for example, get out of breath if I ran for a long time."

Mel agrees that is true.

"Will I be able to do all those difficult yoga poses? The ones where you resemble a pretzel with your legs behind your head and other impossible positions? Will my body be that flexible?"

Again, he says this will be so. I'm really looking forward to being able to move like that.

I ask Gaia to speak about the new energy of the 5th dimension with the idea of putting the information on my website.

Her reply is, "As the energy merges more fully, as the sweetness of my spirit catches hold onto the minds of individuals who are awakening to this new transformation, they will have new insights of ways to apply life's measures that are of less stricture, more expanding responses and uplifting, sweet happy endings. There have been very few happy endings in the 3rd dimension and the 4th dimension was somewhat the same. The 5th dimension offers a happy ending, and an interesting journey to reach that. There are many more flavors to choose from. Was this what you were looking for?"

"It is."

"May I give you an insight of what will help make this quicken?"

"Yes, of course."

"All those who desire to have the journey bridge upward very swiftly and in the greatest of harmony need only direct their focus upward. Lift the chin; look higher. Do not look down and see that the path is rocky; walk as if it is the greatest, sweetest path of golden. Uplift, elevate."

"Thank you. That will be great to share."

Two days ago I remember meeting a man who was exceptionally tall. Actually, what happened was that I could sense him standing in front of me and he seemed like a "sequoia" version of a man. Since I don't remember what we talked about or his name, I ask the group who he was.

I learn he is from Adelbar, his name is Coonahtway and, after a moment of consultation, I am told he is at least twenty-five feet tall. My mind immediately thinks of what a great basketball player he would be, and then I immediately realize that, no, he wouldn't fit in any kind of game we have. He would even have a challenge getting into most of the buildings on Earth. His city and world must be gigantic! I decide to speak with him again but not today.

I mention that yesterday I heard Archangel Metatron had recognized a supernova and that someone had "gone into the fire." Tonas explains that the Ashtar Command assisted the people on a star to move to another planet in the Corena Universe before it exploded. This is definitely something to acknowledge.

With the full Joy Councils:

I address Archangel Metatron, Commander Ashtar and all of the Ashtar Command and thank them for assisting the beings whose star went supernova to move to another planet.

"The other people I wish to thank are the indigenous peoples who have returned to Earth from their stars or worlds as well as any other people who have joined our councils. Thank you for coming back to assist us; we are glad to have you."

I explain that the transmission we will be doing today is one that shows people of Earth 5th dimensional energies in comparison to the 4th dimension. That should help them to know the value of the 5th dimension. As soon as I finish explaining that, Charlie says it is ready and we send it out through the Joy Arrows. Ta-da!

In privacy with Charlie and Tonas:

Charlie informs me that some of the other boys would like to be more like him. I realized the other day that the remaining unnamed kids have given themselves numbers and that Number 36 would like a name. Before giving him a name, I'd like to find out more information about him. I ask Charlie what color of hair this one has and he says it is brown for now. Then he adds, and his voice has an aggrieved tone to it, "He's doing a limp, Mommy, and he's making it up!"

Charlie says the reason 36 is limping is because he wants to be like a human. "I think we should help him to feel more a part of the group, Mommy."

That sounds like a good idea but I still don't know why he's limping. Charlie explains it is because there is a character on *Gunsmoke* who is tall and skinny. Number 36 wants to be like Festus? Oh, no, that feels like an old energy name. (Pardon me if that's your name; no insult intended.)

"Would he like the name Toby?"

Charlie likes that name, and, after he asks, he says that 36 loves that name, too.

I ask him to join us. When he does, Charlie says Toby is doing sign language that means, "Thank you for my name, Mommy. Please can I have…"

Charlie interrupts his translation to indignantly say to Toby, "You have a horse, Toby!" To me, "He wants another horse!"

I want to know why he wants another horse and Charlie says Toby actually wants to have five horses. "He thinks that if he has five horses he can be a better cowboy."

"I have to disagree with your idea. I encourage you to really learn about the one horse you have. Maybe you need some extra lessons with Liponie or whoever is teaching people how to ride. Would that be OK?"

Charlie relays that Toby says yes but he is disappointed. And that I'm like a real mom who says no.

This compliment warms my heart, of course. Being a real mom is one of the best jobs there is.

I add that this decision is not necessarily forever, but I encourage Toby to stick with one horse. I let him know that when he gets really good with his horse maybe the Swizzlers can put on a little horseback riding demonstration for us. "Then we'll see if *maybe* you can have two horses."

I learn that is agreeable to Toby. I congratulate him on his name and release him.

"Let's have Jewel join us."

I hear her voice for the first time as she greets me with, "Hello, Sister. Hello, hello, hello."

I never thought I would ever have a sister and I share with her how glad I am she is here. She replies that she never thought she would get to *be* my sister.

When I first came to the council today, I asked Liponie if he thought Jewel might be interested in wearing updated versions of the dresses I wore when I was little. He said he had already made a wardrobe for her but suggested we could tell her these clothes are from what would have been her world.

Now, I ask Liponie to show Jewel the dresses and mention that I wore them when I was a little girl. She sounds uncertain as she asks me if these really were my clothes. I answer that Mom had stored them away for all these years.

"She would have been my mommy."

"Yes, and she was a lovely mommy."

"Can I have a dream about it, please?"

I realize that although she has the energy body of the little girl who would have been my sister, she has no memories of experiencing that. I'm not sure how to provide those for her, but Tonas suggests that perhaps I can get a file from Mom and Dad in the Fifth Realm to give her an appropriate "dream." That sounds like the perfect thing to do!

In the Fifth Realm with Sananda, I show Mom and Dad the information about my sister. Sananda says I was right in assuming that Mom didn't know she had a miscarriage until now; according to her, she would have been born after me. I tell Mom and Dad I've named her Jewel and that she would like to have something from them to help her be their daughter and my sister.

I share with them that what she asked me for was a dream. They both give me something and I sense that a whole bunch of ancestors also stepped forward. I don't know what they've given me but surely they would know the ideal dream for her.

Dad, through Sananda, says they have given her the first six years and then it reflects moving her to the place where she is now. It will be like she's having an adventure and she will have had visits with them. They want her experience to be really balanced because she could become very important to the future. That definitely feels like a possibility to me also. Dad suggests that I visit them every year to get an upgraded file.

Before I take the file Mom and Dad gave me back to the Joy Council, I decide I might as well address the people here in the Fifth Realm that were stuck in the 4th dimension when it released. From this future time they know the way they were extracted.

I ask all of those named on the cards I have—the ones I saw in my garbage bin—to give me their extrication plans and tell them I will give the information to Ashtar to implement. With their plans in hand, I gate back to the Joy Councils.

I intend to work with Jewel and place the file I received from Mom and Dad on her screen. I explain what they gave me for her and guide her through implementing it via SVH. I suggest that she could jump up and down when she gets a yes; Tonas tells me she just jumped.

She asks if she can go to sleep now. After I tell her yes, she says, "Thank you, Sister Joy."

I give her a kiss goodnight; I'm really looking forward to getting to know her better.

I call Ashtar forward, give him the extrication plans and then ask Sananda to assist me in helping Ashtar's ships to bring these individuals out of the 4th dimension. Ashtar says there are only two positions in time and this should be simple. He requests that I join him on his ship and adds that Tonas will also come.

When I sense we're on the ship, Ashtar says the timing for this has been transmitted to me. Here's a place to trust that my Higher Self has a good sense of timing and direction because Joy in this reality easily gets lost. I remind him there are thousands of individuals. He agrees that is true and yet there are specific timings to pick them up.

I turn everything over to my Higher Self and gate Ashtar's ship and all aboard to the first location. He reports that his team is in action and that we will give them a moment. In about thirty seconds, he informs me they are ready to move to the second position. I gate us to that location; this also takes about thirty seconds and then I'm given the OK to move us back to where we began.

I ask if he thinks we've gotten everything. His only reply is to ask me to leave them where they are and return to the council with Tonas.

Once we are back, I repeat my question to Tonas. He advises me that this is in the hands of Ashtar and that there are no mistakes. I'm too dizzy to do anything else but tell Tonas I love him and say goodbye to Charlie.

"Bye, Mommy, and thank you for not giving him those horses. He never gives carrots to his horse!"

I suggest that maybe Charlie can help Toby and he says he will be the "big brother."

CHAPTER TWENTY-SEVEN

March 23, 2015

You know how sometimes you start your day with a very clear plan about what you want to accomplish, and sometimes you even have everything written down? That was my intention for today; you already know that I'm going to tell you that today *nothing* went as I had planned.

I only have six items to discuss with the council and additionally I only heard or saw four things recently that I need to transmit telepathically to the core group. Although one of the items to transmit seems a little ominous, I'm very optimistic that this is going to just be a fun time.

The first item on my list is something I've already spoken with Jill Marie about because she knows quite a bit about people who are tribals. (Tribals can be a member of any race of Earth. At this time, they do not have individual souls—they share Gaia's.) I asked her if there is a way I can assist beings who don't have a soul to have one.

She explained that years ago, when she was at Giza with a group of SVH practitioners, they were able to implement work which assisted many tribals to have a soul. (Because of 120,000 years of crossbreeding they had developed enough master genetics to enable them to become soul-bearing vessels.) Anybody who could have gotten a soul would have done so then. The good news is that we can do that same work to assist individuals in the other universes who are tribals.

I learned that the only thing that might assist them is if Isis or Osiris would go back in time and lend them some of their genetics. I decide to ask them for help when I go to the council.

With the core group at the Joy Councils:

Tonas greets me with, "My darling, welcome. (He's never greeted me that way before; it sounds wonderful.) You were just here moments ago, and you're back."

That certainly puts a new twist on meeting myself coming and going. I just want to stop, sit and talk with him, but there is too much to do right now.

The first thing I do is ask Isis if it is possible for her to lend some of her genetics to people without souls. She answers that this is forbidden. I had a feeling she would say something like that. I try another tack and ask if it is possible for us to help not just the tribals, but all people to experience more of the energy of the angels.

Sananda agrees that I am onto something. He tells me they can't do it but I can and adds, "It could make a tremendous shift in the overall collective."

I ask if it is possible to offer this to the other universes and he says there are angels *everywhere*. He also is disappointed that we can't assist the remaining tribals in our universe to have individuated souls but suggests that this would be possible to do for the other universes using the formula Jill Marie used at Giza. (This had something to do with calibrating the level of genetics within each individual to determine if they were capable of maintaining a soul.)

Gaia says she is infusing the tribals, and all of us, with more love, but assisting them in any other fashion is out of her hands. "Except, of course, to support whatever they choose. I agree with Isis that the rules would be broken if I attempted anything else."

I want to know if there is a way around those rules. She tells me there were enough ways around the rules in the past to allow more than 400,000 beings of Earth to have individual souls. When I ask how many are left without souls, she reveals that there are several million. Ouch.

Charlie's idea is that if they were in a crystal they would not have to worry about genetics, but they would first have to have a soul to be able to do that. "That is so because that is why I got to be in the crystal I'm in. I think that the egg comes first, Mommy, instead of the chicken."

I ask if there is a way to assist tribals other than with the angel's energy. Charlie believes they are happy even without souls and asks Sananda if that is true.

"Yes, they are not aware that they are lacking an individuated essence. Gaia, I know that you have that look in your eye. You have something you are not saying."

I tease her by threatening to wrestle her to the floor. I might even win!

She says that she believes when we are in the 8th dimension, perhaps even in the 7th, it will be possible to elevate their vibration to an extent that will allow them to become a vessel if there are individuals who would offer them their genome. "It would be possible in those dimensions because they would have that same elevation through my own elevation; otherwise, they will not be able to make it forward into the next dimensional leap. If they are a part of me, just as you, it would be possible for me to find some stardust for them."

I don't know what she means about using stardust until she asks Sananda if that was what he used. He admits they added some "sparkly elements" that allowed the vibration of some of the tribals to elevate which then allowed them to become soul-bearing vessels. "Those ones had a higher configuration; it wasn't as if we were trying to exclude anyone."

I'm willing to drop the issue at this time since it seems we will be able to do something in the future that we can't do now.

"Before we do more work I want to double-check something. Is there anyone or anything left in the 4th dimension that needs to be rescued?"

I'm hoping to hear a cheery, "No." Instead, what I hear, which is completely unsatisfactory to me, is Tonas's speculation that, "They are long gone, my dear, if there were."

I never knew it was possible to actually experience something like this, but my heart really does drop at that observation.

"I can't bear the thought of people just drifting off to Neverland without having a chance to be here. I had hoped we got everyone out of there."

"We believed that we did. We went specifically after those that you directed us to."

"But that wasn't everyone?"

"We have a sense."

The easy way to find out about the beings that were left behind is to speak with them in the Fifth Realm. I ask Sananda to accompany me as a translator. In that realm, I call forth any individuals who we or others of our group will rescue because they were left behind when the 4th dimension or the blended 3rd and 4th dimensions left.

Sananda reports that thousands of people stepped forward and I am dismayed. The bright ray to this is that somehow we do rescue them because they are here. We also realize that they aren't from the 4th dimension; they're from the 3rd dimension—which left in 2009.

I move into the SBT to consider what to do now. I used up my "one-time" pass when I gated Ashtar's ships back to pick up people left in the 4th dimension. Before the 3rd dimension fell off it had merged with the 4th dimension. That must have been when we lost the people stuck in the 3rd dimension—nobody thought to check.

I think we can move into the past to fix this because no one said I couldn't go back to pick up things or people in the 3rd dimension. This must be why I haven't been able to relax about the release of the 4th dimension. I just didn't feel we had everything and I am determined to have these people back.

I step back into the Fifth Realm and ask for the people who stepped forward to give me their plans for being extracted. They hand me their files and I head back to the Joy Councils.

With the core group:

"We had a feeling you were going to return very quickly. Did you find them?"

I hand over the plans and tell them that we will need to go back to before 2009 because these are people we left behind in the *3rd dimension.* I wonder what have they been experiencing for the last six years and then decide that I can't think about that right now.

I hear Ashtar say, "My goodness. There are four positions in time and they are all over the Earth. We will need a large fleet."

I ask how many people there are. He says that the list I gave him indicates there are about 120,000 individuals and many of them are children who were indoctrinated. I *knew* there were children but I'm not sure what he means by indoctrinated. He adds that because of this it would be good for us to keep them for awhile.

Ashtar thinks it would be best if I stay with him and Tonas on his ship. Since everyone wants to come, I gate the whole council to Ashtar's ship. I request guidance through all the steps so that we can make a clean pick up of everyone.

Ashtar says, "We are all touching upon your energy. You are our loophole; without you we could not be doing this." He adds that this ship will be the scout ship and all the others will follow us in time. My questions reveal that the other ships are in four different positions and I am to gate all of them simultaneously. I will direct the ships and Ashtar will take over when we arrive.

I turn this over to the Creator and my Higher Self and intend to gate the ships to the divine places and times. All the ships did arrive at the divine positions, according to Ashtar, but it is tricky because in some places we are in January 1st and in others we are in December 31st. I hand the plans from the people in the Fifth Realm to Ashtar.

Very quickly, he says they have collected the children—they are *all* children—and then suggests we create a position for them to be able to learn a wider view of what is possible for their lives. He asks how I feel about bringing the children forward into the 5th dimension. Of course, I agree to this. There is no other place for them and it's the best place for them anyway.

Tonas says the children are quite agitated and asks if they may use the assistance of the angels. I offer the children all the SVH processes that would assist without requiring them to look at a screen, then gate the ships back to the area of our councils. Tonas explains that the children are from third world countries and that they did not transfer into the 4th dimension when everyone else did.

At Tonas's suggestion, we move into privacy at the council to discuss what to do. He believes that these children can be of great assistance to the Earth if given the chance. "We wished to have children. These are children."

I agree that is true; I just didn't plan on 120,000 of them all at once.

Tonas shares with me that none of the children are over the age of seven. I immediately claim guardianship over them; this gives me the right to put all the SVH processes in place for them and I do so. We plan to have Mother Mary and Magdalene, among others, to assist them. Tonas suggests Helena and I think that could be a great idea if it's not too daunting of a task for her. I ask her to join us.

"Helena, we've discovered something wonderful, and also, perhaps, a big task in front of us. We have brought back here thousands of children who were left behind in the 3rd dimension."

I have to stop for a moment to collect myself before I can continue. I'm still trying not to think about what the children experienced during the last six years. Tonas told me they are the same age as when the 3rd dimension left so I'm hoping it was something like suspended animation for them.

She wants to know where the 3rd dimension is and I tell her it left six years ago. Then I explain what we've done so far for them and mention that other people will also be assisting them. I add that she doesn't have to help at all, but if she would like to do anything, we would appreciate it.

"Oh, this would be like a second chance for me. You are thinking of this aren't you? I am greatly honored. Ah! Where are the children now? I must go to them!"

Tonas says they are still on Ashtar's ship.

"Liponie! Help!"

"I am way ahead of you. We have an extension that is part of the council. It is open for them and it is very beautiful. There are waterfalls and it will be perfect. I only have one request for you. Please allow the genies that we have in our ranks to be of assistance. If you allow this it will be good service for them."

That sounds like a great idea to me, but I add that he has to approve them first.

"Ah, I will be the hard ass."

I tell him I agree but before I can say more, he asks, "Is it better to say firm buttocks?"

"No, I think hard ass is appropriate for this situation. These kids have had a rough time and we want it to be smooth sailing for them from now on."

He asks if he may include Cory. I say yes and add that any council members who wish to assist may do so.

His comment is that, "We will be the village. I understand that it takes a village to raise the children."

"We may need more than one village because there are a lot of kids."

Liponie states that no number is too great and adds that the children are a blessing for us all. He lets me know their special chambers are ready for them. Helena says they are tiny children and they are very frightened. She requests leave to assist them and is gone as soon as permission leaves my mouth.

Tonas says Liponie has given him information about the home he made for the children and it is beautiful. "We would want something like this for our children…" Here his voice falters a bit, "should we be so fortunate."

I'm tempted to ask if he has seen our future children, but I hold my tongue. I remind him that even if the place Liponie created is wonderful, it's important that the people who care for the kids are also wonderful and that there are many of them to help.

He lets me know that all of the Earth council members are assisting and they are not allowing anyone from a dual world to be involved in the care of the children. This council is composed of people who ascended from Earth's duality, and so are acceptable caregivers.

With the core group and focused on the Earth Joy Council:

"Let me share a couple of things I heard and saw last night. I first heard, "Bring some of them from the future into the past." No one has an answer for that right now.

I let them know that I saw three cards. The first one was business size and had names and numbers on it. The second was also business size and had just names. Both of them were handwritten. The third one was a 4x6 card that seemed to be typed in small letters and was packed with words. I transmit what I saw telepathically to Tonas. Ashtar returns and Tonas shows him what I transmitted. He tells me they will take care of this and comments that I am a "secret finder."

"Are things settling down in the universes? I'm not complaining, but I wasn't trained in this kind of work!"

Tonas says that Ashtar is gone again and adds that, "As Supreme Commander, I can say there is a tremendous shift. Things are happening very fast in these other universes. They are taking everything that we have done and it seems they are rippling it forward very fast.

I am concerned about this thing you said to me a few moments ago; those words about 'bringing some from the future into the past' bother me."

I need to do more thinking about this situation because if Tonas is bothered, then I am, too. Before I can leave, he asks me to consider doing something special for his special day which is coming very soon. I ask him to share his idea with me.

"I thought how wonderful it would be, during your regeneration, if I was to spirit you away to somewhere wonderful."

"Yes?"

"Where the two of us could spend some quality time eating caramel popcorn and watching sunsets, one after another, on different worlds. The viewing screen from Inishimora is magnificent."

I'm feeling dreamy listening to his plan and before he can say anything more to entice me, I've agreed. I remind him there's something else planned but I'd love to do this with him. He amends the plan by suggesting we take Trifreeah, since Inishimora is so crowded. That sounds even better to me and I warn him that we may have to sneak. We agree not to tell Liponie or Charlie.

With Sananda in the SBT:

I'm sure that the words Tonas and I are concerned about have something to do with the species here on Earth that would prefer humans were not here. After getting a file from my MAPS self and showing it to

Sananda, we determine that they have a plan to strengthen the genetics of those of their species that exist on Earth. The end result of this would be an increase in their abilities which would assist them to control more positions of leadership.

I'm feeling dismayed by these conclusions, but since this information came to me, there must be something we can do. I ask the core group to join us in the SBT and give them an upload of our conclusions. Osiris agrees that this is very clever and that it can work. He says the core group will look for a loophole and he plans to take this information to the galactic councils.

I ask Commander Ashtar if any of the information on the cards I saw last night will be helpful. He says it's curious because these are some of the top families in the world. Although many of them already hold power positions and have lots of money, this would enhance their positions of power worldwide. The cards I showed him are all the bodies of the hybrid women of their species that would be implanted with an ovum. They've been interbreeding for thousands and thousands of years in order to look human, but this has weakened their original genetic strain

Sananda thinks they can do something to forestall this because there are a lot of rules about what the galactic races can or can't do. One of the rules is that you can't evolve someone (or a species) beyond their readiness.

Even though I know that we eventually "win," as shown by the vision of the culmative, I'm feeling just downright put out by this plan. "I'm not sure how much my vote counts, but I vote no!"

The group leaves with a plan to share this information with the galactic councils as we discussed. (I learn later that this was allowed but only for those who have a genetic thread of that species; unfortunately, that is a lot of people.)

In the Fifth Realm with Sananda:

I'd planned to do this work at the beginning of this session, because I've been wanting to assist children. Now is an even better time to do it with the addition of over 124,000 of them to the 5th dimensional Earth.

I ask everyone here to step forward and then ask them for gifts we can carry to them to help them be: better at whatever it was they enjoyed doing, better parents and teachers, coaches, instructors, or anyone who works with or influences children, and also gifts to assist their child within. I let them know that, with their permission, we are going to ask angels to assist them.

Next, I ask all tribal beings to step forward. I offer all of the individuals here an opportunity to be assisted by a legion of angels when they felt alone, sad, separate, different, happy, excited about what they were doing and any time in their life they would like to have had assistance from the angels.

I also ask the angels to step into the SBT, look upon all these individuals and assist them, guardian them, watch over them and help them build incredible pathways of gold so they are able to find their highest and happiest moments in their evolution.

When I am done working, I ask Sananda to step into the new area in the Earth where the children are so that he can describe it to me. All of them have a room of their own, but they are unique in that the walls are clear so they may see the child's room on either side of theirs. There are curtains which may be drawn in case they want privacy. Every child is being held and rocked by a council member. (Since there's 136,000,000 in this council there are plenty of moms and dads to rock them for as long as it will benefit each child.) I hope their recovery is swift, but even if it takes time we will be patient. Six years is a long time to be in limbo.

CHAPTER TWENTY-EIGHT

March 27, 2015

The last three nights I've recorded so many things on the little digital recorder I keep under my pillow that I can't imagine how I'm getting any sleep at all. I've been waiting until I have lots of information and then stepping into the council to discuss and/or transmit it; however, because of the nature of some of the information that's coming to me, I realize that waiting is not a good thing to do. For each of the previous night's information, I've gated to the core group the next day and telepathically given them what I've seen or heard. Now I need to fix things so that I wake up feeling refreshed instead of more tired than when I went to bed. I realize that I've been trying to do *everything*. I also realize I cannot continue to do that and, now that the 4th dimension has finally left, I don't need to.

I go to my MAPS self and ask for a more divine way of receiving information for the Joy Council so that I am able to get a good night's sleep. My intention is to have a system that allows the energy of the transmissions/information to glance off of me and enter a hologram which transmits to me at the council, the CEV and the other four councils there—also incarnated into rocks sitting on my desk. Anything dire will immediately be filtered into myself there and also the incarnated councils so that my core group is able to move into action immediately. This way I should be only receiving the happy stuff and messages of heart. (That was the theory.)

Three days ago I heard, "The 2nd dimension touches the third." My immediate thought was that there must be something *else* left behind. When I remember hearing one of the masters, maybe Gaia, mention that the 2nd dimension contains elementals, I spend some time investigating that bit of information and discover that there are billions of energy masters in crystals in those dimensions. I believe that if I create a bridge of energy, Sananda could assist these crystal masters to leap over the 3rd and 4th dimensions and move directly into the 5th dimension. I create the bridge and place it in a time capsule to give to him when I get to the council.

That same day, I heard myself spell this interesting word, arrognans, and say that it is a system of energy. After tuning into my levels of consciousness, I get that there is a power in crystals that recreates itself when there is light on them. The council must know about this because I also get that this is the foundation for the propulsion of Trifreeah and all the Ashtar Command ships.

Using SVH, I get the systems and principles for every application of this energy in the dimensional frameworks we are in, and for other universes as well, so that it can be discovered and used as a free, safe and clean power source. I plan to transmit this to Earth to individuals who could understand and develop it as well as those who could fund the development of it. I also get systems and principles so that the work will be cloaked from those who would thwart it. The transmission will support and protect those people who can take it, make it and release it to the world so that there is no stopping it.

Yesterday, I heard the word Romans and knew this was a reference to one of the books of the Bible. Then I realized there is a template we can get concerning sacred texts. The only place to get an accurate version of those kinds of works is in the Fifth Realm at the near completion.

After moving into that position with Sananda, I ask authors or perpetuators of all sacred, educational, philosophical and scientific works that have, do or could influence any sentient beings, including tribals, and any and all species in any timeline, dimension, world or universe to step forward. I ask them, "As authors and perpetuators of these works please give us a CD for each universe that contains the files you wish to be transmitted to your worlds so that individuals can hear, sense, feel and know the perfected versions of your works at many levels. The transmission that will be sent out will contain this information and support the higher principles that you now, in your greater understanding, are embracing and wish to share. We will take these CDs with us to the council to transmit the information through the Joy Arrows."

At the Joy Council with the core group:

I address the group to let them know that the part of me there is now empowered to do whatever she needs to do, and they also have my permission to do what needs to be done. Tonas asks me to give this to him as a transmission and I do. With this taken care of, I hope to now be able to get a good night's sleep and just hear about fun things, unless it's something crucial I need to be involved with.

I also inform them about the masters in crystals that were left in the 2nd dimension. I hear an exclamation of surprise and Tonas asks for the transmission. After he receives it, he remarks that there seems to be a bridge of some kind. I forgot that I was going to give Sananda the time capsule I put the bridge in and I hand it to him now. He comments that this was an important find. I agree and say that we need to remember not to leave things behind.

Tonas asks, "What do frogs have to do with this?"

I'm puzzled by his question because I don't remember saying anything about frogs. Suddenly, I realize that even though I didn't *say* anything about the game of leapfrog, the term was in my mind as a description of what the crystals would be doing. I show Tonas what the game looks like and hear him laugh heartily.

"I'm very excited about this next word although I'm not sure how to pronounce it. It's arrognans."

"Yes…"

"I want this and I've got a transmission to give it to the Earth!"

Tonas says they couldn't have given it to me. "It had to be something that you thought for yourself. How you would receive it is certainly not something we could teach."

"I heard myself spell out those letters."

"You are sneaky."

"I put something comprehensive together to help people develop this and also to cloak it from people who would thwart it until there is no way it can be stopped."

"Would you simply give all of us the transmission?"

"OK, there are systems and principles for it, too—here it is."

Tonas remarks that this can be a constant transmission that will inspire people. "The large picture is that we will hold and transmit this through the Joy Arrows. There will be a time when we can assist in other means, but for now we must follow the rules."

"Aton, what was the red blinking light I saw in my third eye two days ago?"

Sananda says, "I believe that it was the reindeer with the red nose."

Both of us begin laughing at his delightful answer and then Sananda explains he only said it because it was Charlie's first thought.

Charlie sounds a little indignant as he replies, "His name is Rudolph. Sananda doesn't know about Rudolph; I will give him the whole story later, Mommy. I think it is!"

Aton interrupts and says, "I am sorry to disappoint you, Charlie. It is a reflection of firing energies within your aura, Joy. This is exciting, actually."

The idea of getting "fired up" this way is exciting to me also.

Now I share with the group information that I recently discovered about artifacts that were used in the ancient academies. "I heard the words Fingal's Cave the other day, and as I investigated why I would hear anything about a cave in Scotland, I realized that ancient artifacts were left there that need better cloaking.

I stepped into the galactic councils and asked for any artifacts that could be used as a tool or weapon to be fully cloaked from those with adversarial or manipulative desires. I chose to elevate all the artifacts into the dragon realm until they can safely be released, maybe when we are in the 8th dimension. I set it up so that you, Gaia, can shift them into the dragon realm, or wherever you think is best."

She says she thinks that would be enjoyable for the dragons and agrees to shift the artifacts there for safekeeping. It would be interesting to know what they are, but I don't have time to discuss that today.

At my request, Helena joins us. I know she has been working a lot with the children we rescued from the 3rd dimension. I want to find out about the kids, but I also want to see how she's doing. She informs me that they have introduced more playtime for the children. I ask her if the stuffed toy animals that I gated there from a store I was in yesterday were distributed to them. She says they were and that Liponie did what he called loaves of fish.

She comments, "I did not think it was a good idea, but he seemed to be impressed with it."

I missed hearing her say the word "loaves" and I'm thinking that he gave all the kids a stuffed fish to play with. Since this seems like an odd gift to me also, I ask her if he gave them an actual fish. She explains that he gave each child one of the animals and told her he was making the loaves and the fish. I finally understand what he was trying to tell her and suggest that she talk to Jesus about this miracle.

I ask how the children are doing and she says that some of them have "hard shells."

"They would need something like that in order to survive. Just give them more love and maybe some ice cream." In my opinion, that can make just about anything better.

Charlie pops in enthusiastically to say that is a great idea, "And if we can have a slide into a pool of chocolate, that would be extra good!"

"They might like to watch someone make an ice cream sundae and then give them a spoon so they can try."

Charlie says, "Yes" but he doesn't sound at all excited about my suggestion. I say that a pool of chocolate might be a little much, but he disagrees and says he thinks it would be yummy to lick off everybody. Uck.

With Tonas, Charlie and Jewel:

"Jewel, do you have good dreams?"

"Yes, and one of my happiest dreams is to play with the fairies."

I'm inspired to offer to take her with me the next time I go there. She's excited and asks me to promise. I don't promise but I do ask her if she's met Sheliah. She says she just has dreams. I ask Tonas if I can take the three of them to meet Sheliah sometime soon and he agrees that would be delightful.

Charlie asks, "But what about me? I know you said I could go, but there are a lot of us that are me."

"All of you can come, and I want you to tell Toby that was a real compliment he gave me the other day when he said I was just like a real mom. Real moms have to say 'no' sometimes."

In a very contemplative voice, Charlie agrees that is true and then adds, "You said 'no' to me. You did, you did. I think you don't want me to have my slide with chocolate."

"It sounded kind of messy and I don't want anyone to drown in chocolate. If we have a chocolate swimming pool lifeguard it might be OK."

Those words are hardly out of my mouth before I hear an almost ear-splitting, "Yippee!"

I comment to Charlie that I've heard he's good at putting things together. He admits he's been putting things together for Jewel and adds that she loves everything. "I think she loves me. I'm her brother now and I told her I would be her big brother. I'm fixing things so they won't be frightening for her."

I know what he's going to tell me because a few days ago I heard him say something about how he could save himself from jumping and being afraid. I then saw a box lid open; there was nothing in the box. I realize he took Jack out of the Jack-in-the-box. I agree it was a good idea to do that because, "Those are scary for me, too. Even if you know when he's going to pop out you're still scared!"

"Would you talk to Helena, please? A long time ago she was going to make us a special thing for cotton candy and now she's too busy for us."

"She's really concerned about the kids, Charlie."

"But maybe she can do it for all the kids and us. We can have a circus with the animals and popcorn. Every kid loves a circus, Mommy, but no clowns, please. I think they're scary."

I agree that clowns can be scary and that they are just too "in your face" for me. I try to explain to Charlie that these kids have had such a hard time that a lot of new things at once might be too scary for them.

"We have to take baby steps with them so that there's not too much new stuff all at once."

He agrees with me and reminds me we haven't done the transmissions. I move into the full council and we send them out quickly since I have an appointment now.

CHAPTER TWENTY-NINE

March 30, 2015

It occurred to me that there is more Fifth Realm work we can do to assist those who will be developing the new crystal energy. I step into that space with Sananda, call forth all the individuals who will be involved with developing, funding or supporting arrognans in any way and ask them to give us gifts that will assist their work.

I also address those who might have wished to keep this energy from being developed during their lifetime. Again I explain that these are just suggestions for gifts, but perhaps they might have been so busy with other things that they didn't even notice this work being developed or maybe they felt tired of doing things the old way and decided to join the "good guys," or maybe they will give themselves gifts to help themselves step a little bit out of their adversarial role.

The final action I'm inspired to take is to ask the angels and guides of all of these individuals ("good" and "bad") to really step up their game and pour on the love. The development of this kind of energy for Earth will be, in my opinion, one of the most magical things *ever* to happen for us. I'm thrilled to have a part in bringing it into our reality.

I recently experienced an interesting dream about a man who had gotten out of a car with a little girl. He was going to put a pacifier in her mouth. She sounded so discouraged when she said, "Oh, no, not again." I know she wanted to be able to talk. In the dream, I offered to carry her into his house and I did. She told me her name and that she was six months old. There were a lot of kids in their house and only one was not a brother or sister for her.

I realize that there might be millions of children who are in her same situation. Perhaps a child is gifted but there is no parental awareness of the child's abilities or no way or time to help the child even if the parent knows there's something special about their kid.

Sananda and I shift into the Fifth Realm and I call forth all children, as well as people involved in their lives, including their parents, guardians, friends, siblings and teachers.

I first ask all these individuals for gifts for the children they knew or were involved with in any way; I also ask the children for gifts for themselves. Then I say, "If you were a caretaker for a gifted child, you might give yourself something to help you recognize they really are special. Of course, all your children would have been special, but you may have had one or more who needed a little something different or extra."

I ask those who incarnated as special children to give us gifts so that whatever situation they found themselves in during their lives they were able to thrive and grow. I also said that if they wished to endure hardship that was still their prerogative, but if not, why not give themselves gifts so that their lives were easy and fun?

At the Joy Councils, Tonas says, "Greetings and welcome to you, my darling."

I love it when he uses that term of endearment for me. It sounds so yummy coming from his lips. I connected with him mentally so quickly that I hadn't even had time to gate into the council so I ask him to let me just zip to him there. He remarks that I am already there; I counter that *this* part of me isn't there. He then agrees that now I am there in "a brighter presence."

I dive right in to business in hopes that maybe I can get it done quickly and then just learn more about fun things that have been going on. The new system I put in place so that information I receive which needs immediate attention is taken care of instantly by the Joy Councils makes me hopeful that fun will be more and more a part of the work I do. I had a list of forty-seven things I've heard, seen or thought about over the last three days. When I sat down and checked, all but three of the items that were crucial, and even possibly "spooky," had already been taken care of. I've already addressed one of those three items by dealing with the dream about the little girl.

One of the two things remaining to address is that two days ago I saw written the date 5/13/12. I know that Ashtar is not allowed to move into the past unless I escort him so I ask if I'm supposed to do something about that date.

Gaia volunteers that this was Mother's Day and that day is associated with Goddess energy. She wants to know if I wish for them to apply something. I answer that it looks like we're supposed to do something but I don't know what. Tonas suggests that perhaps we can make a transmission into the past that supports mothers who are overseeing their little ones and helping them to grow. I like that idea but ask why not do it for every Mother's Day.

Sananda explains that this particular Mother's Day is special because some women will be giving birth to their children on or before the period of new energy that began on December 21, 2012. I'd forgotten all about that day and the wonderful things we hoped would happen. I explain to the group that, like many people on Earth, I didn't perceive any occurrences to be whelmed about, much less over-the-whelmed.

Gaia comments that there are different layers. "Some have a nuance that is a little different than others." I must have missed that layer of nuance then.

When I ask Charlie if he can put together a transmission for us, he agrees he can and suggests we transmit it from Papa Tonas's ship since it's in the past. I mention there's a chamber here that we can use to move into the past.

Charlie sounds a little disappointed when he answers, "Yes, but Mommy it would be so much more fun if we could all go."

I'm laughing as I comment that he loves to travel. He agrees that he's a travelin' boy.

"The next item of business is that we need to do something to assist the Republic of Georgia."

Sananda comments that the people there are quite open-minded and forward-thinking. "Perhaps they have some special energy that is for the world. I see that there will be several days leading into fall when they will be quite important."

"I actually heard, 'The Republic of August is waiting,' but after some checking, I figured out the meaning is that the Republic of Georgia will be involved in something important in August." (Their motto is

"Strength in Unity" and their anthem is "Freedom." Sounds like a great country to live in.)

Sananda suggests we get gifts from individuals in the Fifth Realm to give to themselves if they lived in the Republic of Georgia during this time. We do that at the end of this council meeting.

Finally, I have to ask the group about all the indecipherable, at least by me, information I've been bringing to them for some time now. (Numbers, pages of writing, pictures of objects, cryptic sayings and descriptions of things that are metaphors. Some things I've seen very clearly but many things, for example, the pages of writing, I only have an impression of. The interesting thing, though, is that when I show them telepathically the information that seemed vague or incomplete to my mind, there is frequently immediate action. Many times I'm told that Commander Ashtar's movements seem to be like (my description) those of a cat on a hot tin roof—here one moment, gone the next, then almost immediately back again. I ask if one day it will be safe for me to know about the information I've been bringing to them because it does have my curiosity quite stimulated.

Tonas answers, "You will know all."

I'm satisfied with that answer since it means fewer things to worry about right now.

I announce that I want to know about the kids who have been flying kites. (This morning I felt/saw many children standing on a shore while flying their kites.) Someone suggests bringing Helena into our meeting. While I'm waiting for her, I ask what Liponie is up to because I haven't heard from him for awhile.

Sananda explains that Liponie is up to genie work and over busy with his desires to assist all the stars, moons and suns that are falling head-over-heels in love. He's also working diligently with all the councils.

I remind him that Liponie will never ask for help. "Maybe we need to make sure he has enough of it, because even a genie might think there's too much to do. I don't like to think of that, but we want him to have fun."

Finally, I'm relieved to hear Liponie's voice say, "My dear, I am stretched much too thin. You can see right through me, and it brings me such joy."

"I know, but you can share that joy with other people by asking them to give you a hand."

He just says that this is a pinnacle time.

"You're very important to me, Liponie. A lot of people are really important to me, and I feel like I have to remind them every once in a while to take care of themselves."

"Hmm, have no concerns. I will take care of myself, and you know Cory is watching after me."

"OK, but I think you're quite a bit to handle for just one woman!"

He simply answers that all the work he is doing is important. I agree and thank him for checking in with me.

Charlie and Helena are ready to give me a report about the kids. Charlie offers to go first because he loves every one of the kids. "Each and every one of them knows that I am their big brother and they can trust me! Liponie has been helping me with projects for the kids because Helena says it is very important for them to play. I agree, Mommy, because it is hard work being a kid."

Charlie explains that they have reading rooms and that Helena is always with the kids. She has all the Indian ladies helping because all the kids have projects.

"We fly kites and all the kids have bikes now. There are little bikes. I'm too big for that, Mommy, but there are little kids and there are special things we can put kids in so they can ride behind us. We believe that it's very important for the kids to learn how to have fun in the kitchen because you know how important all the good food is. Food is homey and it makes you feel that way. So Helena and I have been taking them into the kitchen and we give them anything they want!'

Here, I list a couple of foods that many Midwesterners consider comfort foods: mashed potatoes and macaroni and cheese. Charlie is quick to admit that they weren't thinking of any of that kind of food. "We were mostly thinking about candy and ice cream." Then, sounding defensive, he adds that their tummies are good. Next, he relates that he gave some of them a ride on his train and Liponie made him more cars for it. "There are a lot of kids, Mom."

I ask him how many and he says there are 124,310. I knew there were a lot, but it's really difficult for me to imagine taking care of that many children. That's twenty-four times the population of the city I went to school in!

He says that none of them are even seven years old and some of them are only three. "They had things done to their head, Mom. I don't like it that they had these things on their heads and had to wear glasses that put pictures in their eyes. I think this is terrible so we don't let them have television. We're afraid they might have sadness and remember things like that. We made a mistake, Mommy, but we fixed it."

It seems that Charlie and Helena showed the kids a little bit of a cartoon on TV. Charlie thought it would be fun for them but they had experienced having to watch flashes of pictures before we found them and watching the TV made them cry.

I can tell that Charlie is crying as he is telling me that he didn't want to hurt them. He explains that they were very messed up but they are getting better because Helena knows how to love them. "She's learning how to love herself, too."

Helena speaks to confirm that the children were very damaged, just as Charlie reported. She adds that she has seen similar kinds of visual indoctrination on her world. Sananda tells me that the children do not know how to play; they have slides but they're very afraid of everything.

I'm trying to think of toys that little kids might enjoy and not feel intimidated. Charlie says they do love the stuffed animals I brought and Liponie duplicated. My suggestion is that perhaps a little ball might be fun to play with. Charlie agrees and wants to know if he can take them into my special garden because there is serenity there. I approve that idea, of course.

When I mention that perhaps an animal like a kitten might be good, Helena admits they are afraid the children might harm something like that. They're going to wait a bit before introducing any animals.

I tell them I'm going to have some surgery in the SBT after our session; I invite Aton and Mel, but tell Tonas he can't come since I might be naked.

He replies, "Oh, that's distressing."

"I'm sorry. You just can't see that yet."

"And yet, all the rest."

Charlie volunteers, "What if he wears the 3D glasses, Mommy? I snuck back in cause I just want to say something that's very important. Number 57 wants to be like a real boy."

"You mean, Bruce?" (I heard that name this morning and figured it had to be another new Swizzler name.)

"Yes, Mommy."

"Let's have Bruce join us."

Charlie says he wants to introduce me to Bruce, adding that I know him already. "He's the one that always wants to sit on your lap and I let him do it sometimes. He is very happy and he's using his hands to talk. He says, 'Mommy Joy, I am Bruce. I would like to be called Bruce because I think it is a very powerful name and I hope to be of support to you and the worlds.'"

"I congratulate you on picking your own name. Good job! Do you know about Bruce Lee?"

Charlie tells me that Bruce doesn't know about the Lee Bruce, (I should have known that they wouldn't be watching those kinds of action movies.) but he knows about the Almighty Bruce. I manage not to burst out laughing and agree that I really enjoyed that movie. Charlie says that's why Bruce picked that name. Bruce loves his new room and he loves me very much. I tell him I love him, too, and want to know what color his hair is. Charlie replies that it is purple.

Now I make a big goof, but thanks to SVH I am able to fix it. I tell the group that I discovered we're building some kind of underwater palace on Zahseet's planet. There is complete silence so I almost yell, "I'd like to know about these things!"

When Tonas says he is speechless about this, I have a sinking intimation that I was not supposed to say anything about it. I'm right, because Charlie whispers very close to my ear, "Mommy, it's a secret."

SVH to the rescue! I immediately roll back in time to just before I said anything about the palace, mute my words, and then quickly roll back to the present moment. Then I say in a jolly voice, "Hey, Charlie, I'd like to talk with you in private for a moment."

Charlie tells me we're all alone and I ask him about the secret. He says, "Here's the biggest scoop of ever! You and Liponie are working on this as a special surprise for Tonas. You know Papa Tonas always wants to give you everything. The little princess of Horeeshnah said she wanted more than anything for you to have a special underwater place there. Then you got the idea that you wanted to make a big surprise for Tonas and you're going to surprise him on his birthday."

Now, I explain to Charlie that I was just talking about the palace to the whole group, but when Tonas said he was speechless, I rolled back and muted my words about it. Just to double-check that this worked, I ask Charlie if I said anything about the surprise a moment ago. He confirms I didn't.

Whew. I'm really going to have to be more careful about what I reveal in the future. There is so much going on here it's hard to keep track of everything, especially since I'm here but not really here. *Plus*, a lot of telepathy goes on here. It's really confusing when you have secrets from yourself.

I check to make sure that was the big secret Charlie wanted to tell me the other day. He says that he wants to tell me everything and he has so many things to say. After I encourage him to share his thoughts, he says, "I just think it's time for all of us to think more about the importance of the children and how they can affect the world by us helping them to change their lives so that they are no longer being the persons that they were trying to be made into. Nobody knows they're here. It will be a big surprise when they are able to be out in the world. They will be good citizens."

"They're going to need a lot of support."

"We're giving it to them. They know how to make fire and not to touch it. I did not teach them that because I'm not allowed to touch fire either. The Indians taught this and they are showing the kids how to meditate. They said it's very important for them to have their thoughts and when they get quiet they can have their own thoughts."

"You had a chance to experience that when you became an individual. Remember how you always had everyone else's thoughts?"

"That was a long time ago. It was almost forever. I'm a very big boy."

"You are, but you're still my kid."

"I know. I'm always going to be your kid. I don't want to ever grow up. I want to always be your little boy."

"You know what? No matter what age or size you become, you'll still be my kid, Charlie. That's just the way it works. My sons here are in their thirties and they are considered to be grown up, but they are still my kids."

"They're my big brothers."

"They are."

"They're gonna love me, Mommy."

"My son Mike wants to see a dragon."

"Why don't you bring him here? If you bring him here he will *definitely* see a dragon."

"He hasn't read my book yet. He's just beginning to understand things like this."

"Oh, OK."

With the full council, I let them know I forgot to tell them last time I was here that I have, in the fields of my aura, a copy of templates from Jesus, Mohammed and Moses which contain an upgraded version of their life stories. (Upgraded means that *they* rewrote their lives to be as they wished they had been.) Even though I don't know the details of Jesus's new story, I hope it helps to uplift our world.

Charlie says he has made this into a transmission and agrees that these stories are different than their old stories. "You are right. There is plenty of the story that Jesus would like to have out in the world in your energy fields."

I inform the council that the other transmission supports women who birthed children between Mother's Day, 2012 and December 21,

2012. Before I transmit it, Charlie explains it is going to go all the way from Mother's Day, 2012 into the future.

Once that work is done, Charlie mentions it would be good to have stories for the other universes. Sananda and I oblige him by stepping into the Fifth Realm at the near completion. I ask all beings there who wrote stories or had stories written about themselves to step forward. I ask if they would like to share stories that would empower people to be uplifted and joyful or whatever story they would like to have told about them to, "Please give us your real deal, high vibration, lovely stories about yourself. We're going to take them to our council and they will be beamed out to your worlds as gifts for all the peoples of your worlds."

Private meeting with Charlie, Tonas, Jewel and Sananda:

Jewel greets me with, "Hello, big sister."

It's lovely to be called a sister; I can't wait until I can spend more time with her consciously.

I ask Sananda to come with us into the Fifth Realm. I explain to Jewel that it's where Mom and Dad are and ask her if she wants to see them. I hear a bunch of "um's" and realize she's hesitant. Finally she says, "They really don't know me."

"This would give you a chance to know them and for them to know you."

Finally, she says, "OK" and wants to know if Charlie can come, too.

He answers, "Of course I will." He doesn't sound at all like the Charlie I'm used to hearing. He adds, "I will come as a big brother like this. I have made myself very tall. I want your mommy and daddy to see me. They are my grandparents, you see."

Just to make sure, I ask if this is Charlie. Then I hear him say, in his regular but distressed-sounding voice, "I don't like to be the big boy. Can I just be the little boy? I just want to be me."

"Mom and Dad will love you just the way you are."

"But what about my hair? Do you think they will like my hair? It's a little different."

I was warned that now his hair is orange with a little green stripe instead of being all green. I tell him his hair is perfect and hear him giggle happily. With their concerns out of the way, I step with Jewel, Charlie and Sananda into the Fifth Realm to Mom and Dad's place. Sananda says he is witnessing a great homecoming, and, "I think they have been waiting for your little Jewel."

I introduce Jewel and Charlie to Mom and Dad and remind them that they are Charlie's grandparents. Sananda is going to stay with the kids as long as they want to be here. He says there is a pitcher of lemonade with glasses sitting beside a huge four-layer cake with pink frosting and Mom and Dad are pushing the kids on swings. Knowing about what they are doing is a bit sad for me because, although Mom and Dad spent time with me, especially reading to me when I was little, I don't remember experiencing anything quite like this.

CHAPTER THIRTY

April 1, 2015

Fifth Realm work with Sananda: "I call forward all beings that were hungry for good things when you were alive. You were searching for something or feeling lost and you wanted more for your life. I'm asking you for gifts for yourself that will nourish you, your passion, your focus and help you to flourish. These gifts might be people to connect with, books to read or events that will enliven you and help you feel joyful and wonderful. Give yourself whatever gifts that will help you to step into a role of being fed in all areas, physical, mental and spiritual and we will bring them to you.

If you, when you were incarnated, suffered from any kind of addiction and would like to assist yourself to wake up and to find some means, method, person or place that could assist you to release your addictions and move into higher vibratory activities that support your physical body, give us gifts for yourself, and we will bring them to you when you were alive. The world is waking up and if you want to be one of those beings who is also waking up and moving into a life that's fulfilling while releasing compulsory longings you might have had, now is the time to give yourself assistance."

Yesterday, I saw my Grandpa Brummett sitting at a table; today, I got that there's something about transferring his genetics that could assist me. I remember the stories my mom told me about how poor her family was as she was growing up and realize that there must be a chunk of his genetics associated with poverty and the school of hard knocks. I enter the Fifth Realm and call him forward along with anyone else from my genetic lineage with genes that anchored a poverty mentality, as well as other issues not in alignment with the higher dimensions that I'm smoothing my way into. I telepathically transmit my request for assistance with those areas, thank my ancestors and put the files they gave me in place using SVH.

At the council with Liponie:

I've been missing his laugh but I hear it now as he announces. "It is I!"

"Hi, sweetheart, hey, it's time for some fun."

"Oh, thank goodness it is time for fun. It has been so gruelsome, has it not?" (I'm sure he meant grueling but gruelsome sounds interesting so I'm not correcting it.)

"You know today is April Fools' Day?"

He doesn't know about this interesting day, but, after I explain that it's a day of legalized pranksterhood, he's all ears. And I've decided that ears are what today is going to be about—specifically, bunny ears. I transmit a vision of Playboy bunny outfits for the women at our council table. He's enthusiastic about seeing Cory in one.

Then I picture men wearing "regular" Easter bunny costumes with big floppy ears and feet. Liponie wants to know if I have that in mind for him and I advise him to make whatever kind of suit he likes for himself since he'll be making them for everybody else. These outfits will only be for the people sitting at the council tables because I don't want to frighten the new kids.

We consider having an Easter egg hunt, but since Liponie says some of the older children are still very aggressive, we nix that idea for the new kids. Although it was very messy, I remember how much fun it was to color eggs with my kids when they were little so I decide to involve the Swizzlers in coloring eggs for an Easter egg hunt for them. Liponie says he will research this and I remind him to ask Mr. Kennedy. I know he must have been involved with Easter egg hunts on the White House lawn. Thinking about being able to do these kinds of activities again with my kids is so exciting for me!

Private meeting with Charlie:

I heard myself talking to Charlie yesterday and telling him not to forget. Since I didn't hear what it was I was telling him not to forget, I ask him now what it was.

"You told me not to ever, ever, ever forget that you loved me and that you will always be there for me. And you said that I am your big boy and to never forget that I am always in your heart."

"I'm glad I told you those things because they are very true. Are you a juggler now?"

"Yes, and we are doing funny things. Do you know what a wagon with only one wheel in the front is?"

I'm not picturing what kind of wagon would only have one wheel, other than a wagon that's not going to go anywhere. Then he says they are having wheelbarrow races. He doesn't like to be in the wheelbarrow because he keeps tumbling out. Charlie doesn't mention that this is any kind of official event completion; maybe these kinds of activities are to give kids who never sleep something to do?

I explain that the reason I wanted to talk with him in private is so that I don't inadvertently reveal any more secrets. He immediately says he has some secret things to tell me right now.

"We have changed the whole party plan. We've been talking to Papa Tonas and what he wants for his birthday," Charlie begins to whisper, "is to be alone with you. So we thought we would rough him up a little bit…"

Charlie notices that I'm startled by what he just said and asks me if those were the wrong words. I mentally show him a view of roughing someone up and he exclaims, "Oh, Mommy, we won't do that! We want to blow up lots of balloons and have him be celebrating and we have these things you blow that are really fun. They make noise. We will do all that celebrating and then send you two off on a cruise on the boat. Papa Tonas likes the boat and he wants to put you on it. We're OK with it, Mommy, as long as we get to watch."

At first, I'm not sure where we have a boat. Then I remember I asked Tonas and Liponie to make one for us on Hosemelia. I like Tonas's idea and remark to Charlie that it is important for us two to have a little alone time once in awhile. Charlie agrees, but there is definitely a tone in his voice of not understanding the necessity for alone time.

With the core group, Tonas sounds a little bit hurried when he says, "Greetings to you, and my kisses." Perhaps this is how I sound when I come zipping in here with work to do. I advise him to get those kisses in quick before I dive into business.

The first thing I report is that I heard, from an individual who wished to remain anonymous, that we might speed up the evolution of the lower dimensions by anchoring more energy into the 12th dimension and above. "As much time as I'm spending in the 10th dimension, can I get more of me anchored in twelve?"

Tonas mentions that the Atlanteans, although they are not in the 11th dimension, are radiating their energy into it. His idea is that perhaps each day we can take a little ride into the 12th dimension and have a picnic. There's no one on that dimension of Earth to complain if we do. I agree that I love that idea; a bunch of us, including all the beings from the different worlds in our universe, will be picnicking there daily.

"Can we have some educational assistance and maybe some genies assist the world of Delta Prime? I heard that it is a rough place. What is going on there?"

"They are all at war with each other."

My initial suggestion was going to be that someone needs to wade in there and knock some heads together, but before I even start to say that I stop myself and begin laughing. Those kinds of actions are old paradigm ways of dealing with situations and just not appropriate any more.

Sananda suggests an immersion, beginning in the past, of higher vibrational energies as was done with Earth. Although this will stir up some interesting energies, if we send some transmissions showing higher possibilities, that could help to balance their situation. He adds that this place has always been troubled.

The thought I share is that it feels like one of those far from civilization frontier places and in science fiction novels that's always where the bad guys go to raise a ruckus. Sananda says I've described it well and he adds that it's like places in our history where pirates would hide out.

"Aton, please tell me about the deep breaths that I find myself experiencing."

"I'm asking you to take deep breaths and you are also feeling great shifts. Let this other one tell you what else."

I hear Charlie say, "It's when you give me the biggest hugs, Mommy. You just go…" Here, just imagine the sound of him drawing in a deep breath and saying, "Ahhh."

I'm delighted that I'm giving him such big hugs, and comment that I might squeeze him to be even skinnier than he is. He says he's not skinny; he's perfect. Realizing that was an oops, I quickly correct myself and say that he is indeed perfect as he is.

I request an update from Aton about the new happenings going on inside my cranium. He explains that he removed the iris over my third eye and put in a new reflecting iris which is pure crystalline. That explains why I felt something pulled off my third eye and then saw a round, silvery object in that area.

When I show him the green plant I saw inside my head, he laughs. I knew it wasn't really a plant. He confirms that and then explains that it is an emerald which is the color of spinach. It will transmit through my third eye and is a "pass through" for my consciousness levels. I also learn that the emerald is shaped like a half-moon and rests on top of my pineal gland.

Now I know that I have a crystalline third eye and an emerald inside my head, but the functioning of these objects is a mystery to me. Instead of asking him what they do, I'm just going to wait and see what I notice.

Yesterday, I heard someone say the name Carlisle, and so I ask if there is someone new at our council with that name. Charlie speaks up and tells me that he brought Carlissel in with him to listen to me read. I can tell he's worried that he shouldn't have done this because he's explaining that Carlissel is very nice and he's a new friend. I reassure Charlie that it was OK and I was just trying to find out who the new person was.

"It's important for you to know, Mommy, that I think Carlissel can help all of the kids, because he is the one that wants to be loved *sooo* much. That's why I let him sit with us."

I agree this was a good idea and I'm proud of Charlie for thinking of it.

"I heard something the other day about horses and then I heard Tonas tell me, 'Yes, of course. He picked out mine.' What was that about?"

Tonas says that Charlie thought his horse was too fast and that he needed one that was more of a nag. "I do not understand this 'nag.' Do you understand? It is a very slow horse."

I'm trying not to laugh too loudly at the mental picture I have of my dashing Tonas on a plodding nag. Charlie explains he was just trying to help Tonas, because he keeps falling off the horse. Tonas still wants an explanation of "nag." I'm trying to be diplomatic, but that really doesn't seem possible at this moment so I just come out and say, "It's a horse that has seen its better days and is not going to go very fast." He agrees it is certainly an elderly horse. I'm still trying to muffle my laughter. Charlie reiterates that he's just trying to help and that Tonas has not fallen off this new horse one time.

My suggestion to Tonas is that maybe he can gradually work up to speedier horses. He's not a bit upset as he admits perhaps he is not the best of riders, that he is allowing Charlie to help him and he is learning. I apologize to him because I can't stop laughing.

As we get ready to move into the full council, I check to make sure that Liponie is with me and then we all step right in. Someone gasps in surprise and I can feel astonishment rippling around the room. Oh, I love doing things like this and already I am cackling with laughter.

Tonas says, "Oh, my dear, this is wonderful. It is very pink. (Liponie obviously gave him a pink bunny suit.) Kennedy is laughing and slapping his legs. You look beautiful, my dear. I look ridiculous."

Still gasping with laughter, I admit that that was the idea.

"Osiris is enjoying himself, of course."

I want to know what color his bunny suit is and Tonas says that most of them are wearing either pink or white but Woonfred is the funniest looking of all in a bunny suit with brown and white patches. Liponie is the second funniest because he is very blue.

Still laughing, I ask, "Charlie, isn't this the funnest?"

"Mommy, I think I look like a bunny rabbit."

I explain that today is April Fools' Day and you get to play jokes on people. Charlie is still confused about what is happening until Tonas explains that Mr. Kennedy has transmitted an explanation to everyone. Tonas reports that everyone is bent over with laughter.

He adds, "Marilyn is on the table walking as she does and looking quite gorgeous. She is wiggling her tail and singing a song about diamonds."

I get a really strong sense of what she looks like, and, of course, I know about diamonds being a girl's best friend.

Tonas observes again that Woonfred's costume is the most hilarious.

Woonfred pipes up to say, "You think I look ridiculous. Humph! I have been a cowboy but never an animal that would be eaten by *myself*!"

"We haven't done anything like this for awhile so I was inspired to do something fun."

Tonas admits that I took them by great surprise. With a genie like Liponie there are no limits to fun possibilities; I give my gratitude and love to him.

Charlie says he likes his new clothes—the pink is especially nice with his orange hair—and wants to know if everyone has bunny outfits. I explain that I didn't want to scare the new kids with them. Then he wants to know if he can have Easter, and I say that we are going to color Easter eggs. He asks why we would do that. I forgot he wouldn't necessarily know about that so I transmit to him telepathically information about Easter eggs. Then I explain that the mommy or daddy is the one who usually hides the eggs and the kids get to look for them. He wants to know if they are supposed to hide the eggs again after they find them.

Here I am again trying to explain a tradition that I don't really know about myself, but just take for granted. I'm pretty sure the eggs won't be real, so the only thing I can think of to say is that there might be some treats in them. I knew that would be a very satisfactory answer and Charlie's giggle confirms it.

I got so carried away with the bunny joke that I don't remember if we have a transmission today or not so I ask Charlie. He says we do and then I hear him exclaim, "Wow!" followed immediately by a second, "Wow!" It seems that Pinky and Nicky look really cute. This is followed by his statement that they all look cute, but Nicky and Pinky look different from the rest of them since all the others are boys.

He reminds me that the transmission is for all universes and it allows people to be drawn to things that will nourish them. Now that I remember what we are sending out, I call everyone in their bunny suits to attention. Then I suggest that they could wiggle their bunny noses and flap their bunny ears as we hop down the bunny trail together. Seriousness is just not on my agenda today. Through gasps and laughter I manage to facilitate the transmission. When Tonas suggests we send an extra burst to Delta Prime, I agree to that proposal and say, "Here's some laughter, fun and joy and maybe you want to think about straightening up and having some fun flying straighter."

"And now I want to read something from my son Mike. He's reading my book and he's ready for some assistance. Here's what he wrote me:

'If I have to I will go outside and look straight up into the night sky and plead with ANY of these beings from ANY dimension to stop by, call, text, e-mail, write a letter or ring my doorbell. If they are so intent with us moving to the next phase, then they need to step up their collective game and get things going. I submit myself for further communication. I am ready to communicate with someone from another plane directly and not through any other person or medium. You can let Tonas know this. If he is trying to get with you, then he can have the decency to introduce himself to me. This does not seem like too far-fetched a request.'

I read that because I think there are a lot of people who feel like he does. Tonas, tell me something to tell him."

"That I love his mother very much and that the world will evolve in its own timing. As it rises, it will be on its own wings; it will not be dragged into that new vibration by any of us. We are here to assist; we are here to be an inspiration; we are here to be the voice of wisdom for those who are willing to hear. There are rules and laws and we will not cross boundaries, instead we will inspire. Through you, my dear, there will be great moments on this world where individuals will feel the spur of light that is within themselves and become ready to be uplifted."

"I'm going to write those words down to share with him, but he really wants someone to speak with him. Is it possible that you can make more direct communication with him? Can he visit the ship or the Moon Council?"

"I believe that he will listen more during his regeneration (sleep). Sananda, what are the laws for this?"

"It is possible for him to *feel* the interconnection and bring his consciousness here. Tonas is barred from kidnapping individuals. It would be a breach of every law. We have extrications that are warranted, as you must know. There might be some education."

"I'm going to set up some mastery school education for both my sons. It will begin in the past during every one of their regeneration periods that would be in alignment with that instruction. Sananda, will you be part of that?"

Sananda asks to be put in charge of their education and recommends starting when they were six. I also put energy bridges in place that will make it easier for both of them to visit the ship or the Moon Council.

"Tonas, if they do show up will you give them a tour?"

"I will do so. Let me say that the time will come when this son of yours allows me to be a presence in his life. He will stand his feet firmly within either your ship or mine and he will learn of the great life that is opening up as possibilities for this world. It is only a matter of time."

After today's session, I show each of my sons an SVH screen in order to get their permission for this instruction.

Speaking with Esthra:

"Who was the woman I saw who is an aspect of my soul lineage; she had a dark braid on either side of her head?" I mentally show her face to him.

"Her name is Chotreeuh. She is from an interesting tribe named Sequoia and she is grateful to you. They were an ancient tribe originally from another world and brought to Earth, but were returned to their home thousands of years ago. It is her wish that they return to Earth. Are you available to assist them?"

I ask what star they are on; Esthra tells me it is called Eebra. I zip back to the council and relate this information to Commander Ashtar. He says he will send someone immediately to speak with them.

CHAPTER THIRTY-ONE

April 4, 2015

I went to the Fifth Realm with Sananda and asked people for gifts that would help them to release the past and to move forward with ease and grace. I repeatedly stressed that these were only suggestions, and that we'd be glad to take any gifts they chose to give us and maybe even more wonderful things than I could think of. Some possibilities included gifts to help them be excited about the future and inspired, also to release grudges, revenge, hatred, and the old stories that no longer serve them. I asked them to please give us updated stories that we can take to the council and transmit to their worlds.

With Charlie at the Joy Council:

"The party is ready, Mommy! The party is ready."

Charlie makes a special request not to have to wear a uniform. He explains that Helena has all the kids in uniforms so that they all look alike, and she thinks Charlie should wear one too. He feels this is a mistake because they are all individuals.

Rather than make an immediate decision, I ask him to let me think about this. He agrees to wait and then asks if he can also have a submarine. This is another request to consider, I say. He offers to let Tonas have one first so it will be extra special.

Submarine explanation: When I spoke with Jill Marie on the phone yesterday, she told me that she had Liponie make a yellow submarine for a birthday gift for Tonas. Yes, just like the one the Beatle's were pictured with. Now, perhaps, you have just a small picture of what a wonderful, wacky friend she is for me.

"Charlie, I think you might have seen my son Michael last night."

"Yes, he's pretty. He looked at me kind of funny. He tipped his head and he raised his eyebrow. I don't know if he likes me, Mommy, but I hugged him hard."

"He's never seen anyone who looks like you, and, remember, he's new to these kinds of experiences. Plus, I didn't tell him about you."

"Well, when I hugged him my arms went clear through him. It was like he was a ghost or something."

"That was his energy body; he's not there physically."

"If he's gonna be my brother, he's gonna need a body."

Sananda confirms that my sons started their instruction when they were six, and that he has been working with them quite diligently. I'm not surprised when he describes their heads as being "hard rocks." Even though they have been skeptical about some of the council work I've told them about, they are both giving me the benefit of the doubt. Tonas says that he took Mike on a full tour of the facility.

With the core group:

"Ah, my dear, greetings to you and celebrations to me."

I wish Tonas a happy birthday in Spanish then add that I have a little work to do before we can party. He remarks that there are many secrets being held.

"Aton, did you take something out of my head this morning?"

He jokes that it was a sponge left in there during surgery, then admits there was a little pin holding everything in place that was ready to be removed. I picture things falling apart in my head and say that doesn't sound too good. He clarifies that it was just a new little gauge that I will be able to use for nearly everything. When I ask what it does, he replies, that there is nothing it cannot do. Since that answer didn't help, I ask him to give me an idea of something it *can* do.

"It is a gauge that you will be able to use to direct energies just as Tonas and all of us."

This reminds me that I did experience aiming a silver object and moving energy through it this morning. "Was I aiming through my third eye this morning?"

"Yes, are you impressed with yourself?"

"I am! Then I also saw a piece of pretty crystal; what was that?"

"That is simply a piece of your new aura."

"Does it have a specific purpose?"

"It has many fractals to support your continued evolution. We are preparing you to be as if one of these others, Osiris, Isis. You simply cannot see it within their bodies. Soon you will have a perfect match to Isis."

That sounds wonderful to me. I think it would be interesting to be able to experience her color of light blue skin.

This morning I had a sense that one of the little kids is sick. I heard him say that he wanted to go home and I heard myself answer that I loved him. Sananda explains that the moment the little boy began to open his heart he wanted to go home to his mommy; unfortunately, there is no home for him to go to. I ask if he's better now and I'm told he is evolving nicely.

We move to a discussion of Helena after Sananda informs me that she has made caring for the children her mission. She's asking to be multiplied so that she can care for more of them, but this is something we agree is not in her best interest. The women of the tribes are assisting her because the color of their skin is acceptable to the children. It seems they respond nervously to fair-skinned people.

The next item to discuss is the uniforms that Helena suggested; I'm told that it has helped. I mention that Charlie doesn't want to wear it and ask Tonas if he is wearing a uniform like the kids are.

"Of course not, my dear, I *do* have my robes." That was said very regally, but I know he's joking. "Helena thought it would be much easier for them if they all wore the traditional garb."

I answer that I understand that clothing would be of value for the children because that's what they are familiar with, but I'm not sure that dress is required for Charlie and the gang. Tonas agrees with me. Since I don't feel like addressing this issue with Helena now, I suggest to Charlie that maybe he can wear the outfit sometimes, but not every day. He volunteers to wear it just when he's around the kids, and that settles the matter for me for now.

With the full council:

"We have some really marvelous transmissions to do today. There's one about releasing the old stories, and Charlie, did you do anything with the vision of unity idea that I gave you?"

"Yes, you got a vision from your MAPS self of the beautiful picture of their own journey from the hearts of everyone in the Fifth Realm. The transmission will show it to them and we are sending it to *all* the universes so everyone can see the picture of their own journey."

"Before we do this we have to sing 'Happy Birthday.'"

Now, Charlie asks everyone to put out their hand because they are going to get a big surprise in it. "Ta-da! It's licorice."

"Good, I was afraid maybe it would be a frog."

"There are some of my brothers who like frogs."

This morning I saw a skinny, yellow arm reach into a little bag, pull something out of it and then hold their open hand with a frog sitting on it right in front of my face. Yikes! What is it with boys and frogs?

Charlie informs me that Jory has a name now. I offer congratulations to the former Number 47. My plan is to sing "Happy Birthday" to Tonas and then to Jory, but we end up singing just to Tonas. Charlie and I could have used a little more rehearsal because our parts of the song had more of the flavor of a round.

Tonas's reply is that he is truly "over the whelmed." He thanks all of us for this celebration and the new custom of celebrating a birthday. He adds that he feels very special.

Before we send out the transmission, I say, "Every day is a new beginning, and this is another one." When we're done, I add, "Now we know who's who and what's what. Hooray for that!"

I can't say much about this, but we are now able to detect a certain group of individuals whose identities have previously been undetectable. Charlie adds that we love *everybody* and I agree.

At this point, I dub Charlie the master of ceremonies and turn the proceedings over to him.

"Mister Ashtar will be taking all of us to a very special place for a picnic. It's going to be an exceptional one but you have to have your own picnic basket. It is not up to you what you get to eat; we decided for you. Tonas is now giving you your basket. You all are going to get special costumes that I designed myself so that you will look like angels. All of you who are angels, we have you looking like humans, so it's a little switch."

Charlie asks everyone to get on Ashtar's ships. I'm not ready to go yet because I heard Charlie say something about Earth angels, and I want to find out what he was talking about. According to him there are Earth angels everywhere.

"They walk around and look like human beings, but they are angels for real! They make miracles and some of them look like those people who don't have homes. You can tell they're an angel because they don't smell funny or stinky; they sometimes smell like cookies. You can't make an angel stink, Mommy."

I admit I don't usually get close enough to smell homeless people. Many of them around here are standing next to a busy intersection with cardboard signs that say something like, "Homeless, anything helps, God bless."

I thank Tonas for showing Mike around the ship. He replies that my sons are quite welcome and they will be treated with gloves that are for children. He says that Michael was in a dream state, but even so they handled him with gloves for children. I try to explain that the term would be "kid gloves" and Tonas says, "Yes! We did." It's just not worth the effort to explain it again.

I mention to Tonas that I hope to taste some of the foods he likes and spend some time snuggling. He admits his birthday wish is to spend special time with me after our picnic.

"Charlie, do I have my basket?"

"No peeking, Mommy."

"Not even one little peek?"

"OK, because one of the things I got you was that mud pie. I did, I did, I did."

This immediately brings to my mind the actual mud pies I used to make for my Grandma Crystal. They weren't totally mud, there was quite a bit of sand mixed in. I'm sure that is not what Charlie means, though. Well, I'm reasonably sure.

"You mean the S'more Pie?"

"Yes, it looks like mud, but I'm gonna have a bite."

"If you haven't tasted it, once you do, you won't think its mud."

"I've tasted mud and I don't think it's good."

Charlie feels we need to be the first ones at the picnic so that we can have our kites in the air when everyone else arrives. I didn't know we were going to be flying kites but that does sound like fun. I thought we were going to take my ship, but Charlie wants to go to Hosemelia via gate so I oblige. I do love to hear his, "Wheeeeee!" when I travel with him that way.

Tonas informs me there are thousands of kites lying on the ground. Charlie hands me my own kite, which, he says, is a princess one. Then he must be addressing Tonas because he says, "Yes, go ahead and look. Mama says I might be able to get one too."

Tonas stutters a little bit and then admits it is quite unique. He says that he is aware of submarines but has never seen one that looks like a "yellow tadpole."

Charlie says he can wait until tomorrow to ride in it because he doesn't want to take away from Papa Tonas's special day.

Then he casually adds, "If you tell Liponie, he will make me one; I'd like one the color of my hair, please. We need to get our kites in the air because they are coming any minute! OK, run! Run! Here they come; act natural. Papa you can kiss her. I won't look… I might look a little. I'm learning about romance, you know. I don't know if I want any, but I will watch. OK, I'm turning my head now. I will get everyone going and you can do your smooching thing. You go play."

"You made him the master of ceremonies. You are a goodly mother."

"Will you just hold me for a moment and let me whisper something in your ear."

"With pleasure."

"Ooqwa, I hope it's a special day for you today. You'll have to tell me all about it next time I'm here."

"I have a dream of us on the top deck; the ship is piloted by my consciousness so that we are alone. As it sails with its billowing sheets caught in the wind, we simply float on this beautiful water and watch this world go by. It is quite beautiful here, my dear, and it is a time for doing nothing, just relaxing. I have a lounging deck chair that is made for two and there are many pillows on it as if for an Egyptian princess."

To me, this sounds like the perfect thing to do.

"And so, perhaps we can spend a little bit of time here and then I can spirit you away. If you close your eyes you will come directly back to me on the ship and I will be waiting."

And that is exactly what I do.

CHAPTER THIRTY-TWO

April 6, 2015

"Hello, my dear, what a *wonderful* gift you gave to me; the gift of your presence. We did *nothing*, and it was heaven on the Earth. I should say it was heaven on Hosemelia. Everyone had a wonderful time at the party and it was delightful for this little one to be the head of ceremony."

"Did he ride in the submarine?

"Yes, Liponie has already made him one, and then, because he must see something when he uses his submarine, we have an underwater extravaganza. We have quite a course for him to follow."

"Are we spoiling Charlie?"

"What does spoil mean?"

"When you give kids so many things they sometimes don't appreciate what they have and they expect that nothing will ever be denied them."

"That is the non-dual way, my dear. This is how we teach that anything is possible."

I realize I'm going to have to do some rethinking about this concept of giving your children everything they desire. It's always been the idea here that you don't really appreciate things unless you've done without them; that kind of thinking does not fit in a reality of instant manifestation.

With the core group:

"Charlie, thank you so much for my Easter eggs. They were beautiful." (This morning I saw two pretty eggs pop into my view as I was waking up.)

"There was one from me and then one from all the other kids. Mine was the pink one and inside," here he begins to whisper for some reason, "if you open it up, there is the yolk and there's white! We cooked it, Mommy."

He says they had a lot of fun coloring their eggs. Even though I don't remember helping them do it, I'm determined that *next* year I will fully experience having my fingers turn purple and blue from coloring the eggs. Or maybe I'll just wear gloves.

"Liponie, there are trees I want to bring up. Can I do that?"

"Bring them, bring them!"

"They're going to be big. One is in the city where I used to live and is probably seventy-five feet tall. Can I just intend to gate there and gate it to you?"

"Simply do that. When you are there, put your hand upon it and move it directly to the spaces we have on the Moon and in the Earth.

"Do you have a big enough place for things like that?"

"The sky is not the limit."

I gate to Rockford to a huge oak tree I've admired for years, put my energy hand on it and send it on its way. I wonder what that feels like for the tree. The last few years when I visited the city and drove on the road that goes underneath its canopy, it did not look well. Maybe this will help to perk it up.

Liponie asks if there is any special place I would like it positioned in my arboretum. I answer no and warn him to be prepared for a lot of big trees to come his way.

After our work today, I visited our public library and checked out some books on famous and big trees. I also spent an hour or two searching on the internet for pictures of trees. It takes me a few hours but I follow the procedure I did with the first oak tree and gate them to the Moon and Earth. I hope Liponie has been able to keep up with me in placing them in our gardens; otherwise, he may be buried in trees.

"The other thing I realized is that there are lots of people at our table that should be included in our core group meetings. I just didn't want the dual worlds to hear about some of the challenges we've been dealing with. How can I fix this, Tonas?"

"You are correct in that those of dual worlds are privy to what we discuss around the Round Table. It is possible for us to let all who are seated at the table (They are all non-dual.) know what is occurring so that they may step in and assist if they have relevant information. It is like having an internal radio so that they know what we are speaking about and can immediately be in presence."

That seems like a good plan; Horus, Hathor, Mr. Kennedy and Mr. Lincoln, as well as all the others at our table should definitely be kept abreast of what's going on.

This morning I heard someone singing, "I brought something for you. My heart is true." After spending some time wondering who this was, it comes to me that Changkolar was speaking to me. I know he would like to assist Helena and that he gave me something he feels will help her. Sananda has been assisting Helena, so I let him know that I have something from Changkolar and hand it over to him. He comments that this is a delicate situation, but he does agree to take the information. He's going to focus more on neutrality and assisting Helena to release the past during his weekly study with her.

"I think he really would like to help his kids. I know we haven't said anything to Helena about this, but I'm hoping she can become involved with them at some time. Maybe if she gets comfortable with these children she will be willing to assist her own."

"I must explain to her a little more about ascension, the academies and training. Perhaps give her a chance to do the Five Star Send-off for those who have died that she was involved with. I know they already have this but I think it would be very healing for her. We can take a journey to show her the transformation of these individuals who were angry and not kind. Leave this with me; I will apprise you at some point."

"I've been thinking about the solstice party for this year. How about forty-six ships surrounding our ship; one from each universe with all their special entertainments, foods, artists? We can have a big *get to know the other universes* party and when the party is over the ships can circulate through the universes to continue to share information.

Liponie exclaims and says, "Oooh! The goose bumped me! Ah, this is delightful. It should be no problem, of course."

"Do you think that would be fun, Tonas?"

"I am aghast; I cannot imagine how magnificent this would be. This would be a great study and we could supply the ships so that it can be managed."

"We could have quite a party that way. That's down the road a ways."

I continue to speak but suddenly Tonas asks, "What road? What road is it down?"

"That's just an expression for in the future."

"Oh, thank you, I thought I missed a piece of communication."

"Let me show you this road that I saw this morning. What's that about?"

"It is funny that you would ask this. It is as if there is a need to find a space that is quiet for yourself."

"Yes, I look for those kinds of places and I haven't found one for awhile."

"I can tell you, my dear, that there will come a time when all the works will be over and we will find a most calm space. That will last a minute and a half because you will wish to stir up energies on something. I know you, my dear. You think that you are exhausted but your heart and mind will never stop."

I've been giggling as he tells me this because I realize he's probably right.

"Charlie, did you taste the pie?"

"Yes, and I love it, Mommy. I think it is the bestest pie I ever ate in my life. I only want that pie always now."

"I'm glad you said that because I would have been seriously worried that you might not be my son if you didn't like that pie."

"Yes, well, I didn't fall very far from your tree, Mommy. It's a chocolate tree."

We are both laughing about our mutual love for chocolate.

"Thank you, Mommy, for letting me have my beautiful submarine. I love it very much and I'm giving rides."

Although it's orange, Charlie did acquiesce to having green fins for it. I bet it will look darling snuggled up next to Tonas's yellow one. Tonas is going to bring it to Hosemelia the next time we go there.

"Tonas, did we eat anything special?

"Yes, Liponie left us with an exquisite buffet. We had waffles with whipping cream and chocolate, many pies and cakes. There was the most delicious, he called it, quiche with spinach. There was a fountain of champagne. We never left the top deck."

The boat description that Tonas furnishes is that it has red and green sails that have a golden stripe running through them. I gather this ship is like an Egyptian luxury barge that might have sailed the Nile during ancient times. I like the idea of something like that, but I also like the idea of a ship that will go fast. I need to make time to talk with Liponie about a real sailboat.

CHAPTER THIRTY-THREE

April 7, 2015

At the Joy Councils, Tonas confirms that the core group is bigger and I apologize to all of them for not including them from the beginning. I can't imagine what I was thinking not to include Kennedy in the group.

Now I ask Liponie if I've swamped him with trees because I've gated several hundred to the councils. These have been trees I've seen as I'm driving along, trees I remember seeing at different locations, copies of famous trees of Earth and trees I've seen pictured on the internet. I'm a big fan of trees, and the bigger the better; however, I'm still a little nervous about the size of some of the trees I've been flinging at him. I've even sent groups of trees, because many times it just didn't seem right to send one little tree and leave its brothers and sisters behind.

Liponie confirms that we have forests now and asks me to have a greater vision of his abilities, saying that even a thousand trees wouldn't give him a moment of thought.

Tonas comments that the trees are so beautiful he would love to have millions of them on Hosemelia. My concern is that they might cause problems there since they are not native to that world. Tonas explains that since Hosemelia is non-dual even if the trees had diseases or pests they would have none once they were on Hosemelia. That allays my fears of introducing something that would decimate Hosemelia's ecosystems.

"Would any of the other worlds like to have some Earth trees?"

"Oh, this is a wonderful idea! We could make a catalogue and offer individuals an opportunity to select trees."

I explain to the group that I sent the Hitching Post of the Sun here yesterday—that's the name for a sacred hunk of rock on top of Machu Picchu—and ask Charlie if he can draw a picture of Aton sitting on it.

I can barely manage to get that sentence out of my mouth before I start laughing. I've been to Machu Picchu in person, and as I was looking through my photo albums for pictures of trees to send to Liponie, it occurred to me that the rock needed to be somewhere where Aton could enjoy it.

I encourage Tonas to share with other worlds the trees, artwork and other objects I'm going to be sending to both councils. Then he mentions that they have been expecting some of the obelisks.

"I've been a little hesitant about sending some of the bigger things, but I guess if I can gate the General Sherman Redwood tree I can do some of the obelisks, right? Do you think I could throw the pyramids up there?"

"What an endeavor! Especially if they are the original version."

I ask if I can just travel back in time to when they were the most beautiful, but Tonas suggests we have Liponie get copies of them at the height of their glory. They are magnificent even now, so having the original versions would be amazing for people to see.

Liponie lets me know he is already making extensions to fit them in. I joke that we may run out of Moon and he explains he will simply make it bigger.

Sananda agrees that it would be wonderful to bring back beautiful objects that were ancient wonders. Mention of ancient wonders prompts me to ask about the Colossus of Rhodes, the Roman and Greek temples, the library at Alexandria and all the temples along the Nile. I've seen those temples and even with the colors almost faded away and the defacements that they have incurred over the centuries, they are still magnificent. Osiris vouches for the beauty of those temples as well as the ancient academies.

"Is this something that Liponie can do on his own?"

Osiris suggests I might add these things to a list. I've been thinking on a pretty grand scale working with forty-six other universes, but trying to visualize a shopping list with the pyramids, the Sphinx and the temples on the Nile is still a staggering thought.

I mention that the beauty of the temples is that they are on the Nile. Osiris answers that then we must have the parts of the Nile that they like. I ask where the best location for these objects is and Tonas suggests we just spread them around.

"So, a temple here, a temple there, a temple everywhere?"

Tonas advises me to just make a list and let Liponie make it all happen.

"Here's the beginning of the list. I want all the temples along the Nile, the pyramids and the Sphinxes (There were three originally.) at the height of their beauty, and that includes the temples of Isis on Philae, the Colossus of Rhodes, the library at Alexandria, all the temples of Rome and Greece, the original temples in Thailand, Machu Picchu, the Mayan, Incan and Mexican temples. Name some temples I've missed."

Tonas lists the temple at Lake Titicaca, Akhenaten's temple, the great Lemurian temples of the South Seas and the Atlantean temples. The temples of Atlantis! Wow! I'm really in the swing of this now and I say, "Yes! Let's have some restoration! I want to see all these beautiful structures. This is a big list, but I'm ready for it. I knew at some time we were going to see all those temples restored, so why not now? If somebody thinks of anything else, send me a memo when I'm sleeping."

We've discussed new clothing for the children we rescued from the 3rd dimension, but nothing has been decided yet. When I broach this subject, Tonas starts talking about an outlet mall for children. He explains that they made copies of cute clothes for children from someplace called California Clothings. It seems that he and Liponie took it upon themselves to materialize there and that they had a great deal of fun walking through the stores in order to identify "age relevant clothing."

"I'm still confused. You mean you went to California to look at clothes?"

"To San Francisco, California."

"You were just strolling around one of the malls there? How could you do that?"

"It was not forbidden!"

"Remember when I asked you to come to my concert and that was a big deal for you to do. Are you able to come here more easily now?"

"In California we were not invisible; we were in our most comely presence, as you can imagine."

"No, I can't imagine! You were walking around a mall in San Francisco, California, looking at children's clothes…"

"It was called Gilroy and then we went to a place called the Premium."

"So you're dressed in California clothes and strolling around with your gorgeous long hair and people are not even looking at you. Is that right?"

"Liponie was in his cream-colored face and they assumed we were a couple. We were not bothered and we were not breaking any laws. No one knew who we were; we were simply walking around and looking in the Petaluma. There were all of these little outlets."

"Darn! How come you can't just come and visit me?"

"Because you would know it was me. We can all be on Earth in different places. We can have a coffee and now that we understand about the banana splits we can have one. No one will know who we are. It is only required that our skin colors match."

I've been feeling disgruntled throughout this recital of events, and I've also been challenged with feeling left out and possessive. *My* sweetheart was walking around in California without me. It would have been so much fun to do this shopping with him.

He reminds me that their shopping was an important mission but that doesn't placate me at all. I do feel a little better when he offers to let me join them the next time they shop. Before I can ask more about that, he informs me that they have created an outlet mall in the Earth's Joy Council, plus an ice rink for skating and a roller rink for rollering. There are bicycle tracks for the children and there is the "ball of roll."

"You mean bowling?"

"Are you sure it's not rolling?"

"We call it bowling, but bowling balls would be heavy for kids."

"These are children sizes and weights and also we have the shoes. Liponie has moved beyond all my ideas."

The kids haven't seen any of these things yet because Tonas says they are watching programs that will accustom them to some of these new activities. Charlie has insisted that there be a cake place, a pie place and cookie stores. I mention that they will need to know about regular foods and am assured the kids are receiving a balanced diet. Tonas starts to say something else then stops.

"Mommy, Papa Tonas almost told you my secret. It is a surprise for you. We have ceramics, painting with the hands and with brushes and there is a place that you can make your own cup!"

Charlie sounds really excited about this and I am, too. I did quite a bit of ceramic painting years ago and I really enjoyed it. And who doesn't love finger painting? I remember doing that, and, although my pictures never really looked any good, it was fun to smear the paint around.

"They can make their own cup and their own plate and it's going to be wonderful for them. I get to be the one to lead them in and show everybody how it's done. I've been doing my research. Also, I think it would be good for the kids to have a place where they can lay down and rest. We made little spaces so they can have privacy, because, Mommy, sometimes people can get whelmed."

"I know. I've been whelmed lately myself."

"They have special little beds and we made all the colors of the rooms happy. There are no colors that are unhappy, Mommy."

"It sounds like wonderful things are going on and I'm pleased with what you are all doing."

I have some concerns about security for the solstice party this year. Of course, the non-dual worlds would present no problem, but many of the universes have dual worlds and a few universes are composed completely of dual worlds. It seems like with so many people involved, there would be some who might want to cause trouble. I ask the group what their thoughts are about this.

Tonas feels the Ashtar Command can manage it and it would be a great inspiration to all the worlds. "With the rulings of the councils overseeing Earth, we would need to make sure none of these other worlds have even the smallest possibility of creating imbalance on the Earth. These rulings have been in place for a very long time."

"There are people who don't care about rules, Tonas. We have to plan for that."

He agrees and adds that we have time. He feels that if the command is in full charge of security, there will be no imbalance.

I suggest that the party lasts for forty-eight days. That way each universe has a day to show their stuff and then we have a final day for a last big hurrah, like they do for the Olympics. Finally, we decide to have everyone in position on June 20th and have the opening ceremony on June 21st. That means there will be forty-nine days of party. Wow, as Charlie would say.

Osiris asks us to imagine all of the universes wishing to be as fully evolved as they can be. "To watch Earth is to see many in their different stages of evolution. It is a magnificent opportunity for others to feel exactly where they are in comparison to Earth and how that appears within the full spectrum of all that exists."

I suggest that we send out notice now because there's really not a lot of time before the solstice. My idea is that what we're looking for from each universe are things they want to show off; their stories, artists, foods, dress, talents and the things that they feel best exemplify as many of their worlds as possible.

Private meeting with Charlie, Jewel and Tonas:

"Mommy, Jewel says she loves me."

Rather than comment about that, I ask her if she's been able to visit Mom and Dad again. She says they only went the one time, but she would like to go again.

"Do you have fun playing with Charlie?"

She whispers, "Yes, he loves me."

"Charlie is a love bug."

He sounds indignant and denies being a bug. I explain that is just an expression of endearment and he agrees that he is indeed an endearment. After I show him a Volkswagen Beetle, he giggles, agrees that is a love bug and that he is also a love bug. "I'm never bugging anyone, but I am always love."

I have a plan for something I would like Charlie and Jewel to experience, but first I need to check with Mom and Dad to see if it's possible.

In the Fifth Realm with Sananda who vocalizes my parents' telepathic answers:

"Dad, this is close to the time of year that we always went hunting for mushrooms. Can you create woods like we used to walk through? One that has the dead leaves and branches and spring flowers like you'd find in our woods so that Charlie and Jewel could hunt for mushrooms."

He says he can and it would be a delight. He wants me to bring all the Swizzler children. I ask if he knows all the names of the spring flowers so he can talk to Charlie and Jewel about them. He says he does and it will only take him about a minute and a half to create the woods.

Imagine having a place where you can create, look for and find mushrooms any time of year! That would be heaven for those that, like me, love searching for and eating them.

While Dad is creating the wooded setting for mushrooms, I ask Mom what she's been doing. She says she's been helping Dad with a song that he's rewritten five times; it's about the dreams in his life coming true.

There's something that's been bothering me for awhile and now I ask Mom why my Grandmother Nancy has not bothered to say hello to me. Mom explains that at this time I have more in common with her than they do and she suggests I visit with her.

I ask her to join us. After she does, I say, "I am just a little bit out of joint that I haven't heard a peep from you after all those years I prayed for you (at her request) every night and made all those cards to send to you when you were in the hospital. I've been sorting through some of your old letters that I found at Mom and Dad's house, and it would be nice if you communicated with me sometime."

She answers that she has never lost sight of me and that she's not missed me because she always sees me. Years ago, I saw a vision of myself when I was little; I was following behind her and we were connected by a silver cord. She explains that represents a heart connection and she is always watching over me.

"I still miss you. I'm glad you haven't forgotten me, because I haven't forgotten you."

I check with Dad and find out he's done creating the woods. Sananda returns to the council and brings Jewel, Charlie and all the other Swizzlers to join us in the Fifth Realm.

When I sense they are present, I say, "This is about spring on the farm, Jewel. You're going to have a chance to find some things we always looked for when I was a kid."

Before I can say anything more, Sananda informs me that Jewel just took off running and is chasing a butterfly.

"Charlie, this is the time for you and your brothers and sisters to learn about the farm and have fun."

Sananda whispers to me that Charlie just put his hand in my father's hand and he's just standing there looking up at Dad. My tender-hearted son—I'm grateful my parents love him.

Dad begins to lead them out into a meadow and Mom hands each one a basket as they pass her.

"Mom, since the mushrooms won't have bugs in them, you can just cook them up!" (In my dimension, mushrooms come with bugs. You have to soak them in salt water overnight to kill the critters. Then you rinse them, pat dry, dip in flour and fry. Yum.)

Mom agrees to cook any mushrooms they find and they're also going to have a picnic. Sananda reminds me, even though there is nothing there that would hurt them, that this activity is worry free since they are with him.

CHAPTER THIRTY-FOUR

April 13, 2015

I recently realized that I should have set up parameters for duplicating and sending objects to the Moon and Earth Joy Councils. I started out with copying and gating an oak tree in Rockford that I really love, if you remember, and I branched out to trees and gardens all over the world, two parks I enjoy, the farm my brother and I own, the property where Sheliah lives, the Morgan Monroe State Forest, the rainforest of the Amazon, uninhabited parts of Madagascar, and lots of other places and things I can't remember. (Later today, Liponie reports that we're not running out of room. That's good; I thought the rainforest might have taken up a little too much space.)

I visit my MAPS self to get a file so that anything I copied and transferred that shouldn't have been transferred will not have been moved; this file also covers future objects I choose to transfer. Also, I make it so that from the very first time I transferred anything, my Higher Consciousness and soul transmitted a message asking all objects and areas that I intended to copy and send to the Moon/Earth Councils if they would like to co-exist in those places. Only the objects or areas that accepted were transmitted. No people were transmitted, and if a dwelling place chose to be duplicated, the energy of the copy did not interact with or affect the people living in it. After I put this file in place, I feel certain that everything that has been transferred wanted to be and that I created no imbalance or harm in doing so.

This morning I heard myself talking about our boat and that I needed a fail-safe. That sounds like something Esthra can tell me more about, so I intend to speak with him. He says that even though I don't remember it, I became really involved when Tonas and I were celebrating his birthday on our boat. Before I can express my alarm, he assures me that this was not sexual involvement. It seems that while I was on the boat there was a time when I could have become fully aware of my presence with Tonas, and upon realizing that, my biggest concern was, why would I come back to Earth?

I have to think about that for a moment and my rather weak reply is, "Responsibility?"

Esthra replies, "Not when you are looking in the face of that one and you realize you are head over your heels in love. You also know that you can still work from that dimension. The fail-safe we were discussing is so that if you wish to return to your current Earth dimension and location, you will."

I realize that I don't really trust the part of me that Tonas is with all the time. *I* want to be the one deciding if and when to stay with him, and I don't want to do that until *this* part of me feels that all-encompassing love for him that he feels for me. I also want to be sure that the work I'm doing here will not be disrupted and that I'll be able to visit my family and friends living on Earth. Finally, I want to be completely happy with my life, my body and fully embracing my master abilities before I move in with a man as wonderful as Tonas.

The best person to ask for a fail-safe is my MAPS self. I'm going to ask for everything that will assist me to be able to make the most of the moment when I come to my full awareness of Tonas; I don't want to be afraid of that eventuality or confused about what to do. After I get the file, I step into the SBT, have the Creator and the masters assisting me add to it and then put it in place for myself using SVH.

I did my first expo as author Joy Elaine this weekend. The lady in the booth next to mine had a gorgeous, eleven-inch Tibetan bowl for sale. I played it several times over the weekend and knew I had to purchase it even though it was very expensive. The only thing she knew about it was that it was about three hundred years old.

Intent upon finding out the history of the bowl, I ask Esthra to step into the Fifth Realm with me. Once there, I request the maker of the bowl to step forward; when no one does, we know we will have to visit an ascended master temple in order to speak with him. According to Esthra, he is located in an important place in the Himalayas; the temple does not have a name but the name of the area is Fweese. I intend to gate to this temple, and, since I find myself bowing in this reality, I assume I am also bowing there. Esthra explains that the individual I am standing in front of is a man named Koormah.

"What can he tell me about the bowl?"

"It is called a bell, not a bowl. It was made specifically for a particular monk that is of Bhutan."

"What is the monk's name?"

Esthra laughs and then says the man is telling him something quite fascinating. "Conch is and was a very famous Tibetan monk who lived in an important cave. He is one of the ancient ones and his purpose is to anchor the energies of truth and wisdom; he reached greatest enlightenment at the age of twelve. In this enlightenment, he moved to the cave as a boy and lived there. Many came to hear the wonders that came from his speaking. He lived to be one hundred and forty."

"Where is he now?"

"He is ascended and is at this temple."

"What does the inscription on the side of the bowl say?"

"The truth that brings greatest wisdom can be found in the innermost part of self."

"What year was the bowl made?"

"The bowl was made when Conch was thirty-three in the year 1720. He received the bowl as a gift since the speaking of his wisdom was important."

"Do you think I could speak with Conch for a moment?"

"Yes, we have him here."

Conch's presence is so profound that I feel myself bowing very deeply. Tears spring to my eyes and I am barely able to speak. Finally, words tumble from my mouth that are not English; I know their intent is to honor him, to thank him for his service to humanity and to convey my gratitude for the bowl I have that once was his.

"He has told me that he has a lineage that follows in the prints of his feet, and he offers his wisdom to each of these. He is important through these individuals even today. There is always a Conch."

His name makes me realize I have something I'd like to give him. I gate home, pick it up and bring it back to the temple. As I hand it to him, I say, "This is a gift from me to you. My parents had it for years and years and all that time it sat outside. As you can see, it's a very white and weathered-looking shell that housed a sea creature we call a conch. I think it's very beautiful and I wanted you to have something from me."

Esthra says that Conch looks Mongolian and has a great smile with no teeth.

Addressing Conch again, I say, "I'm honored to meet you and to have your bell. It is very special to me and I will think of you when I play it."

Esthra informs me that Conch is "pleasured," and I return to my home.

At the Joy Councils:

As soon as I'm there I hear Charlie yell, "Yippee! Hi, Mommy!"

"Do you like it when I play my bell wearing your ring?"

"It makes me tickle."

I telepathically transmit what I learned about it to Charlie; his only comment is an interested sounding, "Oh."

I've been curious how the mushroom hunting went, but when I ask Charlie if he found any his "yes" does not sound the least bit enthusiastic. It turns out he didn't like the taste of them. I assure him that not everybody likes them and he makes sure I know how he feels about them by saying that he doesn't have to like them.

It seems he also didn't even have fun looking for them because they "hide." My suggestion that looking for them is like hide-and-seek doesn't work either. Charlie says they cheat, "because they cover up and you don't know that they are there. I think that they should come out and play."

Then he changes the subject by telling me he can see fairies, with his eyes open, everywhere there is grass. He says that he loves them and wants to squeeze one, but they won't let him.

"Mommy, you got them in your garden. They peek at me sometimes through the windows (of my house on Earth) and I see them!"

During a brief discussion we have about Jewel, I learn that she wanted Charlie to ask Mom and Dad if he could be their kid. He lets me know he doesn't want to be their kid, he wants to be mine. I agree that he will always be my son but remind him that my mom and dad are his grandparents.

"Jewel said to me that we can't ever be together in the ways of boys and girls because we're related."

This casual statement catches me completely off-guard; when did he start thinking about the ways of boys and girls? I tell him that's not true because they are not related by blood.

His "Oh" sounds very interested and he adds, "Because I love her."

I answer that I know he loves Jewel and explain that the human rule about not marrying someone to whom you are closely related is meant to prevent babies that might not be healthy.

"I thought you were going to say it's because I'm so much *older* than her with all my millions and millions and millions and millions and millions of years old. I have wisdom but I am still just a kid! My body is young, Mommy."

I agree and can't resist adding that mine will also be young soon.

When I ask to speak with the Moon, Liponie agrees it is time. Then he adds that she is waiting to be named. *Oh no*, I do *not* want to have to pick out a name for the Moon.

Osiris answers my request for help by explaining that, "It did not matter before and then you started pairing every one up and problems began to arise. She has never truly had a name that she felt comfortable with. Our little one has suggested Carla; it did not resonate with her."

"Does she have any suggestions?"

"She had a thought eons ago that perhaps she could be the lovely, Q. I thought it was less than attractive. I suggested to my beloved that perhaps the name Jimbo would be nice. She is not prone to striking me but she looked at me with a look and said, 'The name must be Radiance.'"

That seems a possible choice, but then anything would sound good after Carla and Jimbo. I mention we've always called her Luna and Osiris suggests we ask her if she likes Luna Radiance as a name. Liponie offers to bring her before us and says he will give her a body.

I hear a woman's voice say, "Oh, I am looking quite interesting."

"If Liponie designed your body it has to be lovely."

Tonas interrupts to say that there is a great beauty before us and since this is her first time to be embodied, "Please, let us give her a moment to come into some kind of feeling about her physical presence. Let me show you how to sit, my dear." He tells me that she is looking at her fingers and explains to her that they will be useful when she wishes to put something in her mouth.

I mention to her that it was my understanding she would not be able to walk upon herself. She replies that she is not walking upon herself since she is in some structure of mine. "It is quite beautiful and I have very much enjoyed being host to your great works. I am grateful to be selected to be such an important role player. I do love these fingers."

I suggest that maybe it's too soon to talk about a name for her. She says she already has a name she would love and it is Shasmeah. She adds that it is a name she pondered long ago when she was considering having a name.

Isis comments that it is a glorious name and adds, "It is the sound of you. Is it not?"

The Moon agrees that it is and whispers her new name several times. I'm so delighted I didn't have to pick a name for her and that she chose a lovely one.

It's interesting that things I found or made a long time ago are turning out to be perfect gifts for the monk, celestial bodies and ascended masters I've been encountering. I gate to my house and bring back a gift for her of a large, silvery representation of the Moon that I made several years ago. It has lovely peacock feather eyes, one of which looks like it is winking. She thanks me and asks how she will keep it. Liponie speaks up to say she will have quarters here on the Moon and in the Earth if she wishes to remain embodied.

She remarks, "Moon, what a silly name."

I explain that we've been gazing at her for a long time as the Moon and add that people will be reluctant to use her new name. She is unconcerned and asks if she may see her quarters. Liponie volunteers to take her there by way of the kitchen.

I ask what's been happening with the Lowmeesha Universe and Tonas tells me it is a work in progress. Charlie volunteers that the problem is they have so many different people who want to remain dual and others who want to be non-dual that this is creating a rift.

He explains, "We took all the potentials for what could be and offered this yesterday as a special school for individuals so that they could see possibilities. These schools are not to make anybody do anything. There are a few people that put their finger in the ring, or maybe it was their hat, and they are going to try it. Then they will have a meeting and talk about it."

We're just going to wait and see what happens.

This morning I heard Woonfred say he really would like to say goodbye. I know he must have a good reason for leaving but the thought of losing his presence here saddens me. I address him to ask if he wishes to speak with me in private or can the others hear our conversation.

"All can hear my thoughts and they have been aware of my growing interest to return. It is for Kira, who is my mate. My place was on the council, and yet my heart draws me to return to be of assistance to all those of our realm so they might be ready to join that world and dimension where humans exist. Kira is ready to become with child. The body of a female dragon has a period of preparation for this which is sometimes hundreds of years. She is reaching her time of readiness."

"You must go to her then. I'm so happy for you; your news makes our parting bearable for me."

"First he will be a prince; then he will be a king among us."

"You already know your baby will be a he?"

"It was always written of my sweetness, Kira, that she shall be, through me, the bearer of the future of all dragons."

"Wow, you need to go, but can I have a hug before you go? I do love you, Woonfred."

I visualize myself rising up and giving him a big smooch on his snout. He laughs and then says, "If you have need of me, I am yours. It will be possible for me to hear you. The birth will be a great moment in the new history. We will summon you to be present for it. I wish for you to know we will be in Scotland."

When I remind him I'm going to be there this fall, he says he will make himself present for me to see. I ask where exactly in Scotland they will be. He tells me they will sit with their egg in a place that is deep underneath a large castle. I ask him the name of the castle, but he isn't aware that castles are named. Osiris volunteers that it is Edinburgh Castle. I say that is an important site and it is on my list of places to visit.

"Woonfred, I'm happy for you. Thank you for being part of my life."

"You have given us life and a future. It is us that are of gratitude, my dear. I will continue to be in communication."

"How are the kids coming along?"

Tonas says they are doing well with a few exceptions. There is a little girl named Abira who is sickly and they cannot find anything wrong with her. Tonas feels it is in her mind. When I ask if she has a friend she is close to, Helena tells me she stays off to herself, she is very shy and she is only three years old. Helena says they have tried many things to help her.

Charlie pops in with, "I think we should give her a dog, Mommy; dogs are good." I want to check with Liponie, but Charlie says he is still with the pretty lady. I agree that a dog is a good pet, but they also poop. Charlie says Abria needs to get used to poop and that it's a good job to have to watch after that.

I've just spent too much of my life watching whatever dog I had at the time poop and picking up its poop. I'm through with dog poop! I remind him that three years old is too young to be responsible for picking up dog poop and he volunteers to pick it up. It occurs to me that the other kids will want a dog, too. We could be overrun with dogs, and, worse yet, dog poop.

Charlie says, "We could also give her a teddy bear, but they don't snuggle. They just lay there."

Tonas suggests we start with giving Abira a dog and see how it works. "If it draws her out, it may be the answer for all of them. They have their own quarters."

We settle on a Shih Tzu, and if the dog helps Abira, Tonas is going to provide a catalogue of dogs for the other kids to select from. His thought is that Liponie can create an ethereal dog that doesn't poop. I agree to this dog without the poop plan.

"I need to talk to Number 21."

Charlie says that is Chuckie. After he joins us, I congratulate him for making a telepathic communication as an individual. This morning I heard him relay, "We'll all benefit from a happier dream." (He meant by being individuals.)

Charlie explains that Chuckie is communicating right now that he wants to be a real boy, too. I assure him that I love him and Charlie says Chuckie wants to know if he can call me Mommy. I answer that he and all the Swizzzlers can call me Mommy because that's what I am to them.

Now Charlie says, "I'm your little boy and I've been your little boy all along. So can I be the older brother?"

"Yes."

Charlie says Chuckie wants to start using his mouth to talk and he has something to say. "Can we have the drum rolling, please? Chuckie, you can talk."

After a few seconds of silence, I hear him say, "Mom…my…Mom…my…. Love…Mommy."

I compliment Chuckie on speaking his first words.

"I'm going to teach him some more words, Mom. He did that all on his own; I did not give him any help."

I thank Chuckie for speaking and tell him he made my day. He says a few more "Mommy Loves" then Charlie dismisses him in a very business-like manner. "You go away now. We're busy here. I'll teach you later, bye."

This morning I saw myself holding up an ametrine crystal to my third eye. Don't ask me how I knew what kind of crystal it was, I just did;

however, since I don't know how it might assist me, it's time to find out what Aton knows about it. He explains that there are certain crystals that are quite stimulating to my orbs and ametrine is one of them. He adds that he can also speak highly for several other crystals beginning with amethyst, which can be held to the heart and the throat. "Rhodolite is good for giving you energy. Another crystal that will help you to release water and to access more of your knowledge is verdite. Variscite will assist your urination. Orange calcite will help your tummy and several of your other issues. Peridot will create more balance for you, not that you are out of balance; it is as if you are longing for something that is just out of reach."

Although the sense of waiting has lessened this last year, the longing he refers to has been with me my whole life. I feel like saying "no kidding," but Aton probably wouldn't get that slang expression.

"Charlie, can Jewel see the fairies here like you can?"

"Oh, this is exciting. I will show her and then she will like me ever more so."

"Charlie, are you in love with Jewel?"

"Yes, I *love* her, Mommy. I love her and someday maybe she will want to be married to me. I will be a good husband to her. I told her we could have striped babies, but she said, 'No.'"

This ancient/young kid of mine is amazing. Where did he come up with the idea of striped babies? The only thing I can think to say is to tell him that I love him.

"Mommy, I love you, too. You're Mommy love to me. I don't want you to think that I don't love you because I didn't say baby words. I learned all my words, and then I talked to you."

"I don't think that, Charlie!"

"You got emotional. I saw it."

"I've been waiting for one of the other kids to speak for a long time, so it was an emotional experience for me." That explanation seems to satisfy him because he agrees it was good for Chuckie to speak, says he loves me and adds a cheery, "Bye!"

CHAPTER THIRTY-FIVE

April 17, 2015

The energy of the ascended master temple in the Himalayas that I visited last time was so wonderful I've decided to go there again. Esthra accompanies me as translator because Conch only communicates telepathically. After stepping into that space, I find myself again bowing to Conch and speaking very softly. I feel profound reverence for him and this temple. After a moment, I ask him if there is some way we can assist each other. Esthra tells me Conch believes that there are many ancient teachings about becoming still that will be very helpful to teach the world and he's willing to offer me something I can transmit. As soon as I hear what the teachings are about, I know that's the main reason I came back here.

"Does he have another name besides Conch?"

"That is his name, but it was originally Conchaka. He didn't keep any other name. It's not that he left his family; he said that it was his destiny to step away and become who he is."

"How can I transmit the information about being still?"

Conch hands me a stick with all the information in it and I ask him if he would be willing to teach me about stillness. Esthra relays that Conch says he would be incredibly honored and he agrees to come to the Joy Council in the Earth when I'm there.

I want to know if it would be possible for others to experience his teachings since I think the children would benefit from this kind of knowledge. Esthra reports that Conch says it would be an honor to teach them.

I'm thrilled to have this teacher's assistance. Stillness is something I've read about and sporadically tried to cultivate for a long time. With the SVH work I've done over the years, my mind has become quieter and lately I've found myself frequently moving more and more often into a calm observance of my surroundings.

At the Joy Councils:

I'm greeted by Charlie with ten "Mommy's" in a row.

A couple of days ago I heard someone, Chuckie, I believe, say, "Hey, Mommy, I several was good." Charlie confirms it was Chuckie and reminds me that although Chuckie is just learning his words, he's doing well.

Next, I ask Charlie if he's going to be doing some kind of cooking. The reason I ask that is, this morning I saw an outline of the United States, but instead of a map of the states there was a pretty picture of a kitchen inside it. This had to be something Charlie was showing me.

"I have a whole feast prepared, and everyone promised to come. I am learning how to be a professional since I might need a job."

"Who is teaching you?"

"I wanted Mr. Puck; he's not interested because he's not dead. If he was dead he would say yes automatically; dead people are very kind, Mommy. He's famous for his chowder."

"If he's not your teacher, who is?"

"I got this one guy and he is a woman named Julia."

I *know* this must be Julia Child, and, sure enough, Charlie says she is his coach. I am amazed at Charlie's interests and abilities. Julia Child!

"She's teaching me everything, Mommy, and I am very happy about it. I feel like I'm going to be incredibly successful. If *anybody* wants to give me a job, I will be the best!"

"I'm thrilled for you, Charlie. She's really an interesting lady. I didn't realize she was dead."

A short explanation about my lack of interest in current events is that I'm just not interested in the drama. I don't watch the news or read the paper and there's only about three or four TV shows I ever sporadically watch. People close to me are frequently amazed about what I *don't* know about current events. Not knowing helps me to stay focused on the positive changes I'm working to help manifest.

Charlie says that Julia Child is a little bit crazy and then he giggles.

"How is it that she's teaching you if she's not dead?"

"Because Liponie said we could do it and when she's asleep she comes and helps me."

"What have you made that you really liked?"

"We've had all kinds of onions and we've been doing lots of work. One of the things that we have made is quiche. She understands that we don't want to eat things that were animals. We made a dessert that was the most delicious one I ever had in my whole life, and you know I am almost a year old, Mommy.

What she told me was I could have something called a crepe, and I made it! I had it with cherries in it, then I had it with some strawberries and then I had one with just whipping cream. Then we tried the ones with chocolate and I never want to have any of them ever again except for the chocolate. People like all different foods so she's teaching me many different things. I have a hat and a white jacket and checkered pants. I'm wearing my Mickey shoes because I think those look the best."

Checkered pants and Mickey Mouse shoes… The hat would have to be very thin to stay on top of Charlie's head. I'm trying to picture him, pencil-thin body, orange hair with a green stripe, wearing this outfit, and not having much luck.

"She lets me call her Julia. Do you know her?"

"I saw a movie about her several years ago. She is very famous; you're very lucky that she is willing to teach you."

"She stays here to teach me at night when she is sleeping; when she wakes up she feels really, really good because we kiss her all over her face. We thank her *so much*. When she dies maybe she will come here and be my teacher all the time. We're doing the work in the past because the only time she can work with me is when she's alive."

I'm beginning to get confused because I'm not sure if Julia is currently dead or alive.

"She's very busy right now and she says when she dies she will help me. She's been dead for a long time, Mommy, but she only will work with me when she's alive. She doesn't want to work with me when she's dead. That was what Liponie said because he interviewed her. It's possible she will help me when she's dead *later*."

My confusion is getting very deep—dead later?

Charlie is not going to drop this subject, although I suggest we cross that bridge when we come to it. He persists because he wants me to talk with her where she is in the Fifth Realm to try to persuade her to work with him now. He adds, "She told me when she dies she will. She just doesn't know that when she dies she gets difficult."

She must feel what she's doing in the Fifth Realm is important and I tell Charlie I'm not going to bother her now. He agrees to continue studying with her in the past. God bless you, Julia.

This morning, I experienced telepathic communication with a man who, according to Esthra, is an aboriginal elder living in the Australian outback. The elder said he has something that will assist to balance the Earth now; the aborigines used it twenty thousand years ago when there was some upheaval on the planet.

After relating this information to the group, Sananda says, "Gracious!"

"I know. I'm astonished myself at the things I tune into. This elder said his name is Ahkahmah."

Sananda asks for a moment to check and verifies that the man is indeed a great elder with much knowledge about the Earth. He explains that Ahkahmah suggested that Gaia can slow the pulse of the fluids of the Earth. This would create a state of calm as if the heartbeat of Earth is slowing. He said this is something the aborigines willed into being in the period after Atlantis when there was a darkened time.

Sananda suggests creating an illusion of this since, "It is best to have the speed and momentum continue. Gaia can give us a vision of this slowing down for those it would benefit and we can transmit it directly to each of them. Charlie, please take what she has given me and prepare it for us."

I add that I have something else that should fit nicely with this work. "It's a stick from an ascended master named Conch and it contains teachings about being still. He will be coming to the Earth Joy Council to teach me and anyone else who is interested about stillness."

"How are the kids doing?"

Tonas reports that they are settling in and that the new clothing has helped. "Each of them is advancing at their own pace. We believe the skateboards, the bicycles, the clothing, the roller-skates, the three wheelers, and all of the things Charlie has been convincing everyone that the children need have helped."

"What was it like when they saw the clothes?"

"We showed them some television first. They watched the Rogers gentleman with the sweater fetish and it was very calming for them. Naturally, we had him speaking in languages that the children knew."

A vision of Mr. Rogers in his sweater speaking foreign languages refuses to lodge in my mind. It doesn't fit at all and it makes me feel disoriented.

Tonas says that the manikins of children modeling the new clothes were also very helpful. Helena suggested a style show and the children were excited to pick out their own clothes; they had a good time walking up and down the runway to cheering and clapping.

I ask about Abira, and it seems that having a dog—a poodle, not a Shih Tzu—has helped her quite a bit. She is teaching it how to do tricks and she has become more sociable.

My next question is about how the children react to me; I wonder if they are afraid of me because of my skin color. Tonas explains that they aren't afraid; it is more that they consider me to be famous. "They are very excited to be in your presence and when you walk through their living area they are very respectful."

I suppose that's a good beginning, but it isn't exactly the friendly, mom-type relationship I'd hoped for.

I learn that Mike visits the ship every night when he sleeps and Tonas escorts him around. I'm surprised that John has only visited twice. The good news is that they are still involved in the mastery instruction I set up for them and although they are, according to Sananda, still hardheaded, they are also very respectful.

"How is the Moon getting along?"

Tonas answers that she is enjoying her legs and her stomach. He makes a joke that she is eating and eating and is now as big as the Moon. "She is eating like she has not eaten in… Oh, well, she has not."

I inquire if any of our planets besides Jupiter and Saturn have embodied and chosen names. Tonas says they haven't, although he thinks there will be a lot of requests, especially after Shasmeah puts out the word about our commissary.

"Liponie, did you get the Washington Monument I sent the other day?" He says he has it. When I ask him what the benefits of obelisks are, he explains that they are energy transmitters and receivers; it would be beneficial to send him as many as I wish. He updates me on the Nile temples by saying that he recreated them in their greatest splendor!

"Are there temples I haven't thought of that would be good to have on the 10th dimension?" Liponie says that there are temples that no longer exist. I hadn't thought about that, so I ask if someone can do a survey of all the temples that exist or have existed. Charlie volunteers to do that and the group will discuss ideas about what to do with them.

I request that Jewel joins us. After we exchange hellos, I ask her if Charlie has been able to show her any fairies. She says that he showed her how to see them with her eyes wide open. That sounds like something I'd like to be able to do, but when I ask her to explain that method to me, she says that she just holds her fingers on her eyelids and makes them stay open. Although that must work for her, I had hoped to get information about a little more elaborate technique.

I have questions about fairies that Jewel and Charlie can't answer. The logical place to get answers about fairies is in a fairy garden, and, since I think Jewel and Charlie would like to visit the fairies that keep peeking in my windows, I gate the three of us to the fairy garden at my house.

I intend to speak with Chulee and say, "Hello!" She returns my greeting and I comment that I know she's been peeking in my windows. She admits that she and Bobo have been doing that.

"Would you like to come in my house?"

"No, it feels like a prison in there."

I explain that the reason I know she's been peeking in my windows is that my son, Charlie, has seen her. She says he is very, very cute. My next question is if my greenhouse feels like a prison to her. She says it doesn't and the fairies are doing what they can to help my plants. (Many orchids are still dying.)

"We are asking them not to die, but if they do, I promise to take them to Fossie."

I thank her for that and ask her if she and Bobo are happy.

"Yes, we are so happy and we are very much enjoying his penis and my vagina. We think that even without the penis and the vagina we are very well matched because it's a perfect fit. It got stuck in there once."

At this unexpected turn of our conversation, I wish I hadn't brought Jewel and Charlie with me. I hope they don't understand what she's talking about. (When I realized later that I could roll back and mute these words since I'm Jewel's guardian and Charlie is my son, I immediately did so.)

"He said he wanted to hold his breath. He was—here she makes huffing sounds. It got really big and then it stuck in there."

She's giggling; I'm laughing and trying to think of something to say.

"Everybody looked and tried to figure out how to stop it. Then somebody said he should let go of the breath in his mouth and that made it smaller."

I'm left wondering just how long a boy fairy can hold his breath. If something like that would work for a human man, I'm sure it would have been discovered very long ago.

I focus back on our conversation and check to see if Chulee has the book Gaia gave the fairies. She answers yes and I mention that there are things that probably aren't in the book. She agrees that that's why Bobo was experimenting with, what I've decided to term, "the huffing approach."

They don't have a baby yet because they are so much in love. Chulee says, "I just don't know how I could possibly love anybody *more*. He says the same to me and that I'm very pretty. He said he would love me even if I was ugly, but there is no such thing as an ugly fairy."

I ask her if she's noticed any difference in the Earth since the work we've been doing to connect us to the 10th dimension. She says they can feel it outside the bubble of their world.

"We come out sometimes, but we only come out to see you. We like the little girl (Jewel) and she likes us too."

"I'm sorry that you can't come into my house."

"We could, but if we got stuck in there it would be terrible. You house has seals on things and it is all solid. If you leave the windows open then we could stick just our heads in."

I remark that I have screens on my windows. She says she knows that and they could be trapped! She adds that I don't have any "yummy, yummy, yummy" in my house. I'm sure my concept of yummy must be different from theirs and I'm right. She says they don't eat anything but sparkles of dew; if they got stuck in my house they would get very hungry.

Before we leave, I thank her for helping my orchids.

In Sheliah's garden:

After I hear her say she is so excited that I am there, I introduce her to Charlie, Jewel and Sananda. Sheliah asks who Jewel is. I explain that she is my sister and Sheliah wants to know if she would like to play with some of their children.

"We have four hundred and four now and Rosebud is so busy."

I'm laughing but it's mostly from shock. That is a *lot* of babies and I bet Rosebud fainted for each of their births. I ask if the older babies are talking yet; Sheliah says they can say "mama," "papa," and "Joy." She adds that they have lots of joy in their garden because all of her babies are named Joy.

"How's the queen thing going?"

Sheliah says she's conkin' lots of people on the head and tellin' them to be happy. "Even though they are outside my garden, they are in my garden, and so, I conk 'em."

"I know that the fairies take things we kill and keep them safe. Humans are still killing cows and other animals for food, so I'm wondering where all the cows go."

"We send them and the chickens to a special garden so that they can eat grass and have a happy life. There's a stream and it's beautiful there. There are more chickens than anything! They have all the food and water they want and there's nothing to eat them. They live for as long as their body normally would have lived. Then they close their eyes and go sparkly. We don't have to conk 'em; they do it."

"Do they really need to eat?"

"They like to do it so we let 'em. It's their job."

I'm ready to leave, but she wants me to meet their babies. She also says that Rosebud wants to give me many kisses. I wonder how Rosebud can do that since he doesn't have wings. She says she can give him wings by conking him.

"He's a good daddy. He wants to have more babies because he loves them. It's a very special ritual for us now in the garden. He still faints, Joy. (I knew it.) He falls over and we just laugh and laugh. Then I conk 'em and say, 'There's work to be done! Get up! There's new babies.'"

I'm ready for fairy kisses; I hear lots of little smooching sounds since Sheliah kisses me first. Then she gives Rosebud a conk and after he kisses me she says, "Oh, that was very tender, dear. He kissed the end of your nose. He said to tell you… OK, I will let you tell her yourself. Jeepers."

"Joy, I want to thank you. I have a wonderful family and you have such a pretty nose. I want all of our babies to have your nose."

Although I'm thinking, "Please God, not *my* nose," I remark that my nose is definitely striking. Tenth dimension Joy's nose must not resemble mine in any way.

"People can now read about Rosebud and Sheliah in the books I'm writing."

"You have told them about me?"

"Yes, about how you love it when Sheliah dresses you like a flower."

"I do love it. Sheliah is so wonderful! Thank you for our wedding."

I agree that was a very special day. Sheliah has reached her maximum amount of listening time and says that now it is her time to talk. She says she likes my nose too. I ask her what color her hair is today and I'm not surprised when she says it's pink. Rosebud has red hair today.

I'm ready to leave and since Jewel and Charlie want to stay longer, Sananda offers to stay with them. I explain to Jewel that the fairy garden we're in now is located in an area where I played until I was almost nine years old. The last thing that I tell Jewel and Charlie is that someday I'm going to have a house here.

Charlie wants to know if we will live in space, too. I explain that we can have more than one place to live. He answers that he will live wherever I want him to live because I'm his Mommy.

I return to the council, but then realize I need Charlie to be here in order to send out the transmissions. I move with Tonas into the future when Charlie and Jewel have returned.

Charlie says he has a vision of the Earth being slow and relaxed in a transmission for the aborigines that would best benefit from that. Since the stick that Conch gave me had many thousands of teachings in it, Charlie says he put them all into sequence for those wish to listen to it.

There are many transmissions, but Charlie put them all in one orb. Although these are for Earth, he will contact the other universes to explain what we sent out and calibrate for them any of the work that they would like to have.

CHAPTER THIRTY-SIX

April 20, 2015

I've been thinking about a way to anchor sacred sites, temples and crystals to the 10th dimension and I believe I've figured out a way to do it. I'm going to include crystals that were taken off planet that would have preferred to stay here. Holograms will be in place so that they were never stolen.

Archangel Michael is going to assist me by communicating with the crystals to find out those that might wish to be anchored into a higher dimension than the 10th; he will also offer them the SVH process Sovereign Space. I move into the SBT and choose to have a list of every sacred site, crystal and temple of light and love that ever existed on Earth or could be elevated to light and love from Earth's 10th dimension. I specify that this list is only to include those that in the present moment would be honored and in alignment to be sent to the 10th dimensional Moon.

I get another list of these same kinds of items that exist on Earth's 10th dimension that would also like to exist on the Moon's 10th dimension. I ask Liponie and Charlie (Maybe I should start thinking of them as the dynamic duo.) to join me in the SBT and hand over the lists to them. This work feels like a really important piece that will assist Earth's smooth elevation.

(Two days later, I asked Gaia what moving the crystals to the 10th dimension accomplished. She said one of the things it did was to anchor the crystals' connection to their old position with a rainbow arc into the higher dimension. It also anchored Earth more into the 8th dimension.)

I also have an idea about the "seedpods" of cosmic information that might be ready to be released in September or October. (The last time I was at the council, Osiris said that there is a great body of information stored in different pockets from the ancient academies throughout the world. He asked me to imagine that there are little jewels of information ready to be released like a seedpod that opens and floats, instead of seeds, cosmic truths throughout the Earth.) Although Osiris wouldn't say how to go about preparing them, I think a net around the world needs to be created; the easiest way to do that is with the SVH process Mission Link.

I activate that process, step onto a map of the world and split my energy body to move to where all the seedpods are. I hold my energy arms up in the air to connect with the upper grids and choose to receive and anchor the encodements that will prepare and nourish the seedpods. This is something I plan to do every morning until the pods are ready to pop.

Two days ago during my morning reverie, I saw a humanoid skull that had huge teeth. Although it could have been just another one of those weird things I occasionally see, I think it signified a genetic issue for me. Sananda is the one to assist me if it is. He reveals the surprising piece of information that I have a little bit of Neanderthal genetics from my dad's genetic line, and he suggests it could be fixed. That sounds like a good idea to me and we move into a chamber in the SBT. He guides me to stand on a golden disc that will scan my body. It occurs to me that I would have passed these genetics to my children, so I ask him to assist me not to do that. He agrees to move me and the procedure to when I was in Mom's womb. In a moment, he says that those genetics are now deactivated and that they wouldn't have served me in any way. Goodbye, Neanderthal, and God bless.

Yesterday morning, I saw three needles on a rug. These are the kinds of hints I'm given about things and then I have to try to figure out what the heck they mean. What could three needles on a rug be about? I remember speaking with my mother about this vision and hearing myself ask her to give me a clue about what it meant. I don't remember what, if anything, she said, so with Sananda in tow, I step into the Fifth Realm to speak with her again.

"Mom and Dad, thank you for showing me that beautiful picture of how you are now. You looked so youthful and wonderful that it took me a few seconds to recognize you, but I was glad to see it. I saw something that I hope you can help me figure out what it means." I telepathically show them the rug and needles I saw.

Sananda explains that Mom is showing me how tightly things can be sewn together and that things can stay with you a very long time; for example, old stories about struggle and hardship. These can be unraveled and the needles that sew these pieces together that make the weave can be used to unweave. Sananda says she has a very large needle that she is actually using to unweave a rug; the rug needs to be unraveled since all the strips (many holding pain and struggle) are sewn together and stitched to each other.

I ask if this is just for me or if it is also for the world. Sananda says this is for both, and Mom hands me a file that will do this unweaving for me and my two sons. I put this in place for myself immediately and will give it to my sons later. He adds that Mom's desire to assist me sponsored my vision of the rug and needles.

In the early 2000s, I spent several years interacting, on what I assumed was the astral plane, with a man named Jim and another man whose name I never heard. I must have a close soul connection to them because they both spoke to me quite often and frequently seemed to be contesting who would be interacting with me in my dream time. I was very enamored with Jim, and assumed he was a man I would eventually meet in person in this reality; however, nothing ever developed that way and then I shut down my channeling abilities for several years due to fatigue from hearing things all night long. The other day I heard, "His name is Jim." It's time to get to the bottom of Jim's identity. I explain this to Esthra and ask who Jim is.

"It is quite curious how this connection began. You are out of time with them. Jim is long dead. He is a love match from another incarnation. Rahfocco is a lovely individual that also has a close connection to your heart."

I ask what time period I was involved with them. Esthra says I was with Rahfocco in Pompeii prior to the volcano's eruption and Jim was someone from several hundred years back. It seems they still feel a heart connection to me. Hmm, I'm too busy with everything that is happening in my life right now for any reconnection with either of them, and I'm just not interested in anything like that. My thought is, let's let bygones be bygones. Next time I'm in the Fifth Realm, I'll have a chat with them.

At the Joy Councils:

"Liponie, please tutor or give a file about the meanings of names to all the Swizzlers who don't have names, that way they will have a wide selection to choose from. I love the names that have been selected so far, but I realized the kids may not know all the possible names they could choose. Congratulations to Number 23! I heard you speak yesterday!"

Charlie says that Number 23 has named himself Manley and he is learning to talk.

"I know! I heard him say, 'Oh, I love you.'"

Charlie adds that those are always the first words. That makes me glad—I certainly love hearing them said to me.

"Charlie, two days ago I saw the word 'Iamzing.' Was that your writing?"

"Yes, Mommy, I can do anything. I can dance, I can sing, I can do anything."

It's wonderful to hear the easy confidence in his voice.

"The other day you said something about getting a job. I don't know that that will be necessary when you get around to being on Earth."

"I think my biggest job is being your big boy, but right now I want to be your little boy. This is our special time and we'll never have it again; I heard that on the television. It was very sad and I thought, 'Oh, I must keep myself young for a very long time.'"

"We don't really know what's going to happen, but I just want you to flow with whatever you feel is best for you, OK?"

"OK, I love myself and how I am."

Charlie's comment hits me in such a tender spot that I have to think about how many people could say that about themselves. I try to think of the times as an adult when I could say that and mean it. More than I used to, but still not enough.

When I was little, I didn't think about loving myself; I just played. When I entered school, I began experiencing some events that made me start comparing myself to the other kids and I began to feel that I was "less than" some of the other boys and girls. I was not skilled in games the other kids liked to play and consequently I preferred not to play them.

Valentine's Day in first grade came as a shock to me because, in those days, you were not required to give valentine cards to everyone in your class. The kids who were more popular received many cards, others of us, not so many. (I was relieved to learn when my children were in grade school that I needed to provide cards for everyone in the class. At least that aspect of school had improved.)

I'm not going to go into details about the rest of my life. Everybody in duality experiences challenges, but perhaps I can assist some of you who are reading this book by offering you an SVH clearing. For this clearing, your God Self rewrites *every time* through your whole life you felt you were not good enough, smart enough, pretty enough, too old, too young, didn't have enough education, not rich enough, didn't love yourself or your life, didn't have enough time, were not capable or you were just somehow lacking in *something*. This clearing will help you to know you *are* enough, you have enough, you *are* loved and you are *love*.

To access this work, which is put in place by your God Self (your soul and Higher Consciousness) and the Creator, please sit back, close your eyes and pretend to "see" a screen (movie, TV, computer, your choice). Some people see with their inner vision what's on the screen, some people feel what's on the screen or just have an inner knowing. Ask the Creator if it is in alignment for you to receive this clearing, and when you get an affirmative in whatever way you receive guidance, just say or think "Yes!" and the rewriting will instantly be done. By the way, this clearing was calibrated specifically for *you*.

"Liponie, I want to wear something besides gowns!"

He wants to know if I would like a Geisha outfit, including the wig. He even offers to paint my face white.

This is not what I have in mind at all, but instead of saying so, I just ask if he can procure some current fashion magazines. I explain that some of the clothes in them are so ridiculous I would never wear them, but I want to be able to dress casually, too. "I could be a queen in blue jeans."

This statement is met by a period of silence, followed by, "Hmm."

"If I'm always dressed up, that makes me not very approachable for little kids. You know how I dress here."

He dryly replies that he has seen it. I admit that I do frequently wear scruffy clothes, but they certainly are comfortable. When I begin to list things like pants, shorts and sweatshirts, he tells me that these clothes are very curious indeed.

"Your assignment is, if you have time, get some fashion magazines. Then look at that part of me there and say, 'For God's sake, have pity on the part of you on Earth that would like to look approachable and human once in a while.'"

Liponie says it would not be fashionable to wear rags. I agree to that, but insist there are modern clothes that look really wonderful. This statement is met with more silence and so I attempt to telepathically show him an outfit that I thought was cute. He states that you "will indeed stand out as different because all who are in presence here are dressed as you in beautiful gowns."

"I'm sorry. It's just that sometimes *I don't want to wear a gown*!"

Finally, he agrees that I can have whatever I wish.

"Thank you! I want to learn how to roller-skate and ice-skate. I never was any good at those."

Charlie pops in with an offer to show me how, because he's very good. He adds, "If you let me, I will help Liponie because I understand fashion."

"OK, help me Charlie." This might have been a mistake, but I just can't refuse Charlie's assistance. "I'm going to go to a store, copy a few clothes and gate them to you both to look at. There are some modern clothes that are comfortable and comely."

Charlie says he doesn't know what a comely is, but they will get them.

Yesterday morning I saw a Native American man with shoulder-length hair wearing a headband who said he was still coming here most often. I'm not aware of the location he was referring to until Sananda explains there is a portal region in Saskatchewan where the dead Indians meet to hold energy and to assist those who die to cross. This man is from that region and has been coming to our council. I ask Hiawatha to join us. When he is in presence, I greet him and telepathically show him the man I saw.

He says, "I believe this individual is from the Katahkewistahaw. There is a portal of great importance in that region of Saskatchewan."

"I heard someone speak called Grand Heron. Do I need to do something there or here?"

"There will be important works you can apply to assist those who are struggling to acclimate to the new energies. They are stuck in the past in their mind."

Hiawatha adds that the portal in that region is very expansive; it can reflect inward but it can also amplify outward.

"It can disperse from that position to the whole world anything that you send to it. If the Heron is in sentinel in that position, talking to you, the time is coming for this to be applied. It is not necessary any longer to die to cross through the portal. It can be a portal to ascend."

"Grand Heron told me that 'all beings of Earth have moved through a portal of time,' and he also suggested that 'allowing divine timing to unfold would be the wisest course of action.'"

"It is a time on Earth when all is moving as if in streams crossing over itself and struggling to find the direction that is of more ease in the travel upward to the higher dimensions. This is perhaps something that is not to be done today, only to prepare and consider and for you to receive more information."

Hiawatha is going to observe the changes after the transmission and says it is more important to prepare and guide rather than to rush in. "We are a people that are greatly patient."

I thank him for coming and then speak a farewell in the people's language.

"Let's move into the full council and zip these transmissions in place."

Charlie says he doesn't know how to zip but we can do the transmissions. I briefly mention the things that will be coming to the

Moon and suggest to Liponie that he might be swamped. After we send the transmissions out, I ask him if we have a bunch of temples here now. He laughs, but it sounds a little more subdued than usual. He then admits he's going to be very busy.

"I'll be back on Wednesday and maybe we can do some Earth work. Earth Day is the one day that more people are likely to pay attention to caring for Earth, so we want to enhance that idea."

"Charlie, why are you dancing?" (I had a hint about guitars and dancing in my morning reverie and figured that had to be another area he is exploring.)

He says he saw flamenco dancing on TV and, "There was a girl with really nice skirts. She was kickin' her feet and I thought, 'Well, I can do that.' I don't have any skirts but I have the Bolero outfit and I am looking pretty good with my hat!"

"You have the right kind of shoes?" I hope he's not going to say he's wearing his Mickey shoes, but, of course, he is. My comment is that I'm not sure it's possible to dance flamenco in Mickey shoes.

"Oh, I can do it. The louder you stomp the better."

"Don't big shoes like that keep you from moving quickly?"

"No, Mommy, I am very quick. I will show you tonight. I think the shoes are very important because when you stomp you're making the noise. Boy, I can stomp good with these shoes."

"I think they have tap things on the shoes."

We decide to check with Liponie about flamenco shoes.

Yesterday, I got that somebody was going to dive into a pool from a structure as tall as the Empire State Building. I shuddered as I tried to visualize Charlie; it had to be him, doing that. An image of him sticking into the bottom of the pool has flitted through my mind several times since then. Now he confirms that he was just going to show the kids how to dive, but adds that Helena wouldn't let him.

"Liponie and I made it exactly as tall as the Empire State Building. I'm very straight and strong when I dive, Mommy."

My suggestion is that he can teach the kids to dive from the side of the pool and then get a low diving board that they can walk out on and jump into the water. He says that is no fun, but agrees with me when I remind him they are little.

"Charlie, when you are up on a diving board, even if it's not a high one, it still looks like a long way down to the water." I'm trying not to think of a board as tall as the Empire State Building. I'm sure he doesn't understand what I'm talking about so I drop the subject. I'm very glad Helena said no.

"We're going to go water skiing next week, but I think we have the wrong kind of boat, Mommy."

I was going to suggest a speedboat to Liponie, but I forgot. They must have been trying to water ski behind the luxury craft Tonas and I lounged around on for his birthday. I mentally show Charlie a speedboat and he yells to Liponie that we need one of those.

"We tried to stand up on each other and make a big tower. It would have worked but we don't float; the bottom person kept sinking."

With Liponie and Charlie in privacy, I ask Charlie about the palace and he says they go there all the time. The Swizzlers are making flowers and working on something which is not finished. Charlie has invited Tonas's mom and dad to the special party they're planning for the next time I'm at the council.

"We're going to have a portal that takes us out into the water. Everybody is going to be doing something that's called, get this, skin diving."

"You'll have to teach me how to do that."

"Oh, maybe we just better take the submarines, then."

"Maybe I can do it."

His "OK" sounds very hesitant.

I try to reassure him that I was a good swimmer when I was a kid, and he agrees to teach me.

"I am constantly amazed by you, Charlie."

"I can do almost anything, but I can't be a real boy yet. I'm making apple pie today, but I'm not going to let Julia know because she might not think its fancy enough. The little kids are going to help because they have to turn the handle to make the ice cream. It's an old-fashioned thing."

"I want to taste it. I love homemade ice cream!"

"After we have the pie and ice cream, they are all going to get to be with us when we read. Liponie made us a big room so that all the kids could be with us. There are a lot of kids, Mom, so I'm making lots of apple pie, and lots of people are helping me."

I wonder how many apple pies it will take to feed 124,310 kids, ninety-eight Swizzlers and the other council members, including me, of course.

"What book are we reading?"

"It's an adventure book that is very dramatic and scary; it's called *The Hidden Staircase* by Nancy Drew. We're not going to read that to the little kids 'cause we have to read things that won't scare them. This is for bigger kids like me."

I'd like to stay longer but I have another commitment to honor. I ask Charlie for a hug and kiss goodbye and leave him to creating *lots* of apple pies.

CHAPTER THIRTY-SEVEN

April 22, 2015

Yesterday, I remembered that when I was at the Cincinnati Art Museum two weeks ago, I blissfully copied several pieces of art and sent them to Liponie, but I forgot to do so from the SBT. I realized that it might be possible for adversarial beings to track an activity like that back to me since I forgot to work in that space. It's time, and thankfully it's not past time, to fix that goof. To do this, I step into the SBT and set it up with the Creator and my God Self that from the beginning of any kind of council work that I have done or will do, the work has been and will be invisible. In the future, I plan to leave art objects and other items in the SBT for Liponie to pick up and transport to the Moon.

In honor of Earth Day, I've decided to get a list from my MAPS self of all the trees, shrubs, grasses, areas of Earth, stones and natural formations that would like to also experience existence on the 10th dimension of the Moon. Before I do that, I call Liponie into the SBT to ask him if we will run out of room on the Moon for all these new items. He explains that there are no limitations because he is expanding the building outward to encompass everything. He adds that he thinks the whole Moon will be the council soon and then he laughs. Liponie knows me very well.

Stepping into the presence of my MAPS self, I ask for a list that includes representatives of *each* of the species of trees, shrubs and plants that have ever existed on Earth. I bring it back to the SBT, ask Liponie to join me and hand the list to him.

In the Fifth Realm, I call forward every person I've ever had a relationship with in any incarnation and say, "I would like from each of you a file containing the ideal version of a man/woman relationship that will assist me in this lifetime. Jim and Rahfocco, I know I had very close relationships with you in other incarnations and I feel like I wasted quite a few years in this lifetime thinking I was going to meet you. No regrets, but I'm not interested in anything like that anymore. My goal is to be able to move into my mastery of being in an intimate relationship with a man. Thank you for your help and the file you're giving me.

Now I'm calling forth everyone at the near completion. Today is Earth Day. For those of you who have a connection with or interest in Earth but are not of Earth, just listen because I'm also going to ask you for gifts for your worlds. I'd like for those of you who have been on Earth or care about Earth in any way to give me gifts for Gaia. Perhaps you might like to give some gifts for yourself that would help you to wake up to the beauty of the Earth. To realize at some point in your life, 'Oh, I'm living on this place and I love it and want to help it. I want to do *my* part to be the best that I can be for Earth, for nature and for all the creatures of Gaia by loving them and honoring them as much as I possibly can. I know that I am one with all things.' I hope you can give yourself gifts that will help you to inspire yourself to leave off polluting or littering and to use products that assist the Earth and yourself rather than harmful products. Remember these are just suggestions; I'm going to give you these gifts for yourself but this will also be a transmission to the Earth.

Those of you who are not of Earth, I would love to take gifts to our Joy Council on the Moon that you might like to give to your planet, sun, star or universe and this will be transmitted to the places you specify. I'm also willing to bring you gifts for yourself. Thank you for these files."

At the Joy Councils with Tonas and Liponie:

Tonas greets me with, "My dear, my dear, my dear."

I take the time to say, "Hi," but I'm anxious to check with Ashtar to see if he picked up three pieces of information I recently received. The words were so silly and enigmatic that I want to make sure he knows they were code. He confirms they are still working on the codes. He also says they received the information about people (Chu) who are being created using false DNA. My comment is that I hope we can prevent that because it doesn't seem right. He tells me it is their right to do this since they are residents of Earth and adds that there are no rules to stop individuals from creating wars or armies of their own.

"I don't want to tangle with these individuals yet, but isn't there something we can do anonymously?"

"The elevation of the collective is daunting to these individuals. It is almost as if someone is scratching a surface and making sharp noises. They do not like the feel of the elevations. They key is to elevate, elevate, elevate."

"We have something to do that today! Is Liponie here?"

He says that he is standing before me with a white flag in his hand. "I surrender!"

We are both laughing about the very large file of Earth trees and plants that wish to also be on the Moon. When I ask, he lets me know the obelisks I previously sent are beautifully placed. I remind him to check the SBT because I'm going to be using it as a safe deposit place.

"Tonas and Liponie, why is Charlie still thinking he is not a real boy or that he can't be one yet?"

"My darling, for some reason he first made himself plastic. To him, a real boy has skin like us."

"He said he can't do that yet. Is he right?"

"He believes he is not quite ready, and he also knows that you are resistant to this, my dear."

This shocks me so much that I gasp and say, "I am?"

"Of course you are. You wish to have him remain as he is."

"Oh, Tonas, I've got to let *that* go."

Immediately, I spend some time doing an SVH clearing to release any attachment I have to Charlie's appearance. "I think I was resistant to him changing because I want to enjoy him for a time as he is now, but I really want to be OK with however he wants to be."

I ask Charlie to join us. I know he recently tried something that didn't work out, but I don't know exactly what it was.

"Mommy, I'm ready!"

"Did somebody make a mistake the other day?"

I hear him sheepishly and very softly admit, "Yeah."

I explain that mistakes are OK and that I've made more of them than I can even imagine. When I ask if he's embarrassed, he says he is. I give a mini lecture about how many times Edison failed to make a light bulb, and add that it's the great inventors who have made a lot of mistakes.

My words don't seem to help. After a little while I hear him, still very softly, say, "I just wanted to poop so much. If I could just do that then I would be a real boy."

"Wait a minute. Tonas pointed something out to me and I have to apologize to you because *I'm* the one who has been making the biggest mistake."

"No, Mommy, *no*!"

It's difficult for me to talk because I'm crying. I finally manage to say, "Charlie, listen, I wanted you to stay the way you are and I'm so sorry because that's not right."

"You mean I can be a real boy?"

"You can be however you want to be and I apologize if I held you back from that."

"Well, if I can be a real boy then maybe your sister will love me."

"Charlie, the one thing I've learned in this lifetime is never to change yourself to try to please someone else."

"I tried and tried and tried and tried to poop and everybody tried to help me to give it up. They said nothing would come out of my bottom. I ate so much and I ate so much and I ate so much and I tried to have food in there so it would come out as poop and it didn't."

"Liponie can help you be a real boy anytime you want, but please don't change just to poop or to please Jewel. If you want to experience a human body, do it just for you, please, Charlie."

"I just want to make you happy, and I think if I was cuddlier then maybe you would really like it even more when you hug me."

"It will be fun to be able to feel myself hug you even if you are still a Swizzler."

"I want you to see me as a real boy."

"You must decide what you want to do, but I will tell you one more time to be how you want to be just for yourself."

Charlie agrees to this, but he has one more question. He wants to know if he eats lots of chocolate when he is a real boy, will he poop chocolate. I laugh, say no and that I can't wait until I don't have to poop. I do a little explaining about the nature of poop which Charlie finds very interesting. I should have done this when he first mentioned poop, but I thought he'd forgotten about it. After my explanation, I ask him if I've cleared up the poop issue for him.

He agrees he will not be so focused on it, and says, "I sat there and sat there and I just wasted so much time, Mommy." I hope that means we can once and for all move past pooping.

"How did the pie and ice cream affair turn out?"

He says everybody loved it and that people made an assembly line to help him. The kids loved making the ice cream and eating it. Liponie made cherry trees so that the kids could pick the cherries, and they also had to pit them. Charlie made both cherry and apple pies. I ask him if I got to eat any.

"You didn't want any because you were too busy with a project that is very big and takes a lot of your time. It's a project about all of the things from Earth that you are bringing here."

I apologize to Charlie that I didn't eat any of the pie and ice cream. Being upset with myself takes on a whole new meaning in a situation like this. If I could, *I* would shake myself and say, 'Get a clue, you idiot! Leave off whatever important thing you're doing for a few minutes and eat a piece of this kid's pie! For Pete's sake, it's homemade ice cream which Earth Joy hasn't had for years!'"

Tonas explains we were quite busy and I had previously enjoyed the au gratin potato dish Charlie had made. The only way I can think of to vent my frustration is to growl, "Arrrrrgh!"

Tonas tries to placate me by reminding me that I had the beautiful potato dish and Charlie enjoyed that I liked it. OK, I *do* like potatoes, but, in case you haven't figured this out yet, I *love* pie and ice cream. Tonas adds that if I taste everything Charlie makes I will be quite busy eating. I decide to drop this for now, but if I find I missed another chance for homemade ice cream, heads will roll. (Later, I realized that *this* me wouldn't have tasted the food, but it's still the principle of the thing. You take time to taste something special your son makes.)

Last night I gated to Liponie and gave him a current fashion magazine with a few pages marked to show some outfits that might be suitable for me to wear on Earth. The other day I realized that my wardrobe is sadly lacking in successful author clothes. Look in my closet and you will see casual pants, tops and sweaters, and, in some cases, casual verges on worn out. I rarely have a need for any dressy clothes and comfort has been my priority for years. I know it's time to add some dress up clothes and I dread having to go shopping. Most department store clothes seem too young-looking, ridiculous or mundane; if something does look nice it's probably polyester, which I refuse to wear. My hope is that Liponie can help me.

I ask him if he got the magazine and he says he can do better than those clothes. He also agrees to make beautiful pants for me to wear when I'm learning to roller-skate, so I drop the whole idea of wearing other casual clothing at the Joy Council.

"I know I'm going to need to wear better clothes in this reality. Is it possible for you to sneak into Indianapolis, find some clothes for me and then give me hints about where I could shop?"

"I will be pleased to do so; it will be delightful for me."

Wow, now I'm feeling hopeful that shopping won't be too terrible of a chore. I tell him that I usually like Liz Claiborne's brand of clothing, so she would be able to give him some tips.

"I'm not saying that any of the designers I'm going to name are better than you, I know you're the best, but if you can consult with her and two others, Yves St. Laurent and Coco Chanel, I'd be so grateful. Those last two were high fashion designers. I don't want to spend money now for the kind of clothes they have, but I might sometime in the future. Can you consult with them and not be offended that I asked you to do that?"

"My dear, I am thrilled to be of service to you in any means you wish."

Before we join the full council, Gaia says she has seen Charlie and the others practicing as a brass band.

"It's true, Mommy. We all have outfits and we're going to do marching. Pinky and Nicky have little clothes that are like cheerleaders and they are going to do cartwheels in front of us. They have batons and it's so fun! We're going to all sing "God bless America," land that we love, because that is my country. Gaia, could you please go away just for a moment, thank you. We have a special guest; it is a volcano and it's going to erupt for us!" This sentence is followed by a squeal of excitement.

I'm stunned just for a moment as I try to figure out if he actually said we have a volcano for a guest. A *volcano* for a guest?

"It's my idea and it's going to erupt."

"Wha, wha, what volcano do we have here?"

"Kilauea, and it's going to explode champagne."

Oh well then, it's only going to explode champagne. *Explode champagne*? My son is so innovative I'm constantly caught off guard.

"Charlie, I just can't keep up with you. Who brought the volcano here?"

"It was my idea so Liponie brought it. It was his idea to make the champagne come out of it. I wanted to have the fire."

Champagne sounds better than fire, of course, but I'm wondering how that's going to work out. Sounds like it could be messy.

With the full Joy Councils:

I'm feeling really smug as I announce to the group that I received gifts for Gaia from people in the Fifth Realm. I explain that I asked people there who lived on Earth to give themselves gifts so that they would wake up, see how beautiful Earth is and start loving and honoring her in whatever way they could. I relate that I also received gifts for all the planets, stars and suns in all the other universes from people who had lived there to assist them to love and honor their own special places.

"Oh, this is so delightful. What a beautiful gift." Gaia says.

I ask her to please tell me what she feels when we put this in place, "because people are gonna be lovin' on you."

We send out the transmission in honor of "Earth, Star, Sun, Planet Day," and Gaia reports she can feel the work.

With the work done, it's time to party. Charlie asks everyone to make their way into the presentation room, adding that there are many gifts there for Gaia. He announces, "We have a very special presentation that is going to happen; when all the cymbals *crash* get your glasses ready for a surprise."

As Charlie moves into place, Tonas says he is the leader with a long baton. When the music is finished, I hear Charlie yell, "Everybody put out your glasses, quick!"

The result of the volcano explosion is just as I thought. Tonas corroborates my premonition by admitting, "We are all completely soaked and there is only a little bit in my glass."

"It's supposed to be good for your hair. No, that's beer."

This is my kind of party; I love it when goofy things like this happen. I'm still laughing at the calm dismay in Tonas's voice. He thanks Charlie and tells him it was very exciting. I observe that this was like one of those science experiments that does not go how you think it will.

"Papa Tonas, we have a very special surprise. We're going to take Mommy's ship to a special destination and then we're going to get into your yellow submarine."

I turn over the helm to Charlie. Tonas whispers, "Ooqwa," to me and says that Charlie is up to something. When Tonas says we are at Horeeshnah, I suggest to Charlie that perhaps Tonas needs a blindfold.

"How do we fold him to make him blind?"

Whoops, I immediately show Charlie telepathically what a blindfold looks like. Tonas briefly has one in place, but when we move into the submarine, Charlie asks him to take it off because the palace is so pretty.

"We all worked very hard. It is a special place for you and we hope that you love it. What do you think?"

Tonas says that the colors are beautiful, and it looks, to him, a bit like a massive jellyfish. That must mean it's dome-shaped; maybe there are tentacle-looking structures coming off of it? (I learn later that it is just a luminous and glowing bubble.) I want to know how we get into it and Charlie says there is a docking station. He's a little reluctant to take us into the dock because he's having so much fun driving Tonas's yellow submarine. After he docks, he asks to be able to drive it again later. It's more fun than his submarine—naturally. Tonas gets blindfolded again before we get out, then Charlie asks him to take it off once we are inside.

Charlie is giggling as he says, "See Grandma and Grandpa!"

Tonas remarks this is a lovely surprise. Then I hear Firona say to him, "I hope you don't mind, dear. We brought your grandmother and grandfather here. This is a very special offering because it is the first time any world has offered a place for your council members and for Joy."

I ask if Zahseet is here and Firona says she is waiting. Then, referring to the stature of Isis and Osiris, she adds, "Mother and Father carry a large wave, do they not?"

I hear Isis welcome me. Osiris clears his throat, then says, "My dear grandson, you are the best and most magnificent of grandsons ever and I wish for you to know I am greatly proud of you. Every council in every universe wishes for you to have some beautiful facility in presence for your pleasure. It is for you, my beautiful grandson, our dear Joy, and you, my little great-grandson, to have someplace special in every universe. They are creating it for you."

Osiris explains that he has already created several different positions throughout our universe with this same kind of facility. He adds that Sirius is very much a water kingdom and there is a great deal of water on Andromeda. "It is my pleasure to have created additions to the structures being created for you in the universes. These are gifts to you from my beloved and me."

I'd like to be more eloquent, but, "Wow," is going to have to do right now. I keep thinking I'm going to get used to surprises and then something like this happens.

"I was told a long time ago, Firona, that Isis was your mother, but I forgot. Am I marrying, wait a minute, let me correct that to, I might be marrying into quite a lineage."

Emmon answers that I am welcome in any state of my relationship with them and with their beloved. Tonas comments that what he has seen so far of this place is amazing and it looks like it is alive. "The colors are liquid and moving in all directions. It is the most grand palace of all."

I want to know what Charlie has planned and his response is that he very, very, very much wants to ride around in Papa's submarine. We are going to do scuba diving later and Zahseet is going to take us to special caves. After checking with Tonas, I release Charlie to go drive the submarine, but not before reminding him to be how he wants to be.

"OK, I'm going to be a submarine captain! Bye, bye, Mommy. I'll be back in a little while."

"Let's have Zahseet join us because I want to thank her for her graciousness."

I hear her small-sounding voice tell me I am very welcome. I ask if she has a mate and children; she says she has several mates and several children. I invite her and her family to come any time they would like to visit. Then I ask her if she will show us around, but she says we are supposed to show them around since it's our facility. She plans to show us her world when we do the scuba diving. I hope Charlie was able to give me some lessons, but I'm sure no one will let me drown. I thank her and ask to speak with Emmon, Firona and Tonas for a moment in private.

I let them know I'm glad they came and Firona says they would never miss an opportunity to celebrate my and their delightful son's great accomplishments. I agree that he is quite something.

Tonas says, "We have quite a budding romance, Mother, Father, Grandmother, Grandfather. These are strange names."

"Were Isis and Osiris around when you were growing up, Tonas, or did they just stop by occasionally?"

"It was a romance between all of us; they have been a constant in my life. Did you truly not know that they are my grandparents?"

"After I first heard that, I just pushed it to the back of my mind. Actually, it's staggering for me to think of you as the grandson of Isis and Osiris."

Isis replies, "You must know that it is destined for all of us that are of the Origin to come together. It is a great honor for us to be in your presence, you see?"

I answer that I don't quite get that yet, but I'm working up to it.

CHAPTER THIRTY-EIGHT

April 27, 2015

I'm still not sure I'm transporting objects to the Moon in the most divine way possible; plus, I want to make sure there is no way to track any object to me. Sananda suggests that all I need to do is create a holding room for the objects in the SBT. That way when I manifest an object in the SBT, it can stay in the holding room until Liponie picks it up.

With those parameters in place, I choose that anything I've previously gated to the Moon or other locations be manifested now in the SBT for Liponie to collect and transport to our council. I also set it up so that this will always be the way I transport. Now it is safe for Liponie to share with the other worlds all the objects I have gathered or will gather in the SBT since they are untrackable, pristine versions that have *no connection to or impact on* the original object.

Since in previous work I forgot to do anything with Earth flowers and water, I now choose, in the SBT, that every species of flower, past, present and future manifests here for Liponie to pick up. Since it would be nice to also have some water, I do a quick internet search for waterfalls and create these in the SBT for Liponie to pick up: Sutherland Falls, New Zealand; Plitvice Waterfalls, Croatia; Dettifoss, Iceland; Yosemite and Yellowstone waterfalls; Kaieteur Falls, Guyana; Angel Falls, Venezuela; Niagara Falls and Victoria Falls in Zimbabwe. I include all the water animals in these waters and just for fun I throw in Lake Titicaca, Hacker Creek and the little pond at my future home. I call Liponie in to pick them up and Sananda remarks that he is wearing an old-fashioned golf outfit. Liponie is either playing golf on the Moon, making a fashion statement or just having fun—probably all three.

I ask Sananda to come with me to visit Mom and Dad to see if they have anything new that would assist me. Dad has a final draft of the song he's been writing and he wants to know if I will critique it. Here are the words to the song:

Dreams in my life, they came and they went,
Ever changing with the directions of life's breeze.

The dreams of my heart developed through the life
Deeply planted, growing sturdy and strong.
No burdens were these, the dreams of my heart,
Never broken, never lost, ever there, sweetly being, gently
Growing, heart-renewing, spirit-lifting, freedom home.

"Oh, Dad, that is really nice. I'm crying just a little bit because it's beautiful, and, you know, I still miss ya."

Dad says, through Sananda, that he doesn't miss me because he sees me all the time and he loves me. "Thanks, Dad. Mom, I started thinking about Mother's Day coming up and it's the first time since I can remember that I won't send you a card."

She suggests, via Sananda, "Don't send a card, just come. I'm baking cookies."

In reply to my question about what they do all day, I learn that "they are ever busy being, and that is a great help to many."

Sananda explains that being in the Fifth Realm is a big transition for many people who come in via the Five Star Serenity Send-off because they don't have a foundation, for example, of studying and personally evolving and elevating from their studies. It makes sense then that the mundane activities Mom and Dad offer would be comforting, at least for those beings that lived on Earth.

Three days ago I heard the words, "Gathering May 29th where the coil thingies are." What did I mean by coil thingies? At first, I think maybe this has something to do with Tesla coils, but that doesn't feel quite right. Hoping that Sananda can give me some information about coil thingies, I ask him what they are.

He says they are energy spirals that can be connected to the cosmic grid; this would connect all the universes and make it easier for all the worlds to elevate in their own timings. He also says that this is like grids within grids that will be dedicated specifically to Joy Council elements that will be brought through from my Higher Self. I learn there are pieces I need to get and give to Charlie.

Using SVH, I choose to have all the steps and stages as well as systems and principles for this plan. I put this in an orb, call Charlie into the SBT to give it to him, roll forward in time to May 29th and step into the council:

Tonas greets me with, "My dear, you are here and you feel different to me."

"I'm in the future."

"In the future of what?"

"Of my reality."

"You are on the day of ours."

"But I'm not on the day of my day. I've got some work to do with universal grids and I've already given it to Charlie."

Charlie hands me the orb and says that all we are doing today is activating them; we'll use them later to do something. This transmission takes thirty seconds or less to send out and then I move back to today.

Maybe I should make myself a badge for when I do things like this because I bet I'll be doing more and more work in the future. The badge could say something like, "I'm Joy from the past__________ (date)." Hmm, maybe even "Joy Blast from the past_________." No, I'd probably have to explain that too often. Then I remember that only the English savvy people would know what the words meant. Maybe I could have the words in Andromedan and Sirian also. Something to consider, anyway, because explaining when I'm from could get tedious.

Also, three days ago, I heard Osiris say, "A lot of you are a symbol of peace now. You are complete." This must have been part of a future speech to the 124,310 children we have been assisting, because currently they are still in the early stages of recovering from their previous lives. My thought is that the progress the children make, could, at some future date, be an inspiration for dual worlds everywhere. I bet Charlie will want to do something with that.

I intend to speak with Charlie and move to the position of entry into the Joy Council where the children are now a symbol of peace. Sure enough, he is in mid-sentence.

"...and I know it will be true, Mommy, because if we make it so that everybody can see it, it will be beautiful. There are people who are struggling even on Earth, and if they saw what it was like to go from where these kids have come, it would be amazing for them."

"Charlie, can you tell me what year and date we are in?"

"Right now in our world?"

"Yes."

"It's March 7th, 2017."

"I'm from the past."

"The past of what, Mommy?"

Yes, I definitely need to make some kind of badge to explain *when* I'm from.

"I moved forward to this time from 2015. Let me do the work and then I'll move back to my regular time."

Charlie tells me it is almost ready and he was hoping I would say yes because he's been doing lots of work for the Earth. "I think it will help everything move really fast forward for us."

Since Charlie and I were speaking privately, we now move into the full council where Tonas greets me. I explain that we're going to put a transmission in place, and then I will move back to a position two years in the past, because that's when I'm from. Osiris speaks up to say he is viewing the transmission; he is in favor of it, but perhaps we should ask the children's permission.

Charlie immediately says he now has their permission and he apologizes to Osiris for not getting that first. We send out this transmission quickly and I am ready to return to my time. It's not that I'm uncomfortable in the future, it's just that there's so much work to do in the *present* that I don't feel like dilly-dallying here. Before I can leave, Charlie says he has new shoes he wants to show me. I just say I'll be back soon, and hope that my future self will admire his new footwear.

Two nights ago, before I fell asleep, a Native American spoke to me for some time. I enjoyed listening to him and did not interrupt his conversation by trying to record what he said. I decide to connect with him now to listen again to what he wishes to say.

He says his name, Toemuhway, and that he's not choosing to go anywhere or be a part of any council. He prefers to stay on the land. Although he's dead, the area where he lives—perhaps resides is a better word—is close to the Four Corners section of the United States. He feels it is important for the individuals there to be supported because they are in upheaval; he wants to know if there is something we can do.

He says, "The land here is very sacred. All land is sacred, but these are healing lands and the highest energies here are not enough to help your people to find their balance. Perhaps there is something that your connection with the planet can do to help them, for she is powerful."

"I will speak with her and the council that I am working with on the Moon. Thank you for speaking with me the other evening."

At the Joy Councils:

After Tonas and I exchange greetings, I ask him if he has something for me. (Napping yesterday afternoon, I picked up that he was going to give me something that would transmute.)

"It is a special necklace with geometries that will assist you to transmute energies that are conflicting, and it will cloak you more efficiently from prying eyes. Let me place it around your neck."

"Thank you, Tonas." I've done quite a bit of SVH work to cloak my activities from those who oppose Earth's and humanities evolution, but the council must feel more assistance would help. I gladly accept it.

"The next thing on my agenda is to tell you that the women of the Inzleeookeerah Universe have voted to postpone their ascension until May 2825. Will you do some negotiating with them to see if they will modify that date?"

Tonas agrees that I may leave this in the council's hands.

"Three days ago, I heard someone say, 'We're ready for your plan.' I heard myself answer, 'If I knew what it was, I'd help.' Charlie, do we have a transmission for this plan?"

"We do have a transmission, Mommy. It's about all the colors of the worlds and the beauty of all the people with all their cultures. I made a recipe book and we're going to send it out so that everyone from all the stars and worlds can add it to their own recipes. I've been working on this for several days and I'm very proud of it because our universe has many recipes."

I'm not sure I understand why Charlie is sending out recipes. I ask him for more details and he says the recipes correspond with the different colors of the peoples of the worlds. Then he asks if I know that people of different colors like different foods. I reply that I do know that and that his idea is a good one.

"You said something about the delicious and absolutely spectacular meal that I prepared; you told me that everybody has their likes and their dislikes, but you love everything I do. That's what gave me the idea."

I repeat to the core group Toemuhway's concerns about the difficulties the Native Americans living in the Four Corners area are having, and ask Gaia if she can do something to help.

She says that is a very beautiful energy area and suggests perhaps that is amplifying some of their issues. She believes that toning down the vortex energies in different areas might help them because the indigenous are feeling the energies of Earth even more than they used to. Gaia adds that if they are consuming alcohol they will experience even more trouble since it affects their clarity.

I ask if it would be possible for us to get something from the Fifth Realm to help with that, and Tonas informs me that we can now connect with the Fifth Realm from our council. Sananda advises me to first define when I wish to connect with the beings there, at the near completion or now. I decide to connect with people in both those times. Sananda says that the Joy Arrows are now connected to the Fifth Realm at those times and individuals will be present.

"I'm speaking to you from the Joy Councils on the Earth and the Moon. Those of you that are indigenous people, please give us gifts for yourself that we will give to you throughout your life. My suggestion is that since alcohol consumption is causing many of you great difficulty now, perhaps you might want to give yourself gifts to help you with that.

I also hope your gifts might help you to, with clarity and ease, be more in tune with your divine path.

I ask you and charge you to remember that you are people I love. The Earth loves you and we are streaming that love to you; we know in our hearts that you will find your way. You are on the path. We ask you to open your eyes and to feel the grace that we now give to you."

When I have finished saying these words, I passionately address the people in their language and know that I am speaking words of encouragement.

"I think I was giving them a little bit of a pep talk."

Tonas agrees with me and says that at every level they recognized the words were coming from me. I ask if anybody knows what I actually said.

Charlie volunteers, "Mommy, you did *not* say get with it! What you said was, 'It is time for everyone of this world to remember that they are more a part of the greater whole than they can imagine. When you allow yourself to rise up above travail and let it move back and past you, then you help everyone to see that it is not necessary to be in the midst of travail.' It was very beautiful, Mommy, and I could feel them accepting your wisdoms."

I ask Gaia if she thinks this will help the people in the Four Corners area and she answers that it is already helping them. I connect with Toemuhway, who says, "We are most grateful to you, Father. We can feel the lessening of the struggle. If the firewater is to leave us forever, *then* we shall know greater peace. Thank you, Father."

"You are welcome."

Charlie hands the transmission to me and says he put love, hugs and kisses from us into it. We send it out through the Joy Arrows.

It's time to speak with Cory about a bit of information from the future that I heard four days ago. I heard myself saying that I was concerned about the wedding and then I saw the words, "wedding cancelled." At first, I thought perhaps Charlie had embodied, proposed to Jewel, they were going to get married and then they decided to cancel the wedding. Then I realized that even though Charlie is very speedy, that sequence of events would be too fast even for him. As busy as I've been keeping Commander Ashtar, I don't feel he would have set a wedding date yet, let alone cancel one, so it must be Cory and Liponie's wedding that could be cancelled.

When I am alone with her, I mention that I have some future information about her wedding, but I'm not going to discuss it with her now because I believe we can solve it. Hoping my inner guidance isn't steering me wrong, I suggest to her not to wait for her mother to wed because I believe Zeezzz will follow her lead.

"You think? Perhaps she will see how happy we are and she will wish for some of our happiness for herself."

"I think she looks up to you because you took the plunge into being human before she did. She's got to admire you for that; I certainly do."

"I am very busy and I cannot imagine being married anytime soon, and yet I would enjoy it."

"Perhaps you might consider marrying when we take our trip in September."

A few of us in SVH will be traveling in France, England and Scotland this fall to do some energy work.

She tells me they haven't selected a place for the wedding. I advise her not to rush, and I also suggest that when she feels ready, "Don't wait for anybody else. It's your life."

She agrees this is good advice and asks for ideas about wedding locations during our trip. I mention Glastonbury and Edinburgh because those are the only two places I'm sure we will be. She is going to consider locations.

When I ask her if she is still cooking, she says she has developed a cooking school for the children. She also mentions that her mother, Zeezzz is still assisting the stars, moons and suns with finding partners and adds, "She is becoming quite a romantic. She is *so* in love with Ashtar, and I think he is very enamored with her as well. He wishes to be in her presence every minute. Mother is thinking of changing her name, but doesn't have a new one picked out yet."

We exchange a few more pleasantries and then I move back to speak with Tonas and Osiris.

"Osiris, I saw something in the future where you are talking to me about initiating a wave. Your words were, 'Tell this being of light that she will initiate,' and then I saw a hand open up and some kind of particles pour from it." I telepathically show him what I saw and say, "I believe this has something to do with the students in the Academy of Enrichment."

Osiris explains that some of the students have decided to move out from the ship to become more of an instrument. He agrees it is possible we could assist them to do this and wants to know if I oppose that. Tonas and I agree that this is what we were hoping would happen.

"Many of the initiates are from dual worlds and they are evolving to become capable of moving energy and manifesting; this is what you were seeing." Osiris explains. He adds that we have talked about forming schools in the different universes and that he was able to see the bigger picture from what I showed him telepathically; in the years ahead we have actually formed the schools. The schools would be similar to the ancient academies of Earth, but only in the aspect that they would assist people to learn and evolve.

"The other thing I did today was go to our council two years in the future to do some work."

Osiris asks to see a vision of this and I show him the work we put in place concerning the kids. He remarks that it was excellent work. I tell Charlie that he had new shoes then that he wanted me to see, but he wouldn't know about them now.

"I saw them just now, Mommy. I'd like to have them now because they are red and white and striped, and the socks, too!"

Oops, I wonder how this will affect future Charlie, hopefully, not adversely. Maybe that Charlie will just have different new shoes. I ask Charlie how he is feeling about his body now, and if he is comfortable with how he looks.

"I like it very much, Mommy. I'm like all the other kids, not the ones from Earth. I'm from Earth, too, but everybody's different,

Mommy. That's why the recipe book was so important. There's a Swizzler section and we have all the recipes for chocolate."

"I wish I had the book here, or better yet, I wish I had some of the results of the book here."

"You got it, Mommy, because we transmitted it and you are on Earth!"

"Tell me about the party at the underwater palace. Did we have a good time?"

Tonas says it was incredible, but we lost Charlie for awhile because he is now a tremendous water skier. "He likes the new boat. Liponie gives him *everything* before anyone else can do anything for him. I am not jealous; I am simply stating that we lost Charlie for a little while."

"But it's OK because I had fun and being happy is all you ever want for me. I have a new swimsuit, too. It's a Speedo."

"That's good because you're speedy!" I'm trying to picture a Speedo swimsuit on Charlie's swizzle stick shape; it must be just a tiny patch of color.

Charlie agrees he is speedy and then he tells me he had a very good time and Papa Tonas loved being with his mommy and daddy. "I know what it is to love being with your mommy and daddy, 'cause I love being with you."

I ask Liponie to join us so that I can check with him to see if he has found a place for all the flowers and water I left in the SBT. He assures me the Moon is an open canvas.

When I ask what Shasmeah is currently doing, Tonas says she *still* has not left the commissary. I'm not willing to ask her to leave it; if I'd existed for millennia and never had a chance to eat food, especially chocolate, I imagine I'd also be reluctant to quit sampling delicacies.

"Liponie, I suggested to Cory that she not wait for anybody else to marry when she is ready to do so."

"I am forever indebted to you; your advice means a great deal to her."

"You might consider marrying when we are on our trip this fall, but there is no need to hurry."

Liponie likes that idea and says he hopes Woonfred can join us. All of us miss him, but we also know he won't leave the egg. I remind them that Woonfred said that in the time when dragons existed before, gestation took ninety days, but since we are in more elevated dimensions, it might not take that long now. Tonas comments that if the wedding is in the fall he believes the egg will have hatched and maybe Woonfred and his family could be present. He adds that this is another golden egg.

"Charlie, did the other Swizzlers have a chance to water ski?"

"Yes, and we know how to do the pyramid and how to fall at the same time. We do that on purpose. Whoever hits the bottom and then comes all the way back up to the top first is the winner. I win almost every time because I make my legs very long."

"Do you know about the jumps you can do when you water ski? Let me show you." I telepathically transmit a picture of a ski jump to him and immediately hear him say, "Oh, Mommy, bye!" I had planned to also show him about parasailing, but I know he's gone. After I show that activity to Tonas, he agrees this will be the next thing.

CHAPTER THIRTY-NINE

April 27, 2015 part 2

The muscles in the middle of my back have been extremely painful, and this morning I finally remembered that my back was sore like this years ago. The healer I was working with at that time told me I had been practicing flying with a new flight instructor named Jake. When I ask Esthra if I'm taking flying lessons again, he confirms that I am. I ask him why.

"It has something to do with awakening a part of the spirit of you that wishes to be more fully involved in your gifts and abilities. This is your idea, not mine."

"May I speak to Jake?"

I hear the voice of someone small say, "You can speak to me."

For some reason I feel better, at least emotionally, already. Jake's voice is very pleasing and he sounds just a little bit like Charlie only in a slightly lower voice register.

"Hi, Jake."

"Hello to you."

"I love you."

"I love you and we are spending a great time together. It has been too long."

"I'm going to have to do something different, Jake, because the muscles of my back where my wings attach are hurting really, really badly."

"You could have told me."

"But I didn't figure out what was causing it until today. Can we rest for a few days until I recover?"

"We will, of course. I never wished to cause you pain."

"I'm not blaming you. It must be that the part of me there is not tuned into what's happening to my body here."

"We've been practicing in your sleep."

"But I sometimes feel almost crippled during the day! Am I doing different flying than I was before?"

Maybe I'm trying to do loop-the-loops or some other practically impossible flying feat. He says it's just that I'm a beginner again and adds that it's like he is retraining me from "the square of one." We agree to begin again in five days. I hope that's long enough because I've been having to use ibuprofen to get through my days.

After Jake leaves, I ask Esthra what he looks like.

"He is always naked, and he looks to be no more than a human of six years."

I try to find out more about Jake's origins, but Esthra says he is just a cherub. Then he adds, "We must have them, of course."

With Tonas, Charlie and Sananda:

Tonas wonders why I have returned since I worked with the council this morning. When I say I had to sort out my flying lessons, he asks what I mean by flying lessons. Now that I think about it, it sounds really cool to tell him I've been practicing flying. He says he'd like to join me in flying. I reply that he can join me in five days after my back has recovered. I like the idea of us flying together. Wow! I *really* like that idea! And I am *not* going to think about the possibilities of sex while flying.

"Charlie, am I any good at roller-skating?"

"Not so good, Mommy."

Drat, I was afraid he'd say that. Charlie adds that he helps me by holding my hand. I mention that Tonas could help me if he gets bored with trying to help me skate. Charlie says he likes to hold my hand and reminds me that I have to learn. It's not so much that I have to learn, it's just that I'd like to get good enough at *some* activity that Charlie enjoys so that I could enjoy doing it with him.

Next, I ask Liponie if he got the frog boots. Explanation: I was getting ready to go into a store today when I noticed a little boy walking down a small stairway in front of me. He was wearing the cutest little, lime green boots with frog eyes and a mouth on the front of both boots. Immediately, I knew the Swizzlers had to have frog boots; I stepped into the SBT copied them there and called Liponie there to take them to the council.

Liponie agrees he has them. My plan is to give the first pair of boots to the Swizzler who showed me a frog he was holding in his hand, but I can't remember if it was Toby or Chuckie. When I ask which one it was, Liponie says that all the Swizzlers like frogs.

Then I ask Charlie which one it was, and here's his response, "I don't know who it was, but I will tell you right now that if you're going to be giving frogs to anybody, it needs to be to me!"

"It's not a frog, they are frog boots."

I telepathically show him what I saw and comment that I thought they were cute. He agrees they are cute, but there is definitely a tone of disappointment in his voice. I didn't know he liked frogs, too, but I should have guessed he would. He tells me everybody will want them and, for sure, he should have a pair because he loves frogs, too. I just keep digging myself in deeper with the frog boot issue as I try to explain that I just wanted to give a pair *first* to one of the Swizzlers and then to all of them. Charlie is relating the names of the Swizzlers who have names, even Pinky and Nicky, and telling me they *all* like frogs.

"OK! Liponie, everybody gets frog boots right now! Thank you."

I hear Charlie squeal, "Wheee! I love 'em!"

"Hey, Liponie, can I have some frog boots, too!"

Liponie says they are now on my feet. I start laughing because I can see them there.

"Tonas, would you like some frog boots?"

"Clearly, I should."

Picture a gorgeous man wearing stunning black robes with gold trim and lovely accessories of lime green frog boots on his feet. Mmm, adorable.

"Liponie, how about frog boots for yourself?"

"They clash with my color, dear."

I think I'm going to see if I can find frog boots for adults on Earth. Little kids get the coolest footwear, and I'm definitely starting to feel like a kid again.

I intend to work with the council again on May 1st, and suggest to Liponie that we have a Maypole this year. He agrees it is a lovely tradition designed around the penis and fertility.

"All right, but we can have fun with a Maypole, right?"

"Yes, of course, I'm having fun with my Maypole."

"Oh, don't even go there. Tonas might start getting ideas from you."

Charlie says that he already knows about Maypoles. I wonder what he knows, but now is not the time to get into *that* subject. He wants to have a dance that involves the fairies for our celebration. He also wants to know if the fairies can have frog boots. Gaia says there wouldn't be a problem offering them, but adds that she doesn't believe they would accept. She explains to Charlie that the girl fairies like to have little shoes with heels and the boy fairies enjoy little shoes. He sounds disappointed when he says, "OK."

Gaia agrees we could involve the fairies as long as the celebration was in the Joy Council in the Earth. Charlie suggests we have taffy and cupcakes and I agree to that menu.

"Sananda, I want to assist the Native Americans who have prayed to the Great Spirit for help with alcohol problems. Is it possible to do any genetic work that would assist them?"

He says he believes that would not be allowed. His idea is that I could use holograms to appear to them energetically each time they've asked for help and hand them balancing energy that would assist them. I mention that there must be some genetic component that allows alcohol to be such an issue for so many of them. According to him, the aborigines also are very affected by alcohol.

We move into the main council. I tune into the Joy Arrow, aim it into the Fifth Realm and call forward all those at the near completion who ever struggled with any kind of addiction. I suggest this could be any kind of substance that caused imbalances in their bodies and lives. I ask them to hand me their gifts, take them into the SBT and hand them over.

Then I step back into the Joy Councils and call forward all the Native Americans in the Fifth Realm who ever had difficulties with alcohol or any other substance that caused them to stray from their path, to feel despair, to struggle or to call out to the Great Spirit for assistance.

"I wish to offer you that assistance now. As that being you prayed to, I will stand by and with you every time in your life you felt you had to have a substance that would cause imbalance in your life. I am there and the Great Spirit will work through me to hand to you something that will assist you. It will be something divine that you would want at each of those points in your life. I remind you of your true nature, your strength, your beauty, your power, your love and wisdom, your connection to the Earth and that you are strong and worthy. You have prayed for this relief and here it is."

Sananda says he feels this has been very instrumental in assisting and it is a very good start.

"Charlie, before I leave, is everything well with the Swizzlers with the boots?"

"We love them, indeed we do. Mommy, also, I am learning some big words."

"Yes?"

"Indeed."

"You are indeed. Are you still practicing writing?"

He says he doesn't like it and I suggest perhaps he can learn this later. He says there is so much to do now and Mr. Kennedy is teaching him how to whistle songs!

"What story have we read recently?"

"We've mostly been reading the Nancy Drew mystery stories; you only read just a few pages. I like these other ones and I was wondering if we could switch. I think it would be really fun to read about the cowboys and the Indians. We have Roy Rogers' comic books."

I have a little bit of concern because I can't remember if there is any shooting and killing in those comics. Charlie says he sees the shows all the time and he is OK with them because there is no blood. I still want Tonas's opinion.

"These western comics are quite tame, actually. We have the full edition of all the Roy Rogers' comic books."

I agree to read these books and add that Roy Rogers was a hero of mine when I was growing up. As a matter of fact, I'm going to check to see if I have any of those comics myself, although I think I have mostly the Lone Ranger comic books.

"How are the kids coming along?"

Charlie says he is being a big brother to all of them, and there are a lot of them to be big brother to. He gave them a little talk the other day and showed them how to do the Hula-Hoop.

"They weren't very good at it but they kept trying. I think it's important for them to have dexterity."

"Aren't they doing roller-skating and riding bikes?"

"There are some that are good, but many are not. We have stilts, and when you have stilts you are very tall."

That sounds daunting to me and I check to make sure that the littler kids have small ones. Charlie says they do, but the bigger people, like him, get to have the tall ones. Of course, he's really good at using them, and he is showing everybody how to use them.

"Roy Rogers has a horse named Trigger, and I," Here a pleading note enters Charlie's voice and he begins to whisper. "could really use just one…more…horse. If I have just one…more…horse that's like Trigger, then I can do the tricks."

"Can't Skipper do the tricks?"

"Yes, but he doesn't look like Trigger. I could do the trick where you run behind the horse and jump on it by putting your hands on its bottom. Oh, Mommy, if I could just have one…more…horse. I'm very good with the horses; I brush them every day and I even brush yours."

This is every mother's dilemma at some point, I believe. If Charlie has another horse, then ninety-four Swizzlers are likely to want another horse too. We could have a very large herd of horses if that happens. I mention this to Charlie, but he says the other Swizzlers really don't think that they can ask.

"They don't have their lips open much except to eat strawberries and things like that. They're not talkin'. I told them, 'You start talkin', you get your stuff.'"

I suppose he's right. My dad used to say, "The squeaky wheel gets the grease." This might be an incentive for some of them to become more vocal. When I ask Tonas for his opinion, he says he has no issue with this at all because we have room for many horses.

"All right, one horse."

"I can have one more? I can have Trigger? Papa Tonas said I couldn't, and it's really true that if you go to your mommy then you get it."

"Now, wait a minute! You can't neglect Skipper."

"I can't ever neglect Skipper, because if I was to do that, Skipper would be sad."

"And you tell the other Swizzlers that if they want additional horses, they first have to prove that they are as good with their first horse as you are with Skipper."

"That's a good idea. Skipper's a rainbow horse; you gotta love a rainbow horse."

"I'll be back on Friday to enjoy the Maypole party."

And I need to try to remember to talk with Tonas about being on the same page, so to speak, where the children are concerned. He could have given me a "heads up" about the horse issue, or maybe he did and I just didn't pick up on it.

I have a few questions for Aton about things that have been going on in my head. When I tell him that I saw a violet fan unfold in my 3rd eye and then felt very euphoric, he says that was a precursor for the tutorial we had the next day. I felt like it also had something to do with shape-shifting and his reply is that, "Nothing is impossible when you are fully in presence."

I add that yesterday afternoon I felt some kind of liquid being poured into something in my head.

Aton says, "That was me. I was making a salad."

I burst out laughing at this and he says, "Ah, my dear, it is so good to hear your laugh."

"I had quite a vision of Romaine lettuce being tossed in my head."

"It is a worthy bowl."

Grand Heron asks me if I wish to speak about the portal. I answer that I came to visit him so that he could speak about any subject he chose.

"I am impressed with what you are offering the nations. This will, of course, assist the portal. I am here for you."

"You were speaking with me about time the other day."

"Yes, time is a beautiful dance. When I speak of time, it is the fluidity that only the heart can catch and ride as if on the wings of the eagle or the heron. Time is meant to be fluid; it is meant to be open like an egg to find the surprise inside that there is new life. Time is the seed of life, for without it, there is only the void of presence."

"Do you know one who is named He Who Stands?"

"Hmm, yes."

"He was also speaking to me about time."

"It is time to speak about time, for it is compressing."

"What can I do?"

"You are doing it."

"I'm doing many things that I am not aware of, so if there is something that I can consciously do to assist more than I am, please speak with me."

"Thank you, Father."

"You are welcome."

CHAPTER FORTY

May 1, 2015

I've been trying to figure out why the part of me at the council didn't stop flying when my back started hurting so badly. Then it occurs to me that Tonas wasn't aware I had been flying. I might be able to hide something like that from him at the council, but I bet I couldn't hide it from Charlie. That means I've been practicing flying somewhere else, and I think the only other place I could do that would be on the astral plane when I'm asleep. I'm going to choose to discontinue flying until I've recovered.

I ask Esthra and Jake to join me. When Esthra announces they are in presence, I explain to Jake that my back is still sore and that I will have to wait longer before I can practice flying. He suggests we wait two months. I propose letting him know through Esthra when I've recovered enough and he agrees to wait.

"Jake, are all the cherubs little boys?"

"Hmm, all the ones *I* know."

(Don't worry; I'm not planning to ask God to create girl cherubs.)

"What are your jobs?"

"We are always making happiness wherever we are. We like happiness."

"That's a good job. Thank you, Jake."

The second thing on my to do list is to figure out some kind of badge to wear when I time travel so that I don't have to keep explaining when I'm from. The challenge with that is that only a few on the council read English and what will I do when I start traveling to other councils in the future? I don't believe I've done that yet, but I bet I will. I need something like a universal translator that reflects words people can read, hear verbally and telepathically that identifies what time I am from. This would need to be calibrated so it would match the systems of time and date that other worlds use when I travel outside of our Joy Council.

I go to my future self and request a badge that will do those things, but only for people who should receive that information about me. That will protect me from giving information about myself to individuals who shouldn't know about me just in case I encounter anyone like that. I choose the picture of the blue Earth that is on the front cover of *Path of Sweetness* to be the emblem for my badge.

At the Joy Councils, I manage to wait until Tonas greets me and then I call an emergency strategy meeting.

"I'm going to show you what I saw in two books. The first book has a plan that is not good for humans on Earth. In the second book, I saw a picture of a little girl. She is one of the little ones we have here, her name is Sally (not her real name) and she was awake the whole time the rest of the kids were in stasis. She had to have something in place that would assist her to stay awake."

Tonas asks someone to bring Sally to us. When she is present, I speak to her very softly to let her know I'm aware that she was awake while the other kids slept, and I tell her I'm very sorry she had to experience that. She doesn't speak, but I can hear her making whimpering sounds. Tonas asks Helena to join us and I explain to her what we have learned. Helena says that explains why Sally has seemed so frightened all the time. She adds that Sally is seven but she is like a little baby.

"Helena, she is very important for some reason, beyond the fact that she is a lovely little girl."

I ask Helena to take Sally for some ice cream and then come back to us. When they are gone, I show the group telepathically the complete version of the two books I saw this morning. Tonas asks Charlie what he makes of the information.

Charlie answers in his collective voice to say that all of them will be speaking. Their assessment is that this is the story of a planned insurgence. "It was always in the works for the children we rescued to be moles that would be reinserted into the 4th dimension. This little one was to have been the queen bee that all would work around and for. She has been very much indoctrinated, and it was, I am sure, important for her to be awake and to never have lost her consciousness of this. To feel our unconditional love and to also feel herself being drawn to an awareness that one day she must, perhaps, be in a position to cause harm to those who have given her this love may have caused great damage to her. We have just created a program that will assist these children to release this; however, Sally's program must be retained. She is as if a computer that will give us insights; we can hold the program outside of herself and monitor that which is transmitted to her. Transmission to her has never stopped."

I feel greatly dismayed by this revelation; I also feel anger that some beings would use a little girl and all these children this way.

Charlie continues with, "This little one (Sally) is a transmission device. The council is safe, and yet she is in a position, just as the other children, to become a problem in the future. This programming must be brought outside of them. We can place this programming in little crystals in the stasis bubble with each of the crystals transmitting still as if they were on automatic. These children must be set free; their minds do not allow them, at the ages they are, to make free choice. We can assist them."

"Let me show you the information inside the other four pretty books I saw lying on a table; I know they were more than just pretty books."

"It is wise you brought this information to us. We have already seen these books, but not from the mind of reading the encryption. This is very clever; the prettier the book, the less suspicious."

I telepathically transmit to the group a vision of a young man I saw this morning. Tonas says the man has brought them transmissions from council member Kahteem.

Tonas is not disturbed when I show him the paper the man had in his hand. It occurs to me to ask if there are any security precautions taken for people who enter the council. Tonas says there are measures in place for council members, but not for delivery boys or other people who enter. He jokes that the pizza man is not suspicious.

"But the pizza man could bring some nasty pizza. *Anybody* and *anything* that comes into the council needs to be screened. We need heightened security!"

"Perhaps what we need is a field of light so bright that anything entering that is outside of the different grades of love (Interesting that they can define grades of love.) will be recognized as being less than that frequency. This would also be for anything they carry in and would include their clothing."

Tonas agrees to have meetings about this and to set important new guidelines. I ask that the guidelines are very stringent and that the other Joy Councils are included. The discovery of what was done to the children and the new plan for global takeover I saw in the books this morning has me on high alert. I want the Joy Councils to be sacrosanct.

Charlie says the CEV suggests that in the past when we extricate the children, they go through a filter that allows an absolute replica of their presence to be brought through in a crystal but leaves the things that were put in them behind. He says he doesn't think it was an accident that the kids got stuck in the 4th dimension.

"This little girl, Mommy, cries all the time; she shakes and everything makes her jump. She's such a baby, we have to love her."

"Let's fix it!"

"We have to go back to when we got them and we have to put together a very intricate program. It has to be simul and also taneous."

Ashtar says this was a very important discovery. "It would have escaped us, for they are such darlings we only wished to save them. It is important that one of the things we do is set up a living record that we can constantly monitor for the transmissions. We must also learn how the transmissions are received because they have been invisible to us."

Charlie's collective voice answers that the transmissions are not invisible; they are carried on the sound of the children's breaths. "They draw information in when they inhale and then transmit information when they exhale. I do not believe they were being monitored constantly until we extricated them. It would be unthinkable to put them back; however, it is possible that we could make it appear as though the children are still in stasis. I do not believe there is a way for those who left them there to find out if this is true or not."

Charlie suggests a vote about whether we put something in place that makes the children appear to remain in that dimension in stasis or bring them here and allow the transmissions to continue outside of themselves. The only thing I'm sure of is that we can't put them back into stasis permanently.

Ashtar speaks up to say, "From an intelligence view, it would be quite valuable to have a replication of this and to monitor the transmissions, because we are unaware if these transmissions are meant to activate at points when the children mature. And yet, I have the sense that it is not worth this. I believe that the full freedom of these children is more important. Their emancipation must be full and complete."

I agree with Ashtar and Tonas suggests we vote. Osiris speaks up to say he agrees with all of us. He also has the belief that perhaps we can set something in that position for us to monitor. Charlie says if there is something there to be monitored, there is something to be discovered.

"We of the council believe that the freest means is to extricate them, leave something behind to say they are still there and leave well enough alone. These are not unaware beings. (He's referring to the beings that placed the children in stasis). They are very able-minded."

All agree to this plan. We discuss that it will be important to screen the children after they are extricated in order to remove the things that are implanted in them (Ashtar has devices to discover things of that nature.) as well as to watch them as they develop.

I get the fail-safe for the plan from my MAPS self and hand it to Tonas. He says our plan cannot fail. I certainly hope so because I'm shocked at what I stumbled upon. We've had 124,310 potential "time bombs" amongst us in the bodies of our rescued kids.

Tonas reminds me that children have been used from the beginning of time because, in the minds of many, they are useless. "To us they are priceless and it is in our discretion to save them."

I agree with him and tell him I'm ready to move into action. He says they have sent a transmission to the Ashtar Command ships in the past; they are to pause and not do the original extrication. I am to take only Tonas, Ashtar and myself into the past into the lead ship because the plan made by the CEV doesn't include anyone else. Tonas explains that they must first extricate Sally because she is the most dangerous. She is the key to everything because she is the one who is creating the bubble that holds the children in stasis. The good news is that I don't have to do anything to extract them. The council put it all together so that the Ashtar Command can do everything.

The kids are extracted, but then Tonas realizes we need Charlie after all to check to see if this was done correctly. I gate back to the council to get the CEV. When I tell him I need the full council to come with me, he says, "I told them that! I said they would need all of us!"

When we are back with Tonas, he says that if Charlie and Ashtar ascertain the procedure was not correct, we will attempt it again at an earlier time. This attempt does fail; they put the children back and remove the equipment they had put in stasis. Following Tonas's suggestion, I gate all the ships back an additional three hours.

Ashtar moves through the extrication procedure again, and this attempt also fails. Tonas says that with each attempt they discover more of the fail-safes that were in place to keep the kids locked down. I suggest we go back to the divine time for the extrication. Tonas believes that the divine time would be in the moment of the release of the 3rd dimension.

"In that upheaval, the extraction would not be noticed and there would not be a standard set for the stasis bubble they will be in."

Tonas checks with the CEV and Ashtar and they agree that would be the ideal time. I ask the Creator to help me pinpoint the exact correct time for this extraction and then gate all of the ships to that time, sometime between January 10th and January 11th, 2009. Less than a minute after I move the ships, I hear Tonas say that Charlie has given us a thumbs up.

"It is quite a thumb, my dear. It is the Mickey Mouse glove thumb."

Tonas suggests that we allow the CEV to remain for a period of one year in this past time before we return them to the Joy Council. That way the children will be scanned and debugged before they come to us. I agree that can be done in the past because I certainly don't want to be without Charlie for a whole year in our present time.

Tonas suggests we need Liponie to make them quarters on the ships to help bring them into the sweetness of being little non-dual babies. "He will come here if you ask for him."

"Liponie, yoo-hoo."

Since I am a little confused by all the time travel suggestions, I ask Tonas to tell Liponie what he is to do. Liponie says it will be easy to create quarters for each of them as well as programs for them on all of the ships. They are going to reunite children that know each other so they will be together on the ships.

Liponie suggests I move Tonas and myself one year into the future onto the ship where we are now. I gate the two of us a year into the future as suggested. Tonas says the children are now a year older, then adds, "It is a pity we did not have Helena back then, isn't it?"

He's right and I immediately foresee another time travel jaunt. It will be difficult for Helena not to have been with the children for the first year of their new life, and I know the children would benefit from her mothering. I gate Tonas and myself back to the council in current time to meet with Helena. Tonas transmits to her what has occurred and asks if she is willing to assist the children for a year in the past. Then we will bring her back to the present. Liponie will also need to have created new chambers for the children at our council because they will be older and without the problems they are currently experiencing.

Helena is eager to go and Tonas reminds me that I am to gate the three of us back to 2009 just prior to the extraction that worked so that she can be the first person that the children see. After we arrive, Tonas explains to her she is on one of the Ashtar Command ships and, although the Ashtar Commanders on the ships will assist her, she is to be the children's mommy if she agrees.

Helena says, "This is a dream. Little Sally will be safe and no longer in sadness?"

Tonas says we only know she will have a new chance to be herself. Helena says she hopes I come to see her periodically to give her ideas. She adds that she doesn't know what to do, but that it will come to her.

Tonas suggests that she can send transmissions to us through Liponie, and that the Ashtar Commanders on the ships will help her. Suddenly, I come to my senses and realize that there is no way on Earth—well, we're not exactly on Earth, but you know what I mean—there is no way on wherever we are that I'm going to leave Helena here to try to mother 124,310 children with only the assistance of a few men. She's got to have help!

I gate Tonas and myself back to the present time to get reinforcements from the Joy Council. I ask for volunteers of the indigenous women and men who have been assisting Helena with the children. I explain they will be assisting the children for a period of one year in the past and then we will move them back to the present time. Tonas says I have a volunteer to support each child; then he reminds us that if we proceed in this way, they will become the children's parents. Their commitment should be for the child's lifetime.

He suggests we take only 20,000 volunteers and that will provide more of a social network to support the children. I'm glad he pointed this out because I believe he's right. We move to a room with all of these people. Tonas assures me there is room to take them all to one of the ships and they can be transferred to the other ships after we arrive. I gate us all back to the appropriate moment in 2009 so that they will be there as the children are extricated.

Liponie greets us with laughter, says he has everything ready and we can bring on the children now. He moves all the volunteers to the different ships and says, "Let us have the children now, please."

I hear Helena say, "Oh, my goodness, you are a genius, Liponie! They are all coming out of their rooms with their pajamas on and wiping their eyes like they have just woken from a dream. It is perfect!"

I want to know if the children are all on one ship. Helena says they are all on different ships but we are receiving transmissions from all the ships that the little sleepy ones have awakened and their breakfast is ready. Tonas tells Liponie that we are grateful and we will see him in one year. I gate the two of us to this ship one year into the future. Then Tonas asks me to gate all the ships back to the atmosphere above Earth in our current time. They're going to transport the kids into the Joy Council in the Earth without me having to gate them there. I'm glad about that because it feels like I've been meeting myself coming and going. Come to think of it, I might actually have been doing that.

I start to gate Tonas and myself into the Earth Joy Council to see what's happening there, but Tonas asks me to wait a moment because someone wants to hold my hand.

"Mommy, it was a long, long year. I missed you so much; I wrote you many letters. Here they are."

Tonas says that Charlie has handed me a lot of pretty pictures done with crayons. I give Charlie a big hug and tell him that I *love* his pictures and letters. It was a little sad for me when my children outgrew bringing home pictures they drew at school that I could post on my refrigerator.

I gate the three of us to the Joy Council in the Earth. Charlie explains that all of the Swizzlers were instrumental in assisting the kids.

"Every one of them is all cleaned up, and Sally is the cutest little girl. I think I love her, but she's too young for *me*. I thought maybe Jewel could be her best friend because Sally is really good at all kinds of things. She can jump rope like nobody else; she can do two ropes at once. I miss Jewel, too."

"Charlie, you were gone just a minute for me; I'm sorry it was so long for you."

"That's why I wrote you so many letters."

"We were going to do a big Maypole celebration today, but I think we've had enough for today."

"Mommy, can I tell you something about a Maypole?"

"Yes."

"A Maypole is wonderful, but what we did changed the lives of all these kids. They are free now, Mommy. They are free; I feel that this is my greatest work."

Charlie is so young and at the same time so marvelously old and wise. I tell him that I applaud his work and the work of all the Swizzlers.

"What kinds of clothes are they wearing?"

"They wear capris, shorts, skirts and pants. These kids can pee and poop. Did you know that?"

I explain that is just what organic people do. It looks like he is still very interested in those body functions.

"OK, well, they're just normal kids now, Mommy. Liponie gave them everything. They had swings and everything we ever got they had, and they got even better. That's really the truth. They had every advantage and you know what?"

"What?"

"They're happy and they know how to sing, and they laugh all the time. They never used to laugh but now they laugh all the time."

I suggest they go ahead with the Maypole. Tonas says it is already in progress and Liponie has things set up like a carnival. He adds that there will be corn on the cob, everything will be well with the Maypole, and the fairies are involved.

I ask if we've done any planning for the solstice party. Tonas tells me we have had several meetings already. I'm concerned about figuring out how to manage something this huge.

He reminds me, "We have a magical piece. Someone called Liponie."

"Speaking of magic, how are the genies doing now, Liponie?"

"They are supporting in so many different universes; each universe and each council has a genie now."

I ask if they are enjoying what they are doing now. He replies that they have a sense of purpose, and it is not because they are told to do something, it is because they desire to do it.

"I have brought them through many studies; they now know exactly that they are sovereign. All are SVH Level Three Master Practitioners. There was a big celebration and a completing of the study not more than a week ago. There are some that even now are still in the works. They are not all working with the councils; many are working with me with the planets. We are making everyone wedded."

It's time to say goodbye to Charlie. I hear him tell me he loves me then he says, "Thank you for letting me be a part of this very important work. It was important that we were all there, Mommy. There was touching and there was going, and a lot of times it was more touch than go. It was very serious because they had all kinds of things in them and we had to find those things. Then we had to deactivate them without anyone ever knowing. Now they are just real kids. They will grow up to be real people, and then we have to set them free."

We both agree that, no matter what, the kids will always be welcome here. Then Charlie says Liponie is going to have special things for them in a minute.

"I wanna go and find my frog boots, 'cause I wanna be wearing them. Also there's gonna be cotton candy. Let me tell you something wonderful 'cause I am so happy. All these kids, they know how to love. Mommy, they didn't know how to love before; they didn't know how to receive love either. They didn't know how, and now they do! They can do it, Mommy! Nobody ever taught them how, and if you love you can't be doing naughty things."

"Yes, it doesn't feel right."

"Yes, and Mommy, I love you. Thank you for makin' my happy life."

"Do you remember when you didn't even have a mouth?"

"I remember. If you don't have a mouth you can't have cotton candy. Whoever invented cotton candy is my hero."

"Go have fun!"

Mission Participation Directives:

Move into the chair reserved exclusively for you at one or both of the Joy Council tables (Councils are located on the 10th dimension of our Moon and in the center of the Earth.) and add your blessings, prayers, wishes and good intentions to the transmissions we send out. (These transmissions are also supported by the masters and angels overseeing the councils.) The easiest way to do this is to relax someplace comfortable and close your eyes intending to visit the council(s). Your intention automatically transports your consciousness there.

Another option is to choose a specific session to visit while you're sleeping. To enhance your enjoyment, set the intention that you will remember your visit upon awakening.

Here's a peek at some of the events in book 5…

RETURN OF DRAGONS

An intervention to prevent dragons from being lured to their deaths in the past is implemented since that method of trickery could also have been the means to kill the new dragon prince, Joyyah. He is born on Mother's Day, but not in the location Woonfred and Kira had planned. It becomes necessary to create a new world for the dragons (thanks Liponie) to prevent their capture by a relentless tracker. A plot to kill Commander Ashtar results in the deportation of Chu who are not residents of Earth. On the lighter side: Pootie gets a new life; Cardmah, a leprechaun, talks about gold and raspberry pie. The Swizzlers are successful at meditating—on chocolate—and are masters at skateboarding. They are happy to wear suspenders after they learn it is not necessary to expose a certain part of their anatomy.

ABOUT THE AUTHOR

Joy has a Master's degree in music and is a professional violinist living in Bloomington, Indiana. She grows orchids as a hobby, enjoys walks in the woods and playing as well as listening to classical music.

Since 1990 she has been involved with Shaklee Corporation, a company whose philosophy of creating healthier lives matches that of her own. More information about Shaklee may be found at www.joyelaine.myshaklee.com.

She has studied and practiced SVH (Serenity Vibration Healing® and Enlightenment Technique) since 2003 and is a Master Practitioner and an Animal Healing Practitioner in that modality. She credits these studies with assisting her to bring forth the information in the Joy Chronicles. More information about SVH may be found at www.thejoyoflife.info.

18696403R00238

Made in the USA
Lexington, KY
24 November 2018